the GAME and the GLORY

AN AUTOBIOGRAPHY

the
GAME
and the
GLORY

AN AUTOBIOGRAPHY

WITH GREGG LEWIS

MICHELLE AKERS

ZondervanPublishingHouse
Grand Rapids, Michigan 49530
http://www.zondervan.com

A Division of HarperCollinsPublishers

The Game and the Glory
Copyright © 2000 by Michelle Akers

Requests for information should be addressed to:

ZondervanPublishingHouse
Grand Rapids, Michigan 49530

Library of Congress Cataloging-in-Publication Data

Akers, Michelle, 1966-
    The game and the glory : an autobiography / Michelle Akers with Gregg Lewis.
      p. cm.
    Includes bibliographical references and index [if applicable].
    ISBN 0-310-23529-4 (hard)
    1. Akers, Michelle, 1966- 2. Women soccer players–United States–Biography. I. Lewis,
Gregg A. II. Title.
GV942.7.A39 A3 2000
796.334'092—dc21   99-087980
    [B]   CIP

This edition printed on acid-free paper.

Unless otherwise indicated, all quotations from the Bible are taken from the New Revised Standard Version (NRSV).

Published in association with Yates and Yates, LLP., Literary Agents, Orange, California, and Moye Sports Associates, Inc., Atlanta, Georgia.

Interior design by Amy E. Langeler

Printed in the United States of America

00 01 02 03 04 05 06 /❖ DC/ 10 9 8 7 6 5 4 3 2 1

CNTENTS 21551

I have raised you up for the very purpose of showing my power in you,
so that my name may be proclaimed in all the earth.

Romans 9:17

WHILE THE WORLD LOOKS ON

*T*he Women's World Cup was indisputably the biggest sports story in the summer of '99. Never before in America had soccer been so celebrated. Never before in sports history had a women's team attracted so much attention as the U.S. Women's National Team. Never before in human history had a team of female athletes become such sudden worldwide celebrities.

The press quickly declared it a bigger-than-sports story as they searched for words to describe what was happening—calling it an "unprecedented phenomenon," a "historic milestone," and a "cultural watershed." The media just as quickly focused their spotlights on all those people who played significant individual roles in the bigger picture.

Here's just a small sampling of the World Cup media glare Michelle Akers experienced. This collage of news coverage sets the stage for The Game and the Glory.

FEBRUARY 14, 1999
The Chicago Tribune

The best women's soccer teams in the world will get their marching orders Sunday, but that is almost incidental. This weekend's Women's World Cup draw is, simply, an excuse to gather the clans and sound the heraldic trumpet call for what organizers hope will be the most successful women's sporting event ever.

"We're going into the biggest, best-known stadiums in America, and we want to fill those stadiums," Women's World Cup board of directors chairwoman Donna DeVarona said. . . .

May 16
Chicago Sun-Times

They're tough, they're confident, and they're on a mission. Most of us would find the mission too intimidating, but the U.S. women's soccer team has chosen to accept it.

The mission? World dominance.

As forward Kristine Lilly put it, "If we lose, we'll be bummed."

Sure, many of the players are proud owners of a shiny gold medal from the 1996 Olympic Games in Atlanta. They will tell you it's nice, but it's not the same as the World Cup. The United States gave that prize up in 1995, when it lost to eventual champ Norway in the semifinals. This summer the players plan to get it back. . . .

May 17
USA Today

With his introduction of the U.S. women's World Cup soccer team, coach Tony DiCicco has fired off a challenge to the rest of the world. "This is the best American team in history," he says.

But behind his confidence is the undeniable weight of winning back the trophy the U.S. women won in 1991, then lost in 1995. Anything less will be a failure. . . . Some view the women as the greatest American juggernaut since the original NBA Dream Team swept to the 1992 Olympic title. . . .

June 15
San Francisco Chronicle

In February, FIFA president Sepp Blatter declared that "the future of football is feminine."

Well, the future is now.

Beginning Saturday . . . at various stadiums around the United States, the 16 best female soccer teams from around the globe will be contending for their sport's highest honor, the Women's World Cup. . . . And the accolades will be coming from the throats of an anticipated half-million or more people who will attend . . . media are descending in droves, and every match will be televised by ABC, ESPN or ESPN2.

June issue
Elle

If screaming teens and tear-drenched pleas for autographs bring to mind a [rock group's] appearance more readily than a soccer match, this summer should change all that. Welcome to the Women's World Cup, the biggest affair in the history of women's sports, filling sold out arenas across the country beginning June 19. Held on U.S. soil for the first time, this once-every-four-years tournament has more television coverage, more nations participating and far more advertising tie-ins than the two previous contests combined.

"It's a breakthrough event," says Julie Foudy, the irrepressible co-captain of the U.S. team. "I'm not saying we'll convert the whole country, but America responds to big events, and this one is huge."

June 24
The Los Angeles Times

The war horse is being readied for battle once again. The attendants have done what they can to patch her up and prepare her physically and mentally. They have buckled on the armor and wished her luck. There is little more they can do.

Another tournament is underway and she is going out, as she has every year since 1985, to take on the world and show why she still is the finest, the most respected and certainly the most courageous women's soccer player of her generation.

[Michelle Akers] is ready. . . .

USA Today (Cover Story)

Every day for four years Michelle Akers told herself she'd be better off dead than having to endure her living hell.

In late 1991, only a few weeks after celebrating the biggest triumph of her athletic career, leading the USA to it's first Women's World Cup soccer title . . . hammering in 10 goals in six games, Akers was stricken with an extremely debilitating case of Chronic Fatigue Immune Dysfunction Syndrome (CFIDS). And instantly her perfect little soccer world was turned inside out and upside down.

Gripped by overwhelming fatigue, racked with intense migraines and haunted by depression and despair, day after day after day, Akers just wanted to climb into bed and pull the covers over her head, fall into a deep sleep and never, ever wake up again.

. . . Known for her never-say-die training sessions, Akers had to cut back to a bare minimum because any form of exercise totally wiped her out. Ninety minute soccer games became a thing of the past. If she could somehow manage to summon the strength to play 30 minutes, it was considered a huge accomplishment.

And no matter how much, or how little, time she spent on the field, in the locker room afterward, her teammates would always look on in horror as an exhausted Akers lay in a heap on the cold, cement floor, her eyes dazed and full of tears, numerous parts of her ravaged body packed in ice, as team doctors pumped at least two bags of intravenous nutrients into her system.

At 33, the starting midfielder is not only one of the oldest women participating in the World Cup, but according to Mark Adams, the physician for the U.S. women's team, she's also the only athlete, male or female, competing at a world-class level with CFIDS.

"Most people change their lifestyle to fit with the demands of the disease," explains Adams, who has worked with Akers and the national team since 1995. "Nobody [else] would dream of training at a world-class level, much less competing at it."

Chicago Tribune

Trust her, she has tried everything. She used to down the juice from two pounds of carrots daily. She has dabbled with every wild diet, a zillion exercise regimes, herbs and massages and visualization techniques.

In the end, the things that keep working best for Michelle Akers are praying and playing soccer.

"I'm not quite finished yet," said Akers. "While I can play and I feel like I'm being led to stay in this place, I have to bust my butt and do everything I can to maintain my place on this team." Akers' teammates say it over and over: The U.S. team is not the same without her.

"She gives us such a presence out there," said Mia Hamm, who has played with Akers for 12 years. "Whatever amount of time she has to put on the field, we want her. There's no one like her in the world."

JULY 5

The San Diego Union-Tribune

There was a cut on her forehead. Another gash across the bridge of her nose. Scrapes across her left arm. A bandage on her right wrist. A walnut-sized lump on the back of her head. Two bags of IV fluid.

In other words, just another postgame inventory of the injuries for Michelle Akers, the aging warrior of the U.S. Women's soccer team that defeated Brazil 2–0 yesterday at Stanford Stadium to earn a berth in the final of Women's World Cup.

There was one more checklist for Akers: one incredible defensive play; the neutralizing of Brazil's biggest star, Sissi; and the clinching penalty-kick goal in the 80th minute.

This is a woman who last February broke three bones below her left eye in a collision with another player. She has had as many knee operations (12) as she has World Cup goals. Then there is the chronic fatigue syndrome that since 1991 has caused her bone-weary exhaustion, migraines, and low blood pressure.

So there she was yesterday jumping high for a ball in midfield and smashing heads with a Brazilian. Then a few minutes later, pursuing a ball and taking Sissi's full cleat to her face.

"Every time Michelle goes down, we all hold our breath," said forward Shannon MacMillan. "The first thing we do is look for blood. Then we want her to get up. We say, 'Please don't stay down.'"

"She is such a warrior," added captain Carla Overbeck. "Every time we play, we know Michelle is going to leave all of herself on the field. She is an incredible part of this team. She means everything."

Akers has meant everything to the U.S. women's soccer team from the beginning. She was Mia Hamm before Mia Hamm. Before anyone cared about the women's team. She scored the very first goal. She scored two goals in the victorious final of the inaugural Women's World Cup in 1991. With 104 career goals, she is one of only four women on the planet to reach the century mark.

She's not the team's most prolific scorer anymore, but she proved again yesterday how valuable she can be. Her teammates call her Mufasa, after the proud father in "The Lion King," because of her mane of brown curls, and it was that mane that could be seen bobbing all afternoon near the shaved head of Sissi, the dangerous Brazilian midfielder most feared by the United States.

"She was my girl," Akers said with a grin.

Sissi barely sniffed the goal. . . .[1]

The Seattle Times

Michelle Akers looked as if she'd been mugged.

Again. And again.

She had a cut on the bridge of her nose and a scratch under her left eye. Cuts dotted and dashed across her knees.

Had she played a game of soccer or survived a motorcycle wreck?

She wore a bandage on her right hand from the two IV bags she used to revive herself after the game. She had tape around a finger.

"My whole body is pretty much a dull ache," she said yesterday after the United States' 2–0 semifinal win over Brazil in the Women's World Cup.

---

1. Copyright 1999 *The San Diego Union-Tribune*. Used with permission.

Midfielder Akers had taken a boot in the face from Brazilian striker Sissi. She had been kicked in the head—the result of another vicious tackle by Tania. There was a knot on the back of her head and an ache in her right shoulder.

She looked like she needed a medic, or a cut man, or a priest. She looked as if she had gone 12 rounds, not 90 minutes.

"I got my bell rung after that first kick in the head," she said. "I was a little wobbly. But I got a drink of water, took a deep breath and I was ready to rock."

Akers can take a punch.

Between the elbows and the boots, she composed 90 minutes of brilliant, all-purpose soccer. She was the anchor in the American midfield.

"You couldn't have pulled her out of that game with wild horses," Keeper Brianna Scurry said. "She was staying in there. You would have had to cut her leg off to get her out. She's a role model for everybody on this team. Whenever I get a little tired, I think of Michelle. I see her still pushing and that makes me keep pushing."

Akers won balls in the air. She won balls at her feet.

She cleared a dangerous ball intended for Sissi in the 35th minute when the Brazilians were attacking in tsunamis.

Her flick to Mia Hamm set up the run that resulted in a penalty inside the box.

And Akers' resulting penalty kick blurred past keeper Maravilha in the 80th minute, giving the U.S. the security goal it needed.

Imagine playing cornerback and wide receiver in the AFC championship game. Imagine running about six miles under a relentless sun. That was Michelle Akers' Fourth of July.

"You're my hero," Hamm told her as they walked off the field.

Akers, 33, suffers from chronic fatigue syndrome, and there are days she fights to get out of bed. Her body whispers warnings and suggests retirement.

She is playing this World Cup with a bad finger, a sore ankle, and a shoulder that is so bad she played most of last Thursday's game against Germany with her right arm held tightly against her side.

Ice bags and IVs are a regular part of her postgame ritual. She is an episode of "ER" waiting to be aired.

"In the battle, in the game of soccer, there is a high cost for winning," Akers said. "The feeling afterward—the performance of the team, and the unity and the excitement of a final that is approaching so rapidly—of course, I'm sitting back right now and thinking, 'Yeah baby, every second, every drop of blood, every scrape, everything has been worth it.'"[2]

JULY 6
The Los Angeles Times
It can be argued that this World Cup has done more for women's sports than any event preceding it, from turnstile counts to newspaper coverage to office conversation to word-of-mouth wildfire.

"My sense is that it is incredibly significant," says Rick Burton, director of the Warsaw Sports Marketing Center in the University of Oregon's college of business. "My prediction is that this event will be the starburst, the magic mushroom, if you will, that causes Madison Avenue to recognize the power of women in sports. . . .

"Not since the Beatles came here in 1964 have we seen anything comparable in terms of its sociological impact with American teenage girls."

The New York Daily News
. . . Akers manages to persevere as the ultimate symbol of the U.S. Women's National Team.

"It's a privilege to be her coach," U.S. coach Tony DiCicco said. "There has been no other woman who has played the game to her level. . . . She is a champion. Once again she left it all on the field. . . ."

"Every time I think she amazes me just about as much as she can, she amazes me with something else," said (midfielder) Julie Foudy. "It's unbelievable."

At one time Akers was an unbelievable scoring machine.

Before Mia Hamm, Akers was the first women's soccer superstar. . . . Her prolific scoring pace once was a goal per game. . . .

But in [the early 90s], she suddenly developed chronic fatigue syndrome. She had no energy. She couldn't walk, let alone run. She tried diets, various programs, and turned to religion. She is a devout Christian, which has helped her get through it.

"I wasn't thinking, 'Why me, why me? Poor Michelle,'" Akers said. "It was more, 'What does this mean? How do you want me to change?' That was the question I would shout at God."

JULY 7
Memphis Commercial Appeal

They are this summer's phenomenon—the U.S. women's soccer team that will play China for the world championship Saturday before a 90,000-plus sellout at the Rose Bowl.

They have brought fans into stadiums, average attendance 64,000 over five games, and they have brought something badly needed into big-time sports— a sense of fun. The women players genuinely like their sport—only a handful will get rich from it—and they genuinely like each other. Indeed the women mock their own togetherness in Nike commercials.

They are a rarity in the era of free agency, a true team. Sixteen of the 20 players have been together at least four years, and 12 of those at least six. They are patient and good-humored with their fans and, again a bracing change from the general direction of pro sports, remarkably free of egotism and self-absorption.

They are not, unlike the gymnasts network television discovers every four years, pixies. They are mature athletes. Two of the players, Joy Fawcett and co-captain Carla Overbeck, are literally soccer moms. America's infatuation with Team USA may only be a summer phenomenon, and America's growing acceptance of women's sports and the grudging acceptance of soccer as a big league sport is a slow process.

But make no mistake, these girls of summer are a landmark team in American sports, and the reason is in the stands and lined up outside the players' locker room. Those tens of thousands of young fans with the signature ponytails, the Team USA T-shirts, and the red, white and blue face paint are the girls of many summers to come.[3]

JULY 9
USA Today

Thirty years from now, a woman running for president of the United States will be asked about the defining moment of her childhood. She will answer without missing a beat, "The Women's World Cup soccer tournament." . . . [saying] that after the summer of 1999, she never felt silly or unpopular or out of place playing sports. . . .

That's how significant the past three weeks have been to girls and women in this country, and, to boys and men. To think on a scale of lesser proportions is to miss the impact of [this] event. . . .

---

3. Copyright 1999 *The Commercial Appeal*, Memphis, Tenn. Used with permission.

"We are at the epicenter of a big rock being thrown into a huge pond," said Michelle Akers, the 33-year-old heart and soul of the wildly popular U.S. team. "We don't know what the ripple effect will be."

The Arizona Republic

Sure, sports and politics shouldn't mix. But there's too much friction now between China and the United States for their clash in the Women's World Cup final to be just about scoring goals.

For some Chinese, a drubbing of the U.S. women in Saturday's eagerly anticipated match would help avenge the May 7 bombing of China's embassy in Yugoslavia by a U.S. stealth bomber.

"I really hope they lose face," said Wang Zhanjun, a Beijing factory worker. "Economically, militarily, we can't punish America, so we have to use soccer."

The New York Post

Keep a close eye on one player tomorrow. She will stand out.

Look for the one with the fluffy hair that trails out with each bobbing step, the erect 5-foot–11 frame that regally roams the midfield turf and, of course, the bloody scab and green and yellow bruise that spreads down the side of her nose.

Michelle Akers is playing in her last World Cup.

Oh, you'll probably see the 33-year-old in the 2000 Olympics and she might make a token appearance or two in this women's professional league being dreamed up for 2001, but she is stepping down as the dominant figure of the World Cup.

Everyone talks with wide eyes about the offensive prowess of Brazil's Sissi and China's Sun Wen, who lead the tournament with 7 goals each.

But in 1991, Akers scored ten goals in the World Cup including five in one game. She is the all-time leader in World Cup tallies with 12. . . .

July 10

The New York Times

No one could be disappointed by the way Michelle Akers has played in this tournament, and while some of her teammates now get more attention, not one has been more vital to the American success in reaching [the] championship match against China in the Rose Bowl. Akers, the first great star of this team—one who dominated the inaugural Women's World Cup in 1991 with 10 goals—can still control a game in defensive midfield the way she once did at forward. At 33, she is the oldest player on the team, and perhaps the most indispensable.

"She's the best woman that's ever played the game, period," said Tony DiCicco, the American coach.

The St. Louis Post-Dispatch

That's what today's game is. Your average, ordinary world championship soccer game between the planet's two remaining super powers in front of what is believed to be the largest crowd ever to see a women's sporting event. Ho hum.

Part

ONE

Finals Day:
July 10, 1999

Chapter One
WHO WILL
I BE?

$\mathscr{I}$ awakened before 5 A.M. as usual, alone in the quiet darkness of my hotel room. As always, my first thought wasn't about the World Cup; it was about my morning cup—of coffee. Black and strong.

On some less-than-conscious level I guess I was aware this was the morning of July 10, the day of the 1999 Women's World Cup soccer final. But my mind wasn't capable of confronting anything else until I'd stumbled across the room and started brewing a pot of Starbuck's "Gold Coast" from my own personal stash.

Awareness of the rest of the world seeped in only as the first cup of caffeine began to take effect.

I was hardly oblivious to all the hype and the attention the World Cup tournament had generated across the United States and around the world. In the past few weeks I'd talked to more reporters for more interviews than I could count. Friends and family had told me about some of the wonderful media coverage my teammates and I had received. But I hadn't been reading the papers or watching the television coverage.

Of course I realized the significance of playing in the final game at the Rose Bowl in front of 90,000 people with a worldwide television audience tuned in. Getting another shot at a world championship had been my professional goal and a major focus of my life and that of my teammates ever since the '95 World Cup and the '96 Olympics.

Certainly this promised to be a big day.

But despite the grandiose assessments of the media, I wasn't worried about the significance of this game on U.S.–China relations. I hadn't given any serious thought to the possibility of it being a sociological landmark, or a milestone in sports history. The importance of this game for the future of soccer and women's sports wasn't my concern either.

I couldn't afford to think about the day in such lofty terms. For me, the personal challenge I knew I had to face in the coming hours seemed plenty big enough. And the only way to meet that challenge was to begin the morning with my usual daily routine.

Like every morning of my life in the eight years since I'd developed Chronic Fatigue Immune Dysfunction Syndrome (CFIDS), when I woke up I did a mental check. I needed to know, *How am I feeling today?*

I'd felt better. But I'd also felt a lot worse. There was definitely a sense of tiredness—enough that I could tell I wouldn't know until I got on the field and started warming up just how much gas I had left in my tank. *No sense worrying about that now.*

Coffee mug in hand, I climbed back onto the bed and began my habitual quiet time of Bible study and prayer. That done, I pulled out my personal World Cup journal and tried to record my feelings. At the top of the page I wrote:

7/10—Game Day vs. China—The World Cup Final

I'm not sure what to think or what exactly I'm feeling prior to this game. I have a strange sense of destiny, of satisfaction, of call. It's like the calm before the battle, I suppose. All the preparation is behind me. Now it is finally time. Everything I need to give, everything I have to battle and play courageously, is stored inside, ready to be called upon come game time and the 90 minutes that will follow.

Nothing to do now but show up, be courageous, give everything, and see what happens. I have become acutely aware of how a moment can transform . . . or forever alter a person and their life. A collision, cleats to the face, a save off the line, one headball, a car crash, a simple statement, or a conversation with the press or an individual.

Before the Brazil game I stood in front of the mirror and looked into my own eyes to try to see into myself. I wondered, *Would I have the courage required by that challenge?* I noticed the black shadow still around my eye from my broken face back in February. I looked even deeper into myself and asked how different I would be after the game. *What would I find out about myself? What would transpire?*

I came home from that game having fought a valiant battle. Another guts game for me. But I had what it took, and I did not flinch or hesitate.

Today I peer into my eyes and ask the same questions of courage and destiny. Now I also see a cleat mark and a bruise on my face alongside the remaining black eye.

When I stopped writing to think about it, I realized why I felt so beat up. Game after game throughout the tournament, something new had happened to me physically that just added to the burden of my health and my body not working right—whether it was one more blow to my chronically bad knees, being kicked in the face, dislocating a shoulder, or getting my head cracked good any number of times. I'd had to be helped off the field a couple times in the Brazil game alone.

That was all taking a toll. And I knew from experience it was going to happen again. I was already weary and sick and beat up. And there was another ninety minutes to go today—with the entire world watching.

Our team psychologist, Colleen Hacker, who'd been with the Women's National Team for years and had closely followed my own personal ordeal, tried to encourage me. "Hack" (and a few other people closest to me) realized as we progressed through the tournament that, while everyone else's excitement and anticipation were rising toward the final game and a possible world championship, my own personal physical reserves were waning fast. Would I bottom out physically before I reached the summit we'd all been working toward for so long? Would I have the courage to not quit?

"Mish," our resident shrink had assured me earlier in the year when I'd become so discouraged that I'd had to pull myself out of a pre–World Cup game, "rarely in life are people tested so intensely, where everything is required of them to sum up the energy and the mentality to persevere like this. It's not as if you're going to have to train and push yourself to compete at this level for the rest of your life. You need to realize there is a light at the end of the tunnel. And you should recognize that you're going through an amazing period of your life right now that is going to result in a lot of growth."

I knew "Hack" was right. During the whole year leading up to the World Cup and now all during the tournament as well, I'd sensed God doing something very significant in my heart and life. But growth never comes without a price.

Sometimes it seemed like I'd been running this marathon obstacle course forever. Every game, every day was like one more hurdle, one more test placed in my path. I'd faced so many seemingly insurmountable challenges, expended so much of my energy reserves, and endured so much pain that some days I wanted to scream out at God, "That's enough! I can't go on!"

But when I did go on, I realized God was strengthening me, changing me, one day at a time. I was slowly learning that I didn't have to worry about the obstacles, about whether or not I could overcome them, or whether or not I succeeded in reaching my goals, or even whether I ever crossed the finish line. All that God expected of me was to be faithful, to take the next step. That would be enough, because He would make it enough.

Every day, every game I got through, every time of dealing with the media and telling my story, every training session, every physical therapy appointment, every night when I collapsed into bed, I would think, *All right! I've been faithful today.* I would fall asleep knowing I would get the rest needed to be ready to face another day. I couldn't predict what was coming, but I had a growing sense that as long as I was being faithful to what God asked of me—just to keep going—this journey would lead me to some place incredible.

Of course I felt the anticipation and the emotion building as our team sailed through the tournament on the resulting tidal wave of media coverage and public acclamation. Those things alone promised to make the final against China a huge game. But that wasn't what excited me. The usual competitive intensity and emotion hadn't been what had driven me in this tournament. My personal excitement, anticipation, and motivation was somehow connected to this pilgrimage of growth I was on.

I couldn't really understand it, let alone explain it. This drive wasn't an intellectual thing, or even an emotional thing. It was a heart thing. I just knew I had to be steadfast—to step up and step out one day at a time. *Would I be able to do that for one more game? What would happen if I did?* In my mind, those were the crucial questions that made this the biggest game of my life.

I knew in my heart this game would begin the next crucial part of my story—of my purpose. And that wasn't tied to the winning or the losing of a world championship so much as it depended on who I was and the kind of person I was becoming.

With that realization I finished my journal entry:

> Who will I be when I return to this room and look into the mirror after today's game? I don't know. But I think the key is that I'm willing to put myself on the line to find out.
>
> Joshua 1:9—"I hereby command you: Be strong and courageous. Do not be frightened or dismayed, for the LORD your God is with you wherever you go."
>
> Here I go!

Chapter Two

GOOD
TO GO

*N*o sooner had I finished my journaling and answered a few personal E-mails on my laptop, than it was time to join the rest of the U.S. Women's National Team for our traditional game day breakfast buffet in a private hotel dining room. As often happens, I was the first one there, just ahead of the coaching staff and Brandi Chastain. The rest of the team straggled in over the next few minutes, still half asleep. We all wore the same predetermined sweat suits—the usual policy for any required function—so that we looked like a team. Only the pj's sticking out of the warm-ups and the variety of uncombed hairdos poking out from under ball caps hinted at our individuality.

I had my usual water-based oatmeal and, of course, more coffee. Throughout the World Cup, several people would bring morning newspapers to breakfast to read the game reviews or whatever the sports pages carried about the tournament that day. If one of the team was profiled, someone would read that aloud while everyone else would laugh and make fun of them.

But I don't remember any banter this particular morning. Possibly, I tuned it all out to retreat into my own private world. But the more likely explanation is that everyone was quietly focused and ready to get the game underway.

Immediately after breakfast, we all retired to a small, adjacent conference room for a typical morning-of-the-game team meeting. For about thirty minutes Tony DiCicco and the rest of his coaching staff reviewed the game plan we'd talked about and refined in practice all week: possess the ball; change the point of attack often; play tough defense; take advantage of our scoring chances. And *have fun*.

Once that was covered, we signed up for individual meetings with Tony, and then went to get ready to leave for the game. I stopped by the equipment room for my uniform and personal laundry, then headed back to my room to pack my uni, shinguards, cleats, running shoes, game sweats, a change of clothes, and shower stuff. I rounded up a few snacks (granola bars, fruit, dry cereal) from breakfast and brewed some more Starbuck's coffee to pour into my special thermos for a pregame and halftime pick-me-up.

I had this routine down to a science. I could get all this, plus my wristbands, my Walkman loaded with a *dc Talk* tape, and of course, my camera, into my backpack and shoe bag.

That done, it was time to go meet with Tony, who sometimes uses these five-minute game day one-on-one sessions to motivate us. Typically, he spells out what our individual role will be, reviews our performance from last game, says what he expects from us, and then challenges us to step up to that assignment.

But Tony knows how hard I push myself, so our sessions are less motivational and more a quick review of what he wants me to concentrate on in a particular game. We'd played China many times and we'd talked about our strategy all week, so nothing Tony said to me that morning seemed surprising or new.

I understood my role very well. As "holding midfielder" my primary offensive assignment was playmaker, the quarterback of the offense. My job was to control the ball in the middle, to change the point of attack from one side of the field to the other, to get everyone else involved, and to distribute the ball ahead for my teammates.

On the attack, if we had a chance to press an advantage, I could move up, launch an outside shot anytime I got a chance, try to get my head on the ball in the box, and maybe even get a rebound near the top of the penalty box.

But the one thing Tony emphasized most was my defensive role. In addition to dominating the air, winning the 50–50 balls in the middle of the field, organizing the other midfielders (Julie Foudy and Kristine Lilly) into good defensive position, and calling for the forwards to drop in or track back for defensive work when needed, there was just one other challenge: marking up on China's leading striker, Sun Wen. Tied for top scorer in the 1999 World Cup with seven goals, she began a lot of her offensive runs from the midfield. So Tony expected me to know where she was and to track her whenever she came into my area.

That would be one tough assignment. The Chinese players are very skillful, fast, and quick all over the field. Their main strength is possessing the ball—knocking it around, combining with each other, and building from the back through the midfield—which forces opponents to spend a lot of time and energy chasing. If we let them play their usual game, it could be exhausting. And one of the more serious side-effects of my Chronic Fatigue Immune Dysfunction Syndrome (CFIDS) and an accompanying blood pressure disorder is that when I get especially tired, I no longer think quickly or clearly.

I get what they term "shocky"—my body starts going into shock as my blood goes to my vital organs instead of into my arms and legs. As my blood pressure drops, the blood flow to my brain diminishes, my mind gets mushy, and I lose concentration. A tornado roars in my head, my thoughts scatter, and my body feels weighted down and as slow as molasses. Sometimes I've actually gotten delirious on the field and had to be led to the bench by my teammates or the trainers.

I can't afford that this afternoon. If I'm tracking Sun Wen, I gotta be on. One half-second of distraction or a single mistake in judgment could cost a goal, or the game and a world championship.

"How are you feeling today?" Tony asked as we concluded our meeting. He always asks, and I usually give him the short version—leaving the details for the team docs to fill in. I knew my shoulder was in bad shape after falling and wrenching it again in practice the day before, so I had a long, painful day ahead. Yet there was no way that would keep me out of this game.

"I'm good to go!" I tried to assure him with a smile. But we knew each other too well, and Tony had been through this with me too many times to be fooled. I knew that he knew I couldn't be sure of anything until I got out on the field to see how my body responded.

We sometimes refer to game day as our "eat, meet, and eat day." So before long it was time for our pregame meal. And then the short bus ride across town, complete with police escort today, to the Rose Bowl.

Some bus rides are totally quiet, others chaotic. I have no idea what it was like that day because I spent the entire trip with my headphones on listening to *dc Talk*, staring out the window, and remembering my last trip to the Rose Bowl for a World Cup game. That was back in 1994 at the Men's World Cup. I'd seen Brazil win the championship that day. And when their team had celebrated by holding up the trophy and running a victory lap around the stadium, I'd thought back to our World Cup victory in 1991 and vowed to myself, "I want to celebrate like that again!"

Now here I was about to play in my own World Cup final in the same stadium. *Interesting how things have come full circle.*

Arriving at the Rose Bowl, we unloaded our gear and tried to make ourselves at home in the locker room. While my teammates are getting settled and waiting for our last pregame meeting, I routinely hurry to get dressed before anyone else, so I can take a quick jog on the field and loosen up before returning for a stretch and massage from our massage man or trainer.

I go through this whole process to get a feel for how my body is going to respond. Having a slow, progressive, extensive warm-up is crucial to my performance. Without it, I don't start the game feeling right.

I already knew my routine would be altered by the fact that the consolation game between Brazil and Norway was in progress when we arrived at the Rose Bowl. There would be no early on-field warm-ups for me. I would have to loosen up in the tunnel, dodging referees, FIFA bigwigs, and media and security personnel.

But then we got some news that really stunk. A FIFA official informed Tony that because the third-place game was running overtime, and due to the third place medal presentations, the championship game opening ceremonies, and the network broadcasting schedule, there would be no opportunity for *any* pregame warm-up on the field at all.

It wouldn't be the first time during the World Cup tournament our team would have to warm up in a stadium tunnel. *But this is the final!* I told myself. *This is unbelievable!*

Here we were playing a Women's World Cup final game in front of a packed-out Rose Bowl. We'd obviously come a long way since the days of the first National Team in 1985 when we played in used men's uniforms in front of a few friends and family. But we would still have to warm up in a tunnel. *Crazy. Absolutely crazy.*

I was truly ticked.

Our traditional last-minute locker room meeting focused on what to expect from our opponent. Afterwards I drank another half-cup of extra strong coffee and downed a peanut butter granola bar. Then there was nothing to do but go out into the dark, concrete bowels of the stadium and try to find ways to get loose. The team jogged back and forth, went through our stretching routines, and did whatever movement drills we could manage in the tunnel. I took out some of my irritation by repeatedly kicking a soccer ball against a cement block wall as hard as I could.

We'd done it before. Though it was irritating, we were all professional enough to do whatever it took to prepare ourselves to perform at our best.

A few minutes before kickoff we retreated again to the locker room to change into game jerseys. FIFA officials checked our cleats. Everyone got a last few sips of water, a sports drink, or in my case . . . well, you know.

The reserves always go out to the field ahead of the rest of us. But before they do, they file by the starters to dispense last-minute hugs and high fives. Each of us have our own little greetings or sayings that have become like a tradition. Tiffeny Milbrett and I always connect. I remind her to play her game and have fun. She always wants to know how I'm feeling and gives me a big hug. Tish Venturini always comes over and wishes me a good game. CP (Cindy Parlow) does the same.

Brandi Chastain and I had developed a little World Cup '99 tradition of our own. Once I get all my gear on, I have a meaningful Bible verse and the name of a person to whom I want to dedicate that game written on my sock tape just below my shinguards. At the opening game of the tournament at Giants Stadium I'd asked Brandi to write my personal inspirational message of the day on my socks for me. She'd done it every game since, always remembering to come over and ask me, "Who's this game for, Mish? What's the verse today?"

For the final, it wasn't the name of one person, just the Bible reference I'd recorded in my journal that morning. So Brandi took a permanent marker and wrote Joshua 1:9 on each sock. Then she used my camera to take a photo of her handiwork for my World Cup scrapbook.

Shortly after the reserves left, the starters headed out into the tunnel leading onto the field. There the American and the Chinese teams assembled in single-file, parallel lines against opposite walls of the corridor to await the ceremonial procession into the stadium.

I immediately noticed the Chinese goalkeeper, Gao Hong, wearing jersey number 1, and therefore at the very front of their line. She had earned her reputation as one of the best goalkeepers (GKs) in the world. But what intrigued me even more was the fact that she is an outspoken Christian. *How much guts does that take in a country where religion has been outlawed by the Communist regime and where millions of persecuted Christians can still meet only in secret house churches?* During previous games of the World Cup the media had noted her faith—which was no doubt why I'd received countless E-mails on my website telling me, "You have to get with this girl."

What people didn't understand was that there is absolutely no opportunity to interact with other teams during a World Cup tournament. Teams stay in different hotels, sometimes in different cities, and practice on different fields. If you do see each other it's at a press conference—there is no time to chat.

However, I felt a lot of respect for and curiosity about her. I stood midway back in the U.S. line (since my number is 10), looking toward Gao Hong. Suddenly, she turned and made eye contact with me. She smiled in acknowledgement, pointed to her heart, and then lifted her hand with her index finger extending upward toward heaven.

I nodded, gave her a little smile, and repeated the same gestures. To my surprise, she walked back down the tunnel, shook my hand, and then immediately returned to her place at the head of the Chinese line.

Since not a word was said, I can only assume Gao Hong's English is little better than my Mandarin. But that brief encounter meant something to me.

Moments later, the music began to play and the two starting teams marched side-by-side to midfield for the playing of the national anthems. More than 90,000 screaming fans stood to acknowledge our arrival, making it a real challenge for me to spot my family in the stands. I knew about where they were sitting, but with the size of that crowd and all the commotion I feared I'd never locate my dad for our usual pregame salute.

Shielding my eyes against the glare of the overhead sun, I finally saw the signs held by a long row of family and friends—one big bold letter per placard. It was at least halfway up the stands, but I could make out the message: "Pig Farmer #10." I had to laugh—it was an old family joke. For some time I'd even used the name as an alias—for privacy—whenever the team checked into a hotel. My teammates, who used some imaginative aliases of their own, thought it such a hoot when hotel switchboard operators answered calls from my room with "Yes, Ms. Pig Farmer, what can we do for you?" that Brandi Chastain gave me an official team jersey she'd had made with "Pig Farmer #10" on the back.

Now there was my personal rooting section holding their letters high so I could spot them in the crowd. I pointed at Pops and then gave him a big thumbs-up. I couldn't see his face clearly from that distance, but I knew he was grinning back, and his very presence made the game all the more special. Throughout my soccer career, my father's encouragement has always meant more than anyone else's. And I knew I needed that encouragement today.

We stood at attention at midfield as the national anthem played and a squadron of jets roared overhead. During the introductions, Mia reached over and slapped my shinguards—our longtime tradition. I remember a distinct feeling of calm filling me with a heightened sense of awareness: *This is it! The very last World Cup game of my career!* I wanted to soak it all in: the crowd, the anthem, the look on the Chinese faces, Mia and Julie Foudy standing on either side of me, our bench cheering us on, everything.

I remember telling myself, *You've got ninety minutes left. It's time to blow it out. Gotta score early and then hold the lead.*

Play. Score. Win. Go home. That was my personal game strategy.

With temperatures climbing into the nineties and field temperature well over one hundred, the kickoff took place under a clear sky and a blazing midsummer sun. The weather seemed to be conspiring against me.

Feeling near exhaustion soon after the start of the game, I struggled in the heat just to get into the flow of the action. I forced myself to focus on the specific elements of my assigned role one at a time—heading balls in the air, making tackles (stopping an opponent by stealing or knocking the ball away), winning control of the ball, maintaining possession, changing the point, serving the ball forward. But those things took so much concentration I had little left for tracking Sun Wen. *At this rate,* I told myself, *I'm not gonna last to the half.*

For years I had played striker, or center forward. I love to be in the attack. If I have the energy, I can usually create chances for my teammates or just find a shot on my own. But in the past few years, to protect me from the physical beating forwards get around the goal and to save me from the drain of repeated long runs, Tony and I had agreed I could serve the team better playing back in the middle. And ordinarily I enjoy my midfield role—defending, organizing, playmaking, getting my teammates in for a goal-scoring chance, and looking for an occasional long shot.

But as this final game began to unfold, we weren't creating much in the way of offensive chances. When the Chinese had the ball, I had to track their center forward or their attacking midfielder deep into our defensive end. And then, once we got the ball, I had to push up and get involved in the attack.

The effort was killing me. I knew I would soon be in big trouble if we didn't start controlling, maintaining possession, and keeping the ball in the attacking third (the Chinese end of the field), so I could rest a bit.

The pace was too frantic. As usual, the Chinese attack was intense. I was dying. It was as if my reserve tank had sprung a serious leak; I could feel what energy I had left steadily draining out on the turf.

If I'm going to make a difference I need to do it now. *I need to get forward and make something happen. I'm gonna have to score.* If that meant expending so much energy I had to take myself out early, so be it.

I began pressing forward, hoping to get a chance to score, so we could get a goal, relax, hold the lead, and go home World Cup champs. That's why I moved up when, in just the eighth minute of the game, the referee called a Chinese foul and awarded us a free kick from the left side some forty yards out. The moment Mia Hamm's right foot made contact with the ball, I sprinted into the box. No one picked me up. As Mia's shot bent toward the back post, I stretched out in a feet-first slide to try to redirect on goal. My lunging right foot actually contacted the ball in the air just a few yards out. But I couldn't control it. So what was more a deflection than a true shot sailed harmlessly to the right of the goal, over the end line.

I raced back into position for the goal kick thinking, *That may have been my one and only chance to score. If only I'd been a half-step quicker! Oh well, maybe I will get another opportunity.*

Then, in the twelfth minute, I stole the ball in midfield, dribbled past one opponent, ran past another, and saw my next chance. At thirty-five yards I'd created the slightest of openings and took a half-chance—blasting a long shot that Gao Hong easily gathered in for her first save of the day. I had been hoping it would go in or she'd bobble it, which she did. I'd also been hoping a teammate would be there to slot it, which they weren't. But you never know, which is why I'm seldom shy about taking an outside shot.

For the remainder of the first half, opportunities to score were few and far between. I withdrew into my playmaking position, won as many headballs as I could, marked and tracked my girl Sun Wen, and watched the clock tick down to halftime.

⚽ ⚽ ⚽

Neither casual fans nor the most expert observers could tell just how much Michelle was struggling. Indeed, ABC's television broadcasters repeatedly noted her effort—on the day and throughout the World Cup. When she just missed the deflection/shot in the eighth minute, play-by-play announcer J.P. Dellacamera exclaimed, "What a warrior Michelle Akers is for this U.S. team. She's had too many injuries to mention, yet she's been their best field player in this tournament."

Color commentator Wendy Gebauer, a teammate of Michelle's on the 1991 World Cup team, agreed, calling her "the most consistent player for the U.S. She's the heart and soul of the midfield as well. Her performances have been amazing."

A few minutes later, when Michelle took a hard tumble, the ABC announcers noted how she tucked her right arm into her body as she rolled, to protect the shoul-

der she'd dislocated at the North Korea game in Boston just two weeks before. And at another point where they noted her effort, Gebauer referred to her as someone "who has done more for this sport than any player in the world."

Due to a stifling U.S. defense, the Chinese got off only two shots the entire first half—neither of those on goal. Michelle's primary assignment, Sun Wen, seldom even touched the ball. Her only shot all half came on a free kick resulting from a foul. It flew high over the goal.

In the thirty-eighth minute, Michelle broke up China's most serious (and perhaps only real) threat when she sprinted into the goal box and dove past a Chinese player to head a loose ball over the end line and out of play. But that effort sent her sprawling to the turf again, sliding and crashing into the advertising signage at the end of the field.

As she slowly extricated herself from the broken barrier and limped back inbounds, the television commentators heaped on still more accolades. "'The best header in the world,' says Tony DiCicco," Dellacamera informed his viewers.

"Michelle never holds back," Gebauer commented.

Her broadcast partner added, "She plays every game like it's her last."

❂ ❂ ❂

I wondered for a while if that first half *was* going to be my last.

Chapter Three

DOWN
AND OUT

By the time we got to the locker room, I was so exhausted and sick I felt as if I were going to die. I have no idea what Tony and the other coaches told the team in their halftime talk. I had collapsed on the floor in the back of the locker room with a cold, wet towel wrapped around my neck and shoulders. With the help of the team trainer, I refortified myself with a couple of granola bars, some Gatorade, and as much coffee as I could stomach in hopes the caffeine would counteract my plummeting blood pressure. Despite everything we tried, I still had to sit down on the concrete curb of the tunnel as the team waited in the shadows under the stands for the halftime show to conclude on the field.

I had regained just enough strength that there was no way I was going to ask Tony to take me out. I had already decided, *I will play till I drop.* But I didn't know how much longer that would be. *What if I make a costly mistake before that happens?*

While I was sitting there feeling pretty discouraged about my own prospects for the second half, Dr. Mark Adams, our longtime team physician, walked over to me. "How's your shoulder? Did you fall on it?" he asked.

"Yeah," I told him. "That hurt. But it's okay now."

"How are you feeling otherwise?"

"I don't know if I'm gonna make it," I told him honestly.

He pulled me up, put his arm around me, and walked me out of the tunnel. "You'll make it. You're playing great! I know you're hurting. But you're gonna be all right. We need you out there, Mish. You can do it!"

Doc has been a constant source of expertise and support over the years as he's helped me battle through any number of injuries and cope with my

CFIDS. He's not just a medical man, he's often been my advocate and ally. Though I suspected his words were merely friendly encouragement, I chose to accept them as his professional opinion.

Doc is right. I've felt like this before. I am not gonna die. No matter how bad I feel, no matter what happens in the second half, I am going to be okay. At least eventually.

Just forty-five more minutes, I told myself. *I'll play minute by minute if I have to. I've done it before, and I can do it again. If I'm almost done, I'll at least play until I have nothing left.*

Putting on my best game face, I walked out to my position to start the second half—fighting to find that last bit of reserve I knew was there if only I reached deep enough. *Lord, help me be strong and courageous!* I thought.

☺ ☺ ☺

Michelle had spent much of her energy on the attack in the first half (taking two of the U.S.'s four shots, including the only one on goal by either team). Now, in the second period, she found herself in more of the defensive, holding role the coaches expected of her. But she continued winning headballs all over midfield, keeping track of Sun Wen, organizing her closest teammates offensively and defensively, trying to get the ball at her feet and play it ahead.

At the fiftieth minute, just five minutes into the second half, the U.S. took a corner kick. Michelle leaped above the Chinese defenders to reach the ball, but her header sailed over the bar. While that proved to be her last possible scoring opportunity of the game, she continued to make an impact as the relentless American defensive pressure held the Chinese to just five shots (only one of those on goal) the entire second half. Sun Wen's single second-half shot in the fifty-ninth minute sailed wide, and she never managed to get off another during the rest of regulation time.

☺ ☺ ☺

The second half started out even more physical than the first. In separate plays within the first two minutes, the Chinese knocked both Mia and me to the ground in violent collisions. I knew the rest of the way was going to be rough. I was also terrified that as I tired one of the Chinese girls would get loose for a half-step and score.

So my defensive effort was more about dominating the middle physically (so the Chinese would avoid me and my area) to prevent anything from starting that might lead to a goal. I quickly determined that as long as I could stay on my feet, my personal goal was to own the midfield and win every ball on the ground and in the air. Anybody in my area who wanted the ball was going to pay.

But I had to pay as well. In the sixty-seventh minute I took another tumble that sent searing pain through the nerves in my right shoulder. And in the seventy-fourth minute I experienced another memorable encounter when Mia lofted an indirect kick into the box in front of the goal. While she'd lined up the free kick, I'd moved forward and set up to make a run. As Mia's ball flew high into the box, I leaped to challenge for it as Gao Hong sprinted out of the goal to try to grab it. She got to it first, and I clipped her as I flew by and hit the ground.

I wasn't hurt badly. Just a charley horse in my quad. I'd hoped that challenging the GK a little would have made her lose concentration and drop the ball, giving us a chance to score. But she'd held on.

When I stood first, the referee added insult to injury by giving me a yellow card as penalty for contact with the keeper. As I limped to our sidelines for a drink of water, a trainer helped Gao Hong to her feet, and she hobbled around a bit as if she had a twisted ankle. But by the time play resumed a few seconds later, I realized she was fine. I also realized that probably hadn't been the kind of contact my E-mail had been suggesting I make with the Christian Chinese player.

The brief respite provided by our collision and the resulting "injury" time was not enough to dispel my usual late-game funk. Ever since I came down with CFIDS in 1991, I've noticed three crucial times in almost every game I play. It's like I hit a wall fifteen to twenty minutes into every game. If I can make it through that I seem to catch a second wind. But halftime is always another bear. It seems once I've stopped moving, it requires a superhuman effort just to get going again. When I can start the second half, I often actually begin to feel a little stronger as the game goes along until I hit another, seemingly bigger wall, right around the seventy-minute mark.

When that happens, it's like a hole opens up in the bottom of my soul. As the last of my strength drains out, I feel myself slipping away until I'm empty, just a shell with nothing but guts inside. Sometimes they too run out.

So anytime I manage to last until the final minutes of any game, I'm pretty much a zombie on the field. My teammates watch me carefully. When they see my eyes glaze over, Lil (Kristine Lilly), Julie Foudy, or team captain Carla Overbeck will literally get right in my face and yell at me, "Mish, stay in there! We need you!"

I usually respond to them, and I'm able to gather myself for the moment. But then it isn't long before I sink back into my stupor and can barely function.

The only way I can describe the sensation is to say it's like trying to play in a dark tunnel. Awareness of my surroundings fades along with my peripheral vision. All I can see or focus on is whatever is right in front of me—*if* I can just manage to really, really concentrate.

I was playing all alone in that tunnel during the final few minutes of regulation time. Ninety-thousand screaming spectators, the television cameras—everything—slowly disappeared into the growing darkness around me. At the end of the regulation ninety minutes, going into the two minutes of added injury time, I expended every bit of my remaining concentration just to follow the flight of the Chinese corner kick sailing toward me in front of the net. I saw nothing but ball as I leaped to head it away. I didn't notice any of my opponents challenging me. I never saw or heard my own teammate, goalkeeper Brianna Scurry, charging off her line.

When our paths intersected and Bri's arm smashed into the side of my head as she attempted to box the ball away, I had no idea who, or what, hit me.

Next thing I did know was that I was lying on the ground, my face pressed into the grass. I remember wanting to get up, but every time I tried to raise my head I started to pass out. I tried to move, but my entire body had quit working.

I felt no pain.

I'd survived harder blows to my head—that wasn't what kept me from getting back up. The problem was that I was now totally—physically, emotionally, and mentally—spent. Even the guts were gone.

I felt our trainer's hands on my shoulders and heard her voice. I tried in vain to respond. Exhaustion engulfed my entire body.

Eventually someone lifted me up. While I was half-guided, half-carried from the field I thought I heard the word "overtime."

My teammate Danielle Fotopoulos later told a writer that she heard me say, "I'm ready to go back in," when Tony asked how I was. Dr. Doug Brown, another team physician, had to give him the "she's-down-for-the-count" signal. And he was right. I was so out of it I didn't realize overtime had already started.

As badly as I'd wanted to finish this game, my teammates were now going to have to win or lose the world championship without me.

I spent the first of the initial fifteen-minute overtime period slumped on the U.S. bench, my eyes glazed, staring vacantly out from under a damp white towel someone had draped over my head and neck to relieve the heat and shelter me from the relentless sun. I didn't notice the crowd cheering. I didn't hear my teammates around me screaming encouragement to those on the field. I saw none of the overtime action unfolding in front of me.

Doc Brown sat right beside me on the bench, helping hold me upright. He must have kept talking to me, trying to assess my condition. But I don't remember hearing or answering any of his questions.

⊛ ⊛ ⊛

Realizing Michelle was more dangerously dehydrated than she'd first appeared, Dr. Brown summoned the team's equipment manager Dainis Kalnins to help get her out of the heat immediately. "We're gonna take you back to the locker room now," Brown told Michelle, fully expecting a protest. There was none. Probably because his words never registered.

Indeed Michelle recalls so little of what took place over the next few minutes— the next few hours, actually—that she's been able to reconstruct much of what followed that day only by hearing the accounts of others, reading news reports, and viewing videotape of what actually occurred. "It's pretty weird," she admits, "watching yourself on tape and thinking, 'So that's what happened!' But there's so much I just don't remember at all."

⊛ ⊛ ⊛

It was only four or five minutes into overtime when—with my towel-shrouded head down, my unfocused eyes staring toward the grass at my feet—I made the long, tedious trek from the bench to the tunnel at the end of the stadium. Dainis and Doc Adams, who was also on the field, each took an elbow and aimed me in the right general direction. I was somehow able to keep my feet moving—but they were mostly carrying me along the sideline toward the end zone.

I've seen the photos. I was not a pretty sight.

Somebody met us at the mouth of the tunnel and asked Doc Adams what he needed. I found out later that was Dr. Bert Mandelbaum, the chief medical officer for the World Cup.

"Can you please help me get her to our locker room?" Doc asked. He had everything he needed in there.

But after one look into the empty eyes staring out of my pale and pained face, Dr. Mandelbaum said "The triage room is closer." So they took me there instead.

As they carried me in we were met by a team of EMTs, nurses, and doctors, who served as the venue's medical staff. They laid me out on an examination table and Doc Adams quickly began his assessment.

By that time my blood pressure had plummeted to the point that I could no longer control my thoughts or my feelings. I instinctively tried to curl into a ball as my oxygen-depleted muscles contracted in violent cramps. My oxygen-deprived brain could no longer fight the pain or control my emotions.

I nearly blacked out. If that had happened, if I'd been able to relax enough to actually pass out, my blood pressure would have automatically regulated itself again. Instead I felt a panicky, desperate need to fight for breath until someone slipped an oxygen mask over my face.

I wept in agony as someone literally cut off my game jersey and got it out of their way while Doc patiently tried to straighten my arm enough to insert an IV. One of the other medical folks in the room asked Doc if they should transport me out by ambulance, or maybe radio for a helicopter to medivac me to the nearest hospital ER.

⚽ ⚽ ⚽

"I don't think that will be necessary," Mark Adams informed his colleagues. He'd seen these symptoms before. "This is what happens with Michelle after a lot of games." He had already determined that Michelle had not sustained a serious concussion from the blow to her head. He'd treated her for head injuries several times in the past; she presented none of her usual concussion symptoms this time. She knew who she was, where she was, and responded appropriately to what was happening around her. There were no indicators of serious neurological trauma.

"With the weather conditions that day, I was concerned that the heat was exacerbating Michelle's usual exhuastion symptoms," the doctor recalls. "We immediately turned a fan on her and cooled her with cold towels. That's why I cut her jersey off. And we started her usual postgame IV, which would also provide an internal cooling off as we packed her extremities in iced towels."

The doctor soon began a second IV to try to stabilize her even more quickly. He knew the standard glucose-electrolyte solution would quickly alleviate the cramping, and that Michelle's other symptoms would improve with the volume expansion of her blood stream. Her blood pressure was still below a hundred, but the IVs would help that. There seemed to be no indications of heat stroke. Michelle's heart rate was high—but all vital signs were within normal parameters for an athlete who'd just done what she'd done.

Because she looked a lot worse than she was, some of the medical team remained quite concerned. Dr. Mandelbaum assured his staff, "Dr. Adams has dealt with this many times."

Mark Adams nodded. "Once we get a couple bags of fluid in her, she'll stabilize. We have to do this all the time with Michelle."

⚽ ⚽ ⚽

I doubt anyone believed him. They must have assumed he was exaggerating. They looked at him as if he was crazy. Or maybe they thought I was.

With the IV finally in, as I relaxed enough to breathe normally and the fluids began slowly dripping into my arm, the tension in that treatment room also eased. Doc and the medical team turned some of their focus away from me and onto ABC's broadcast coverage of the game playing on a small television set on a table across the room.

Slowly beginning to return from wherever I'd been, I wanted to know what was happening. I wasn't yet mentally alert enough to follow the action on the screen or even to grasp what the announcers were saying. But whenever anyone in the training room exclaimed or groaned, I tried to ask, "What's the score?" I wasn't yet "with-it" enough to realize that in sudden-death overtime, the moment anyone scores the first (golden) goal, the game ends immediately.

I didn't need anyone to tell me the game was still going on. I knew by the constant roar of the crowd, rising and falling in a rumble I could feel as well as hear down in the depths of the stadium. I knew my teammates were still out there playing, and I desperately wanted to know how they were doing.

⚽ ⚽ ⚽

Out on the field, Michelle's team wasn't doing so well without her. As Sports Illustrated's coverage said, "The KO of Akers nearly revived the Chinese, who had entered the final with the tournament's most potent offense. For almost the entire game the Americans had harried China with their version of a full-court press—the 100 defense—which prevented the Chinese midfielders from giving quick support to their forwards. But with Akers off the field during extra time, the Chinese began attacking with greater abandon. After taking just two shots on goal in the game's regulation 90 minutes, they fired three in the 30-minute extra time . . ."

Michelle's teammates clearly missed her physical presence in the midfield—both her defensive dominance in heading contested air balls and her offensive ability to turn the action around and find an open forward to start an effective attack. While the overtime action still flowed up and down the field, once Michelle was gone the Chinese finally took the upper hand. The U.S. managed only a single shot of their own and would have lost except for what turned out to be the single most crucial (and heart-stopping) play of the entire afternoon.

In the tenth minute of overtime play the referee awarded the Chinese a corner kick which was lofted nicely across the goal mouth. As U.S. goalkeeper Brianna Scurry stepped off her line toward the ball, Chinese defender Fan Yunjie leaped high at the edge of the goal box and headed a powerful shot behind and past the charging keeper. For a split second, Scurry, the Chinese, most of the ninety thousand spectators, and millions more watching on television thought the game was over as the header rocketed right toward the opposite corner of the net.

But there was Kristine Lilly holding her defensive corner kick position—standing right on the goal line like a bulletproof wall. She actually got her head on the bullet to send it ricocheting away from the net. Then Brandi Chastain cleared the ball out of the box before there was even time to sigh in relief. It all happened so fast that it wasn't until most people saw the slow-motion replay that they realized the magnitude of what happened.

The Americans recovered enough to hold China to a 0–0 tie for the remainder of overtime play and force the eventual penalty kick (PK) shoot-out. If Michelle had still been in the game at that point, Tony DiCicco would definitely have picked her to take one of the five PKs. Known for having the most powerful shot of any woman in the world, she'd long been the U.S. team's PK specialist. But this time, like millions of anxious Americans, Michelle could only wait and watch how the drama played out.

☻ ☻ ☻

Even then, as out of it as I was, I realized that whatever happened, however this final played out—win or lose—this game wasn't going to be the end of my story. Any more than it was the beginning . . .

Part

TWO

When the Games Began: From Kid to College

Chapter Four

SORE
LOSER

*M*y parents could never tell me why, but the obstetrician who delivered me at a hospital in Santa Clara, California, on February 1, 1966, took one look at me and predicted, "You're gonna have your hands full with this girl; she's a stubborn one." My folks soon decided the man should have been a prophet.

The moment I got hungry or made up my mind I wanted something, everyone within earshot knew it. Neither of my parents got a lot of sleep when I was a baby. But it didn't seem to matter much, because they were young, in love, and excited about having a family. They didn't have much else; they actually had to borrow money from my grandparents to pay for my delivery before the hospital would let them bring me home.

Dad was a twenty-one-year-old ex-Marine and Mom a nineteen-year-old beauty school student when a mutual friend introduced them. They dated only a few months before they married. I was born the following year. Before long, according to my parents, I lived up to the doctor's prediction of stubbornness by showing remarkable persistence in learning to walk. They saw determination all over my face as I refused to quit trying, no matter how hard or how many times I fell down. By the time my brother, Mike, came along to complete our happy little family, I was already a hard-charging two-year-old terror with a lot of high-speed miles behind me.

Looking back now I can see we must have been pretty poor at the time. Pops worked long hours as a meat cutter at a local Safeway store while studying psychology part-time at nearby San Jose State University with the goal of someday becoming a professional counselor. Mom was a full-time homemaker who made most of our clothes on her sewing machine and served delicious made-from-scratch meals we ate together as a family at least twice a day.

We lived in a small subdivision whose developer had packed the cookie-cutter houses so tightly together that when we looked out our kitchen window we could see right through our neighbor's kitchen into the next house two doors down. Our home sat on a corner lot, so we had a larger lawn than most of our neighbors. And Dad built a tree house out back that helped make our big yard the center of attraction for all the neighborhood kids.

So my earliest memories are warm ones—highlighted by plenty of family love and togetherness. To me, our family life seemed every bit as "perfect" as any we saw on Sunday night television every week, when we'd all curl up in the living room to eat popcorn and watch *The Wonderful World of Disney* and *The Waltons*.

Mom regularly took Mike and me to see her parents, who lived in the nearby farming community of Dos Palos, California. We always loved that. Not only would we get to see our grandparents, but they had a built-in swimming pool we could never get enough of. We'd run out to the pool as soon as we arrived—and first thing every morning if we'd slept there overnight. But since we were so small, we could swim only if an adult was in with us. Which is why I vividly remember sitting for what seemed like hours on the edge of the pool, impatiently swishing our feet in the water as we waited for Mom or Grandma or someone to come out of the house and say, "Okay. You can get in now."

The four of us frequently attended Grandma and Grandpa's church with them. But often we went by ourselves as a family. I hated wearing Sunday dresses even more than I dreaded having to sit still through the long, dry services. I believed in God, but it seemed the people I saw at church were about as cold, lifeless, and stiff as the old pews we sat in. And the rules they lived by seemed just as rigid.

I never felt I could be myself in church, where it seemed everyone expected me to be a sweet little girl in a pretty dress who read quietly, played with babies, and always stayed nice and neat. I definitely didn't fit that mold.

Informal family time held much more appeal, whether it was helping Mom do gardening, holding nails for Dad while he tackled some carpentry project, or just watching over Dad's shoulder and handing him tools while he worked on his truck. I enjoyed spending time with my family, especially after-dinner ball games with Pops and Mike out in the yard. We'd play whatever sport was in season.

When we were real young, football was our favorite. Dad would send Mike and me out for long "Hail Mary" passes until his arm got tired. I'd pretend to be Mean Joe Green snaring a touchdown pass from Terry Bradshaw. (I didn't care that he was a defensive lineman; I just figured he could do anything because he was big, mean, and tough.) And I'd lie in bed at night dreaming about growing up someday to play for my favorite team: the Pittsburgh Steelers.

My favorite outfit—which I'd have worn to school every day if Mom had let me—was a pair of dark, forest green, double-patch Tufskin jeans, Keds tennis shoes, and my official Steelers jersey with Mean Joe's #75 clearly visible beneath the braids hanging down my back.

My penchant for sports wasn't always met with the same appreciation and approval at school as it was in my family and among the neighborhood boys who regularly congregated in our yard to play. I remember crying the day a first grade teacher told me, "Little girls don't play football."

But by third grade at Montague Elementary, I stubbornly refused to accept such stereotypical opinions. I remember the day in PE when the boys stayed on the school playground for a kickball game while our teacher escorted all the girls to a nearby park to play on the swings. I told the teacher that, one, I wanted to play kickball, and two, I wasn't going to the park to swing. To underscore my declaration, I promptly plopped myself down on the nearest park bench and refused to move. Three other girls soon joined my little sit-in—not because they wanted to play kickball, but because they just liked me and wanted to be supportive.

The frustrated teacher sent all four of us to the principal's office. When it was quickly determined who the instigator was, the other girls were dismissed back to class. My mother was called and asked to come to school for a conference and to take me home for the day. She showed up a few minutes later. I sat outside by the secretary's desk while Mom and my principal held what seemed like a very long, closed-door meeting.

When Mom finally came out, she took me by the hand and we went home. But she and the administrator had evidently reached an understanding. The next day, and every day thereafter, my teacher allowed me to play kickball with the boys.

I don't know how much that particular incident influenced her decision, but that was the same year Mom signed me up for my very first soccer team, the Cougars, in a local police athletic league, and volunteered to be assistant coach herself. Since I was clearly the most aggressive player on the team and the only one unafraid of diving for the ball in the mud, the coach immediately made me goalkeeper.

I hated it.

Our team wore pink and yellow jerseys. Girlie colors. Yuck!

But what I despised even more than our uniforms was losing every game. Our team of eight-year-olds just couldn't compete with the nine- and ten-year-old teams in our league. I learned right away that there's only so much any goalie can do.

Week after week we'd get slaughtered and I'd cry all the way home, angrily declaring that I was *not* going to play the next week. But assistant coach Mom, and Dad, who came to cheer every game, refused to let me quit the team.

I suspect they hoped this soccer experience could help me channel my intensely competitive nature and learn to better control my anger at the same time. I obviously needed help in both areas.

Even by the age of eight, I was driven by the need to win. Whether it was the family playing Monopoly on the kitchen table or a tackle football game with neighborhood boys out in our yard, I *had* to come out on top. When I didn't, I would pout, stomp off, cry, slug the winner, or simply explode. I absolutely *hated* to lose—at anything.

I remember the day an older boy challenged me to a race at school. I knew I was the fastest kid in my grade, and I could outrun most of the boys in my neighborhood. But even though I suspected Greg could beat me, I wouldn't back down.

The two of us lined up in actual racing lanes painted on the asphalt playground for what was probably a forty-yard sprint. A bunch of kids gathered to watch. Someone said, "On your mark, get set, GO!" And we took off.

Greg beat me across the finish line. But when he slowed down, I tackled him and beat him up. I got in trouble both at school and at home that day. And there were enough other temper-related playground incidents, involving everything from tether-ball to four-square to jump rope, for my parents to definitely know I had trouble losing graciously.

However, my combative nature and experience had its positive side as well. I remember standing in line waiting my turn during a kickball game one day during recess when I saw my first grade brother Michael running across the playground crying.

"M-m-michelle," he blubbered, pointing back in the direction he'd come from, "that big kid over there said he was gonna beat me up. A-a-and he knows karate."

The kickball game had to wait while I marched across the school play-ground to confront the older boy who'd been bullying my little brother. "Don't you pick on my brother!" I told him, punctuating my words with a shove.

I don't know if he'd seen me beat up Greg or if he learned my reputation by talking to kids from the neighborhood. Or maybe he was just a cowardly bully. Whatever the reason, he immediately backed off. Message delivered, I trotted back to my kickball game before I lost my turn.

That wasn't the last time I tried to protect my brother. And some incidents involved a bit more violence. I didn't hesitate to stand up against anyone who messed with Michael. Like the time walking home from school when an older kid taunted my six-year-old brother and made him cry by calling him a vul-gar name. I yelled names back at him and persuaded Mike to ignore him.

Another day, when I was tooling around the school playground after school with Mike on the back of the big banana seat of my red Schwinn bike, a couple older kids knocked us over and snatched a green camouflage cap off my head. "Give it back!" I yelled. My dad had worn that hat in the Marines; since he'd given it to me, it was one of my prized possessions. Making sure to keep Michael behind me, I screamed in rage as I lit into our tormentors—my fists flying. One of them punched me in the mouth, and things were about to esca-late from there, when a teacher rushed over to break up the fight and retrieve the hat for me.

Our family moved to Seattle, Washington, the summer before fourth grade, soon after Dad completed his college degree at San Jose State. He'd found a better job, as manager of the entire meat department for another Safeway. My dad's new position enabled him to work days and attend graduate school classes at night at Seattle University. He also found us a bigger, two-story house in the old north Seattle neighborhood of Lake Forest Park, situated not far from the northern shore of Lake Washington.

I experienced those typical feelings of uncertainty that come when leaving a familiar environment and starting over in a very different place where I had to prove my mettle to a whole new neighborhood and school crowd. I'd made the all-star baseball team in Santa Clara, so I enrolled to play baseball once we got to Seattle, thinking it would be a good way to make new friends. We had, however, moved into a real hotbed of youth soccer in the Northwest. So despite my less than positive first-year soccer experience back in Santa Clara, Mom also signed me up for the Shorelake Soccer Club U–10 Thunderbirds.

The coach let me play center midfielder, where I saw a lot more action than I'd ever had as goalkeeper. I soon discovered I absolutely loved the game. It also helped that the Thunderbirds won far more games than we lost . . . and that the uniforms were a more acceptable color—green.

Mom got me to all my practices and volunteered as team mother. Dad also came to every game, which I appreciated because his approval had always meant so much to me.

Pops did have one habit that drove me nuts. On the rare occasions we did lose, I would get so angry I'd sit in the backseat and fume all the way home. Every time that happened my father would try to use his best (or worst) psychology to lighten my mood. Sometimes he'd try to tease me and make me laugh. That only made me angrier.

Then he'd resort to reasoning. "It's just a soccer game, Michelle."

Like I don't know that. That's not the point.

"Did you have fun, Michelle?"

"NO!" *Of course I didn't have fun. We lost! Losing is never fun!*

For such a smart guy, I thought my Pops could be pretty dumb. *He just doesn't get it!*

But as much as I hated to lose, I loved playing soccer even more. I loved to push myself. To go hard. To compete. To give everything I had. To overcome tough odds. And, of course, to win.

Playing with the Thunderbirds was fun. We spent most of every practice just scrimmaging, among ourselves or against an older Shorelake Soccer Club team. I thought that was a blast. I even enjoyed the running and the basic drills we did to improve our passing and dribbling skills. No matter how often or long the coach practiced us, I always wanted to do more—coming to the field early or staying late to take extra shots or to work alone on my dribbling.

Any day I couldn't persuade Michael and a few neighborhood friends to walk over to Brookside Elementary for a pickup game on the playground, I'd take a ball outside and practice on my own in the yard. I'd use the side of the house or the garage door for the goal and boom shots off it until my legs ached. Then I'd imagine our dog and my pet goat, Peter, as defenders as I dribbled over, under, around, and through the trees and bushes in our backyard. And after I wore out all opposing pets and vegetation, I'd juggle for awhile, always counting the number of times I could bounce the ball with my feet, my knees, and even off my chest and head without letting it hit the ground. I would forever compete—even if it was just with myself—trying to do everything harder, faster, or longer than I had the time before.

⚽ ⚽ ⚽

In the summer of 1975, when she was nine years old, Michelle received a scholarship to spend a week at Northwest Soccer Camp out on Whidbey Island. It was run by Cliff McCrath, longtime soccer coach at Seattle Pacific University. Cliff, a nationally known and respected promoter and pioneer of North American soccer, has been coaching the sport for more than forty years. He's seen thousands of kids come through his program, many of whom have gone on to become successful soccer stars in their own right. But he says Michelle Akers was special. He's compared her to Halley's comet, a once-in-a-lifetime wonder.

"I remember vividly the first time I laid eyes on her," Cliff says. She looked like "a typical, spindly legged, somewhat impish nine-year-old. But that was where any comparison to a typical nine-year-old girl ended. Because she was playing soccer. And she took to the task with a vengeance—make that a fury. She not only despised losing, she hated anything that smacked of mediocrity. She wanted to be the best.

"To be perfectly honest, she was a pest. Because she never got enough of anything. She always wanted to do more—more shooting, more touches, more of whatever drills we were doing. She would wear the staff out.

"For example, her third year at our camp, when Michelle was eleven, she took part in the finals of that week's juggling competition. We made the mistake of starting the contest late on the last morning . . ."

The contestants all started at the same time to see who could keep his or her ball going without hitting the ground for the longest period of time. Each of them had a non-contestant helping them count their touches. This event usually took a very few minutes. And, indeed, on this day the balls began hitting the ground and everyone soon dropped out . . . everyone, that is, but Michelle, who kept going strong. She'd bounce the ball off the top of one foot for a while, then switch to the other foot. Then she'd lift her knees and juggle the ball from one thigh to the other, occasionally lofting it high enough in the air to bounce it off her head a time or two before dropping it and catching it with her foot to start the routine all over again.

Other campers circled around to watch. Before long, the excited buzz drew staff from all over the camp. Some watched in silent admiration, others called out encouragement. Before long a few people tired of standing and took seats on the ground. As amazement faded to numbing routine, lunchtime came and hungry campers went, straggling off slowly in twos and threes, looking back every few steps to see that Michelle was still going, probably figuring they could come back after lunch to see what happened. Somewhere along the line, Cliff McCrath had taken over counting for Michelle. "She'd long since shattered the camp record previously held by a boy who went on to play collegiate soccer at Duke. But she wanted to go further . . . and further . . . and further. After an hour or so, I think I was the only one remaining out there with her," he recalls. "Still she kept going."

All the way to 5,392 touches. "And she didn't miss the ball then," McCrath says. "Her neck got stiff, she got bored and hungry, and simply decided to quit and go eat.

"That was Michelle. From the very beginning she always defined for me what great athletes have that is not coachable. She had it inside her—total commitment, supreme effort, and disciplined determination."

But not all areas of her life were as positive for Michelle as sports were after the Akers family moved to Washington.

✿ ✿ ✿

I guess my parents had some rough times even when we lived in California. I was perhaps too young to notice back then. But tension in their marriage definitely increased after we moved to Seattle. Many were the nights I'd lie in bed up in my room and hear them arguing downstairs.

My mom applied to join the Kenmore Fire Department during my fifth grade year. When I found out what she wanted to do, I was all for it. Other kids' mothers had unexciting jobs like teachers and secretaries; my mom was going to be a firefighter. I thought that was pretty cool. And when she successfully completed her training to become the first female firefighter in King County, Washington, I was extremely proud of her.

Yet the problems between my parents intensified. I'd pull the covers up over my head and try not to listen. They'd be downstairs behind a closed door or two, so I never heard enough specifics to know what they were fighting about. But those arguments grew louder and more frequent. And I didn't have to make out the words to know the anger behind them. The pain echoed through the entire house, up the stairs, and into my heart.

I remember one particular night in sixth grade when I decided I couldn't take listening to them yelling at each other again. I couldn't lie there and ignore it any longer. I climbed out of bed, slipped quietly downstairs, and hesitantly walked in on them in the den.

Everything got suddenly quiet. Mom said, "What are you doing up, Michelle? We thought you were asleep long ago."

"What's wrong?" Dad asked, noticing my tears. "Why are you crying?"

I told them I was afraid because, "I don't want you to get a divorce."

They both gave me big hugs and reassured me they weren't about to break up. I believed them and went back to bed feeling so relieved I fell right to sleep.

But on an even more memorable night a short time later, Mike and I had already gone up to prepare for bed when our parents called us back downstairs. "We've got something we need to tell you," Mom said as they took us into the family room. I remember sitting on her lap in a big old rocking chair. She put her arms around me as she said, "Your dad and I have decided it will be best if we get a divorce."

My first reaction was shock. Then anger. And then confusion. *They lied to me.*

They assured us that it wasn't our fault. That they loved us both very much and always would. They told us they were still our mom and dad and we'd always be a family. They explained Dad was going to be leaving that night, though he assured us he would find a place to live nearby and see us as often as possible.

The more they tried to make it sound okay, the angrier and more confused I felt. Michael and I were both crying as we went back upstairs and Pops began collecting a few of his personal belongings.

A few minutes later I stood with my brother looking out of his upstairs bedroom window. Below in the darkness our father walked slowly to his truck in the rain with a single pillow tucked under his arm. We watched through our tears as he backed out of the driveway and drove off into the night.

Mike and I were still crying when Mom came upstairs to check on us a few minutes later. So she let us both sleep with her that night.

The next few nights my brother slept with me. And every evening for a long time after he'd begun sleeping in his room again, I'd lie in my bed and look out my door across the hall into Mike's room. I'd see him kneeling there in front of his window. His hands folded in prayer, he'd be pleading with God to bring Dad home and put our family back together again. Night after night, I witnessed my little brother's pain as he bowed by that window, watching and waiting for God to answer his prayers.

I didn't bother to pray. I was angry at God. What did He care? Praying obviously did no good.

Chapter Five
WALNUT WARS
AND WORSE

*E*ven if I couldn't pray, I could at least hope that something would happen to bring my parents together again. Perhaps I could do more than
just hope.

For months after our parents' separation, Mike and I carefully watched for
the mailman every afternoon. Anytime we spotted a legal-size envelope with
Mom's attorney's return address, we swiped the envelope and threw it away
long before Mom got home to check the mail. We hated the guy for helping
to break up our family.

Even then I think I knew we couldn't delay the process for long. Still, Mike
and I grasped at any and every reason for hope.

I remember our whole family was invited to some relative's wedding. All
four of us sat together in one pew. Mom sat on one side of Mike and me, Dad
sat on the other. At one point in the ceremony I recall noticing, out of the corner of my eye, that Mom and Dad had reached behind us and were actually
holding hands. Mike and I exchanged looks and I thought, *They're gonna get
back together for sure now.*

But after the wedding ended, nothing changed. We went home with Mom,
and Pops headed for his apartment.

Mike and I both really missed our father. He lived close by so he could stay
involved in our lives. He still came to all of our soccer games and school programs. We knew we could call if we needed him for anything—or just to talk.
But it wasn't the same.

We looked forward to having our once-a-week supper with him, especially
when he'd take us out to eat at the local Dairy Queen. We always ordered the
biggest burgers, fries, Cokes, and, of course, a huge soft-serve ice cream con-

coction with enough extra hot fudge and peanuts that I crudely renamed it Peanut Butter Barf-ait because it contained enough sugar to make any kid sick.

Less exciting than DQ were Dad's home-cooked meals. For the longest time his culinary skills limited him to hamburger, which he invariably overcooked into charred hunks of dry meat you could only barely salvage by drowning them in ketchup and gulping them down with large swallows of water.

What his entrees lacked, however, Dad made up for with dessert. While he cleaned up the kitchen after dinner he always sent us to the grocery store across the street from his apartment to buy a half-gallon of whatever kind of ice cream we wanted.

It would have been any kid's dream, except for one thing: Pops would always pull out an old coffee can full of change, then count out the price of a half-gallon in pennies, nickels, and dimes. Embarrassed to walk into a store with a bagful of change, we'd always complain, "C'mon, Dad. Can't you give us some regular money?"

He'd always respond, "What are you talking about? Pennies are money, too."

Mike and I would finally give up and go to the store. And after arguing over what flavor (I always wanted mint chocolate chip), we'd look for the shortest checkout line and hand the cashier our bag of treasure. The clerks always said the same thing: "We can't take loose change like this. You need to get it rolled."

"We're sorry," we'd apologize. "This is all we have. Here, we'll help you count it." Meanwhile, we were dying a thousand deaths as the line behind us quickly became the longest, with everyone in the store looking at us like we had the plague or something.

When we finally escaped and rushed home, we'd recount our adventure to Dad, insisting that he get his pennies rolled so we wouldn't look so stupid next time.

Pops would just laugh and shake his head. "You got the ice cream, didn't you?"

Yes, we did. And with enough chocolate syrup poured over it we found it an excellent antidote for our humiliation.

This was also about the time Dad started his running career. He'd been a big smoker for years—Mike and I had bugged him to quit for as long as I could remember. We'd toss his cigarettes in the toilet, hide them, break them, or just throw them away. Finally, he decided he'd quit for our sakes and stopped cold turkey.

He began jogging about the same time. I remember him coming back in the house one day to announce, "I just ran a whole mile."

I was like, "Big whoop, Pops!" *One measly little mile.*

I never dreamed that one little mile would lead to marathons, long hikes up rugged mountainsides, and a lifetime trying to keep up on my bike while he cruised roads and hiking trails all over the world.

Every other weekend we'd spend with Dad doing something fun—going to soccer games, hiking, camping, taking a ferry over to Bainbridge Island. He really worked to maintain his relationship with us.

The year after he and Mom broke up, he finally completed work on his master's degree. Mike and I got to see him graduate. I even took pictures to record the occasion. We knew this was a big deal. Dad had been able to go to school only part-time because he'd had to work and support us too. So it had been a long haul. We were very proud that he'd reached his goal.

After graduation, we took him out to celebrate at a fancy-schmantzy restaurant on the waterfront in downtown Seattle. We ordered, and our waiter brought us our food. We started to dig in and, as Pops cut his steak, his knife slipped and dragged the meat off the edge of his plate. We all saw the steak go, like it was in some kind of slow motion. It flopped on the floor, landing right in the path of other diners walking by. People stopped and stared. My dad just casually bent over, picked it up, and set it back on his plate like nothing had happened.

Then he and I started laughing hysterically, but Mike was mortified. He thought it was even worse than buying ice cream with pennies.

Still, no matter how much fun and laughter we shared with him, despite his personal and professional accomplishments, or how hard he tried to act as if nothing had changed, Dad could never quite completely disguise his deep, underlying sadness. I couldn't help feeling sorry for him.

Mom didn't seem to have the same trouble adjusting to the end of their marriage. Perhaps because her whole life was changing at once.

Where Dad made a gradual career change over the next couple of years, continuing to work for Safeway as a meat department manager while simultaneously beginning to develop his career in psychology with a part-time counseling practice, Mom had already made a much more sudden and complete transformation. From homemaker to firefighter.

I was proud of her too. The fact that she accomplished something most women wouldn't think of attempting made me believe anything was possible. As the first woman in her department, Mom took a lot of grief. But she refused to back down. She was passionate and committed—two traits I inherited from her.

Of course I inherited just as much of my make-up from my Pops. The same kind of dogged persistence that kept him pursuing his dream of a career in psychology from the time I was born until I was thirteen years old has served me well over the course of a long soccer career. Dad isn't overtly competitive, he competes more with himself—pursuing an inner challenge and setting his own standard of measurement only he knows if he meets. He likes pushing himself to the edge physically—testing the limits to see what he is made of. When he runs marathons or hikes through the wilderness, he reaches a point near collapse before he allows himself to stop. Sound familiar?

So, in truth, I must admit inheriting a good measure of strength and stubbornness from both parents.

Unfortunately, at the very time I began sorting out who I was and understanding how I was like and different from my parents, they were both gone. At least they didn't play the same role in my day-to-day life they always had. While I never doubted they loved me, I was left to figure out a lot of other early adolescent issues pretty much on my own.

As a firefighter, Mom worked a crazy schedule. She'd be on duty for twenty-four straight hours, then off for forty-eight. She'd leave for the station in the morning before we went to school and we wouldn't see her again until we got home from school the next afternoon. Mom always called in the afternoons to make sure we got home from school okay. And she usually had a casserole or something else she'd fixed and left in the refrigerator for us to heat up for supper. She did a good job of making us feel cared for and accountable.

As a by-product of our unusual new family schedule, I gained a larger measure of independence and responsibility than most twelve-year-olds. And it happened not gradually throughout adolescence—but literally overnight.

We'd always been required to do chores, but when Mom went to work we were forced to step up our responsibilities. I took charge of the household when Mom wasn't there. Mike and I both set our own alarms to get ourselves up and off to school. We'd fix breakfast and pack our own lunches every morning. In the afternoons we usually had a list of chores Mom had left for us—vacuuming, dusting, washing dishes, doing our own laundry.

Worst of all, in my mind, was the gardening. Mom wanted a big garden, whether she was home to care for it or not. So Mike and I watered and weeded and pruned and picked for what seemed like forever every day after school and during the summer. We constantly complained about the hours we spent cutting strawberry runners or thinning carrots before we could go play with our friends. The upside was awesome strawberries and the best carrots I ever tasted.

It wasn't all work. Neither was it all positive. We had to learn to settle our own disputes and cope with our own cuts and bruises. And there were plenty of those since Mike and I were still kids.

One time when we were on restriction and not allowed to go outside, we figured Mom would never know. We snuck out to play on a rope swing our neighbors had attached high in an evergreen tree. Being the daredevil I always was, I sprinted as hard as I could and swung higher and farther out than ever before. When I came down, I crashed into a stump that caught me square on the shin. I fell to the ground screaming, rolling and writhing in pain.

Mike, not knowing what else to do, figured he'd ease my pain by swinging on the rope and making faces to get me to laugh. I was in so much agony I couldn't even sit up, and here was my brother swinging back and forth above me acting like a monkey.

It worked. I told him to keep it up for a while. Then he dragged me back to the house and we waited for Mom to come home. She took one look at my black-and-blue shin, which by that time had swollen to the size of a grapefruit, and rushed me in for x-rays. The doctor told us no bone was broken, but he'd never seen an injury that serious without a break. It seemed to take forever to heal.

We instigated our share of other minor mischief as well. And it seemed we always got caught. Like the time our Aunt Gini down in California sent walnuts to our family for Christmas. We had piles of them. So while Mom was at work one day, Mike and I staged a walnut war in the living room with some neighborhood kids. We rearranged the couch and other furniture as bunkers, behind which we stored our "ammo" in piles and threw them at each other with all our might. Walnuts exploded against walls, shells flew everywhere. Occasionally we even hit each other. When we ran out of walnuts, the war was over.

We were smart enough to realize we needed to clean up after our escapade, so we put all the furniture back in place and started vacuuming up the shell fragments. We noticed the burning smell just before the vacuum quit. Apparently we had vaccuumed up more than just fragments.

No matter what we did, we couldn't dislodge the walnut stuck in the vacuum. So we carefully crawled around on the floor picking up all the bits of walnut shell we could find with our fingers and then stored the machine away in the closet. As if Mom would never vacuum again.

A few days later Mom pulled out the sweeper, and when it didn't work, she took it apart to find the jammed shell and half a vacuum bag full of broken walnuts. She naturally asked us what had happened, and I was such a bad liar that she had the truth out of me in no time. She put me on restriction again and sent me to my room. She says she found walnuts in the furniture, the curtains, and scattered in odd places around the house for months afterwards.

We lived in a cluster of houses on top of a hill with a ledge overlooking 178th Street below. If we ever got really bored, Mike and I would hide along with some of the other neighborhood kids up on that ledge and toss pine cones or snowballs (depending on the season) down at passing cars.

One time Mike and a buddy tossed a snowball that must have had a rock in it because it broke out a light on a vintage Corvette. Fortunately I'd gone in for a bathroom break, because the dude pulled over, ran up the hill, and chased the boys through the woods until he got tired and gave up. I witnessed the whole thing from the bathroom window and stayed inside until the coast was clear again.

I felt a satisfying sense of independence and freedom during those days, not just when we were playing, but also in the duties I assumed around the house. With both Mom and Dad only minutes away with a phone call, I don't remember ever being consciously worried or scared about not being able to deal with an emergency. Only now, looking back, do I realize the responsibility weighed heavier than I recognized at the time. Which may explain why the occasional nightmares I had all seemed to have a recurring theme—I'd be all alone with nobody around to save me.

On the surface at least, Mom appeared to have put the divorce behind her quicker and more easily than anyone else in our family. A year or so after the divorce, she married a man she'd met through work.

The going was pretty tough for a while. Mike didn't like the guy from the start. I figured my brother just resented the idea that anyone else could replace Dad. I thought Mom deserved an opportunity to be happy just as much as anyone else, but I, too, soon decided happiness wasn't going to be part of this marriage equation. And that was the way it turned out for the next couple years, before Mom divorced again.

During this time, one of the ways I escaped the tension and the turmoil of my own life was through reading. I'd shut the door of my room, lie on my bed eating chocolate I should have been selling as a soccer team fund-raiser, and lose myself in the fictional world of the "Black Stallion" series. I loved the adventures of Alec and the black. I used to dream it was me riding the Black Stallion and he was my horse. *Someday,* I told myself, *I want to have my own horse ranch.*

Another godsend during this time of my life was my friendship with Amy Major. Amy and I had met when I first moved to Seattle back in fourth grade. The two of us tore it up on the soccer field, where Amy played left wing and I was a center midfielder. We went to school together and lived in the same neighborhood. I spent so much time with Amy that her house and family became my second home. I ate over there, slept there, hung out there, and grew up there. Her parents and five sisters made it a place where I could get lost, have fun, be taken care of, and not have to worry about the chaos or pain of my own home life.

During those years my most consistent coping strategy for forgetting my troubles and ignoring the emotions eating my insides was to stay active. Whether that meant doing something with friends or just playing in the yard with my dog, I tried to keep moving. And sports was by far the best way I knew to do that.

I spent hours every day either on the soccer field, a baseball diamond, a basketball court, our backyard, or just out on the street—playing whatever sport or activity happened to be going on.

Mom used to have to call me in for dinner and then again at dark. Even then I responded only grudgingly. Better than any other therapy, sports was where I could lose myself and forget about the tough stuff going on in my life, expend pent-up emotions, stretch myself physically and mentally, have fun, and compete.

When we chose sides for neighborhood games, I was usually the first one picked. Often I'd be the only girl playing, which was fine with me; I could play harder against boys. And that made me that much tougher.

The soccer field in particular became an island of normality in the stormy sea of my life. Not only did being a soccer star give me an identity, it provided acceptance and affirmation as well. No matter how disrupted and unsettled the rest of my life felt, the soccer field was one place I could be in control.

⚽ ⚽ ⚽

After moving to Seattle Michelle played four years with the Shorelake Thunderbirds, a club team that won several state and regional championships. By age fourteen she had already made such a name for herself in Seattle soccer circles that Michelle was invited to join the Union Bay Flyers, one of the strongest under-nineteen (U-19) teams in the Pacific Northwest. That meant she'd be playing with and competing against older girls who were much bigger and stronger than she was.

Michelle gladly accepted that challenge. She knew from experience that tough competition would only make her better; it was one of the lessons she had learned playing pickup soccer at Green Lake, a Seattle park where a number of local groups gathered to play. She'd started going there regularly with Mike Koslosky, the coach of the Shorelake Thunderbirds, her first Seattle team.

Often the only kid, as well as the only female, playing, Michelle occasionally had to prove herself to her teammates. But most of the time the guys at Green Lake would pass and play with her because she was just a kid, and something of a phenomenon. They took her under their wing and let her dribble, pass, and play. Once in a while some guy might get a little rough, but if that happened, Mike Koslosky and his friends would usually pull him aside and set him straight.

☻ ☻ ☻

As for my peers at school and in the neighborhood, the guys my age treated me like I was just one of the gang. If I teamed up with boys who didn't know me, I might have to tackle some dude, steal the ball, or score a couple quick goals to show them I could play. It usually wasn't long before I earned their respect and acceptance. If they started playing really rough because they were embarrassed a girl could beat them, I usually knew the coach, or some of the players, or my brother would be there to make sure things didn't get out of hand. It seldom took very long before I could just play and forget all about the guy-girl thing.

Playing with the U–19 Flyers forced me to move my game to a whole new level against physically superior opponents. I had the necessary soccer skills, but where I'd always been able to use my speed and strength to dominate games against girls my own age or a little older, I suddenly had to play smarter. I had to learn the game.

I remember time and again the coach stopping a scrimmage to tell me what I should have done on a particular play. And I can't count the number of times after practices, long past the time the rest of my teammates had gone home, when Scott Hayes, my frustrated coach, would diagram plays in the dust on his car windshield, trying to get me to understand when he wanted me to make a run and how to play off the other forward with and without the ball.

What he never grasped and what took me several more years to learn was that I'm not a very good auditory or visual learner. For a long time I thought I was a slow learner. I now know I just need to see things, walk through them, repeat them back, write them down—or a combination of all this—to really grasp something new. I learn far better by doing. And even then, conceptual understanding comes slowly for me. So some of what my coach tried to teach me about strategy and tactics at fourteen didn't completely sink in until I got to college.

That's not to say my coaches and I were always frustrated with each other during those teen years. Playing with and against older girls very quickly elevated my game. And I remember the satisfaction I felt the very first time we scrimmaged a local women's team called the FC Lowenbrau's, who won national adult amateur championships several years in a row. After stripping the ball from one of their players, I was dribbling down the sideline toward their goal. No one could stop me. And as I ran past their coach, Mike Ryan, on the sidelines I could hear him screaming at his team, "Don't let that little girl beat you!"

I guess I *was* still a "little girl." At fourteen I was only average size for my age—maybe a little small. And playing on a team made up mostly of eighteen- and nineteen-year-olds, several of whom were six feet tall, suddenly made me feel my immaturity in other areas as well. While I couldn't do anything to hurry my physical growth, I quickly made up ground off the field.

Going to parties with my teammates exposed me to beer for the first time. I thought it was fun to try something new and adult and crazy. I wanted to be cool. But since my teammates only invited me to a few parties and my mom seldom let me go when they did, I had to devise my own strategy for acquiring booze.

I remember the first time a friend and I sneaked into Dad's house when I knew he would be gone. The two of us consumed most of a bottle of bourbon and got falling down drunk. I threw up, scraped my knees badly, and ended up feeling pretty stupid. Several hours must have passed before we sobered up enough to call my friend's parents to ask for a ride home. At least I assume we'd sobered up. Her folks never said a word or even hinted that they knew what had been going on.

Emboldened by that experience, my friends and I would frequently swipe beer out of our families' refrigerators. Or we'd empty vodka bottles before carefully refilling them to the same level with water.

Some of my friends got another kind of kick from petty shoplifting, so I went along a few times. I never got caught doing that or another little trick we had of skipping out of restaurants without paying for our meals.

After messing around like that for while, my sense of integrity and personal honor crept in. I'd only wanted to be accepted and liked, but I began to feel ashamed of myself. I realized, *This is not who I am, or who I want to be.* Once I decided that kind of behavior was stupid and could only get me in trouble, I stopped hanging around those friends.

My parents didn't know about any of this, so they never seemed particularly worried about me and this kind of delinquent adolescent behavior. They did, however, know and express concern about my blossoming social life and the sudden attraction I had for a certain nineteen-year-old boy. The five-year age difference troubled my folks. And the red flags really went up when my customary good grades suddenly dropped.

Mom and Dad actually united in their insistence that I was seeing far too much of my new boyfriend. They sometimes refused to let me go out with him and even restricted me from soccer practice because they knew he and I could get together there.

I got into some loud screaming matches with my mom over this. As I always had, I wanted to do what I wanted to do, and I determined that anyone who got in my way would have heck to pay.

I vividly recall one day I got so angry at Mom that I stomped off to my room, pulled a suitcase out of my closet, and began throwing clothes into it right out of the drawers in my chest.

"What do you think you're doing?" Mom asked as she walked in.

"Leaving!" I declared, snapping my suitcase closed and heading out the bedroom door.

As I tried to push past her, Mom grabbed my arm and yanked me back. Struggling with the loaded suitcase, I lost my balance and tumbled onto my bed, which came apart and collapsed with a crack and a crash. It so shocked and surprised us both that my mother and I each burst out laughing. That may be the only argument I ever had with either of my parents that didn't end on a sour note. I never seriously considered running away again.

Mom's second marriage was clearly coming to an end during this period. At the same time, Dad finally seemed to be making progress in his life. He expanded his culinary repertoire beyond blackened burgers to include beef stroganoff and meat loaf, which definitely improved the menu options each week when we had dinner at his house. He had a full-time counseling position and seemed well on his way to becoming a whole new man.

Still, when he teamed up with Mom to express concern over the relationship with my boyfriend, I didn't think either one of them had any right to interfere in my life. I felt like they were trying to control me. So I determined to ignore their concerns for me.

Dad refused to let my obstinate bitterness push him away. He kept coming to my games, fixing me dinner once a week, and having Mike and me over to his house every other weekend. Any day we didn't see him, he'd call to talk. If there had just been another blow-up with Mom over my boyfriend, I wouldn't want to speak to him and was often angry enough that I didn't. He'd ask a question and I'd just hold the receiver to my ear in silence. Dad would say his piece and then he'd tell me, "I love you, Michelle."

When I didn't respond to that, he'd tell me, "I'm not hanging up until you say 'I love you' back to me."

Sometimes I was too stubborn to give in and I'd hang up on him. He'd always call back and I'd know I was in big trouble.

Part of me felt guilty about treating my father that way, but I was too angry about everything that had happened in our family to apologize or admit that I really loved my dad and didn't want to be mad or mean to him. When I would finally give in and say "I love you," I didn't often sound like I meant it.

My confrontations with Dad frustrated and upset my brother. Mike was mad at me because he saw how much my behavior was hurting our dad. Sometimes he'd take out that anger on me by sneaking into my room and turning all my pictures around just to annoy me. And one day Mike found an even more original and memorable way to express his displeasure.

That evening I found a horde of huge, dead grasshoppers strewn all around my bedroom—on my bed, under my covers, among my folded clothes in drawers, even smashed in my school books. For a while I wanted to squash my brother. And for a lot longer than that, I wondered if I'd have a decent relationship with anyone in my family ever again.

Chapter Six

SOMEBODY DIFFERENT

*M*y degenerating relationships at home were a big reason why my new boyfriend played such a big role in my life. I desperately wanted someone who I felt loved and accepted me just the way I was. And he did more than that, telling me how wonderful I was, agreeing that my parents were being unreasonable and that I had a right to run my own life.

When I'd be out with him or over at his house with his dad and brothers, I'd be treated like a queen. He asked me out to dinner, picked me up after school, even took me to some Seattle Sounders professional soccer games. Not only was it fun, but it got me out of the house and away from my family problems. And, of course, all his attention and affection made me feel loved and accepted in ways I'd never felt before. The fact that he was nineteen and good-looking didn't hurt, either.

I'd never had a real boyfriend before. This love stuff all seemed new and exciting and mysterious to me. I just knew this must be love because the more time we spent together, the more I wanted and needed to be with him.

What explained my plummeting grades was the fact that I'd started cutting school and sneaking over to his house to spend the day alone with him. I doubt anyone suspected what was going on until Mom found a note I'd accidentally dropped in the driveway. The handwritten excuse explained that "Michelle has been home sick with the flu this week." At the bottom I'd forged my mother's signature.

That's when all heck broke loose. Mom called Dad, the principal, and finally my boyfriend's home, suspecting I was there. When my boyfriend's dad answered the phone and said, "Michelle, it's your mother," I just about threw up. I'd thought my scheme was foolproof; now it was all blowing up in my face.

When I got to the phone, Mom didn't waste words. "Hang up and get home immediately!"

I did. Terrified, ticked off, and humiliated, I hightailed it home to face the music.

Shorecrest High School principal, Mr. Chuck Taylor, summoned me into his office the next day and demanded an explanation. He was such a huge, bearded man that when I shook hands with him I felt like I was losing myself in his grip. He was not a man to mess with.

My first inclination was to lie. But I was never any good at it. I'd mix up the details, forget what I'd said, and be caught before I knew how. I suspect my face also gave me away. I always felt so guilty about lying that my guilt probably showed. So I simply admitted to the principal what he knew anyway.

"Okay, Michelle," he said. "Now that I know what's going on, the question is, what are we going to do about it?"

Mr. Taylor knew and liked me. I think most of the teachers and staff at Shorecrest did. I was a sophomore who made good grades, never caused trouble, and had already earned Shorecrest state and national notice in girls' high school soccer.

I could have been suspended for truancy. Mr. Taylor might have declared me ineligible to play sports for some period of time. Instead, he did something I thought was much worse.

He assigned me to do community service at a nearby program for people with mental impairments. *No problem*, I thought. *I'll do my time and be done with it. Easy as pie.*

"Somebody will tell you what to do," my mother assured me the next Saturday when she dropped me off at the center. She was wrong.

The extent of my training came from the staff person who met me at the door. She walked me to a dimly lit gymnasium containing a dozen or so mentally-challenged adults of all ages, handed me a soccer ball, suggested I teach my new charges how to play, and left me to figure out the rest on my own.

Looking around, I was horrified. I had never taught soccer to anyone. And all these people who were walking funny, drooling, yelling, laughing, and grabbing at each other scared me. I had no idea what to do. So I began to dribble.

A few gathered around.

"Here," I said, handing the ball to the man nearest me as I casually placed my other hand on his shoulder. The moment I touched him he fell on the floor screaming, thrashing around, and wetting his pants. As I stood open-mouthed, looking on in absolute shock and horror, a couple of the other people got down on the floor with him and began splashing and playing in the puddle of urine.

That ended our soccer lesson for the day. When an aide came running at the sound of screaming, I got out of there without ever telling anyone what happened. And I never went back.

Waiting, or more accurately, hiding, that day in the woods behind the center until my mom returned to pick me up, I had plenty of time to think about what a mess my entire life had become. It seemed I was in trouble all the time and never knew how or when I'd get caught next. My brother hated me and resented my mom for wanting to divorce our dad. My mom was mad and no longer trusted me. And I wasn't even having much fun with my dad anymore. Tension had gotten so bad at home I hated to walk in the front door. My first quarter report card stunk. I'd gotten in trouble with my principal, and my parents had now totally restricted me from my boyfriend and from soccer practice with the Flyers. *Everything I try to do turns out wrong.*

The only adult I felt I could talk to at that time was my English teacher, Al Kovats. He was the "coolest" teacher at Shorecrest; and I wasn't the only one who thought so.

Mr. Kovats coached boys' soccer at Shorecrest. He came to watch all my soccer games the fall of my freshman year, and he'd talk to me about the game when I came to class the next day. He was so nice and such a relief from all the other adults in my life that I just liked hanging out in his classroom.

What I didn't know at the time was that Mr. Kovats had been the first program director at Cliff McCrath's soccer camps, back before I ever went there. We knew a lot of the same Seattle soccer people. So it was our mutual love of soccer that sparked our friendship.

I started dropping by Mr. Kovats's room after school or during his planning period. We'd read soccer books together and he'd draw plays on the board.

What intrigued me most about this man wasn't his love of soccer; there was something else about him that made him stand out. He was outgoing and friendly, but it was more than that. He exuded an air of self-confidence and inner joy that I envied. I felt like such a failure in my personal life that I had a hard time imagining I could ever be happy again. So how did Mr. Kovats do it? What made the guy tick?

After I started to get to know him, I came right out and asked him. "What's your deal, Mr. Kovats? Why are you always so upbeat?"

He told me it was because he was a Christian.

He wasn't like any Christian I'd encountered before. He actually seemed to be excited about his faith.

I told him I hadn't been to church much since we had moved to Seattle, but that back in California I'd found it boring, the people stiff and judgmental, and a lot of their beliefs rigid and confining. For me, religion seemed all about rules—acting and living a certain way. Everybody I knew who went to church or proclaimed themselves "Christians" made me feel I wasn't measuring up to some standard God set. Or they were hypocrites themselves, saying one thing and doing another.

I believed God was probably out there, but all the times I'd ever asked Him for help, He'd never shown up. So He obviously couldn't have cared less about me.

On top of that, the only thing anyone seemed to get out of religion and church anyway was a chance to go to heaven after you die. And that just wasn't doing it for me at that point in my life.

So why in the world was Mr. Kovats excited about God? His eyes actually seemed to light up when he talked about Jesus. I didn't get it.

But then Mr. Kovats told me Christianity wasn't so much a religion as it was a relationship—a personal relationship with God through Jesus Christ. That God was a friend who loved him, and vice versa. That's what he was excited about, that's where his confidence came from. Just knowing that he had a personal relationship with the Creator of the universe was the entire basis of his attitude toward life.

He made it sound so real I could almost believe it. I knew he believed it. And I wanted to trust him.

I began to tell Mr. Kovats about my parents' divorce and the strained relationships with everyone in my family. We talked about school. I even told him about my boyfriend. I talked honestly about things that made me angry as well as those that made me sad. Mr. Kovats soon knew my life was a mess and that I was discouraged about it.

He was as honest with me as I was with him. He told me flat out he thought my boyfriend was taking me for a ride. For some reason, the concern he expressed about my dating relationship didn't upset me the way my parents' did. He also told me that if I would accept Jesus Christ into my heart and life, and let Him take control of my life, that God would help me change a lot of those things that were bothering me and also help me deal with any problems I couldn't change.

I thought a lot about what he had told me. There were days I seriously considered telling him I was ready to do it.

Two factors kept me from it.

First, I worried about what other people would think. Would my friends still accept me if I said I was a Christian? How much would I have to change in order to fit into this Christian thing? I sure didn't want to be a nerd or a religious freak. Would God force me to live a boring life full of rules and laws?

I had no real answers to these serious questions. Except for Mr. Kovats. He was cool, fun, and popular. So maybe this Christian thing would be okay. Just not right now. As a nationally recognized athlete, I was already looked at as "different." Yes, I was different in a good way, but it still meant that I stood out. So being different as a Christian on top of that would just be too much. I'd rather fit in.

The second barrier I faced was actually fear. I was just plain scared to make that kind of commitment. My parents' divorce had rocked my confidence; I found it difficult to really trust anyone or anything. It seemed too big a risk to take to believe what Mr. Kovats said about God being able to help me change the mess I was in. If I committed to Christianity and it didn't work out—if it turned out even God couldn't help me—then where would I be? There might be no hope left at all. What then?

One day during basketball season, Mr. Kovats, who as assistant girls' basketball coach had talked me into playing on his team, offered to drive me home. Since my alternative was walking three miles home in the dark (which I did on occasion when Mom was working), I gladly accepted. He often gave several kids a lift. But on this particular day it was just the two of us when he pulled his beat-up, rusted-out, lime-green pickup truck to a stop in my driveway.

We sat there talking like we often did. This time I broke down and began to cry my heart out. I told Mr. Kovats I hated the person I was becoming. I hated what I was doing to my family. I hated everything going on inside of me.

I was angry. Confused. I knew I needed something or someone. But I didn't know where to turn.

He listened quietly and then he said, "Michelle, I've told you everything I have to tell you. I don't know what else to say."

"I want what you have," I told him. "I need a relationship with God. How do I get that?"

He smiled and told me all I needed to do was ask. It was that simple. And there in the front seat of his old pickup, with rain splattering on the windshield, he took my hand, we bowed our heads, and I repeated a prayer he said. I don't recall the exact words, but I know it went something very much like this: "Dear Jesus, I know I've messed up. I need Your help. I can't do it on my own. I want to know You. And I want to welcome You into my life. Amen."

I don't know how to explain what happened, but as I prayed it was like a swoosh of warmth went all through me. I thought, *Wow! Something is really happening.* I didn't know what. I just took a deep breath and all that stuff that was going on inside me before was gone.

I got a feeling much like I'd experienced many times at the end of a day-long hike through the mountains with my dad and Michael, when I'd finally drop the sixty-pound pack I'd been carrying for miles. Suddenly, I realized the exhausting weight I'd felt and grown so accustomed to wasn't really a part of me after all. I had slipped it off. It was gone. I felt free and strong and good.

Mr. Kovats grinned and told me this could be a fresh start for me. He gave me a hug and said, "You know I love you, Akes. I'll see you tomorrow."

I climbed out of his truck and headed inside to face my angry family and the mess I'd made. I still wasn't sure what had just happened, but even walking in the front door, I knew something was different. I didn't feel like the same sad, lost, angry person I'd been before. The frustration and fear were gone.

It wasn't something other people could see. They might not even realize it right away. But from that moment on, I knew I was a different person inside. That evening marked a turning point in who I was and how I determined to live my life.

The next day at school a couple of the Christian girls on the basketball team came up to me all excited that I'd become a Christian. I knew Mr. Kovats had told them because he wanted them to encourage me and make me feel good about my decision, but these girls were practically yelling the news down the hall. *Everyone doesn't need to know!* I thought. Not that I questioned what had happened the night before—I still felt different. But this whole Christian thing required a little getting used to. I had yet to sort out what a "relationship with God" really meant and how it might affect my life.

I remember a conversation I had standing in the garage one afternoon not long after that, with my mom's new husband. I liked Bob. So did my brother. Bob was a Seattle cop, a nice man who liked Mike and me and seemed to want to be a good stepfather.

He was one of the first people I ever told about my new spiritual commitment. He'd been around just long enough to witness a lot of angry confrontations I'd had with Mom, so I wanted him to know. "I'm a Christian now, Bob," I told him. "That means things are going to be different around here."

He listened respectfully. "I hope so," he responded, not unkindly, but with a touch of skepticism. "I guess we'll have to wait and see, won't we?"

I certainly didn't become a sudden saint. But a lot of things did begin to change. I no longer skipped school, and I soon quit drinking and partying.

My grades came back up. I even broke off the relationship with my boyfriend. And my brother and I got along much better.

Of course, I still had some of the normal disagreements most teenagers have with parents as they work out their own family's definition of independence and maturity. I was still pretty doggone stubborn. But I didn't have the constant, bitter conflicts with my folks that I'd had the past few years. I started spending time with my dad because I wanted to, not because I had to. And I found it easier to tell him I loved him—sometimes without any prompting.

I started attending church with Mr. Kovats and his family, who belonged to a nondenominational congregation. Much to my surprise I liked it, learned a lot, and actually looked forward to going. Unlike my experience as a child, this church seemed neither stiff nor boring.

Still trying to figure what it all meant to be a Christian and have a personal relationship with God, I joined a young peoples' Bible study discipleship class. I even began to understand the Bible a little bit more as I met and talked with other people who said they wanted to follow Jesus.

I got a little disillusioned to learn that some of the teenagers I went to church with on Sundays partied and drank with my old friends on Saturday nights. *How was that? What changes had knowing God made in their lives?* They didn't seem "different" at all. Not in the way Mr. Kovats was different.

I'd always thought Mr. Kovats was a great guy. And certainly he was a Christian. *But, I wondered, if other Christians aren't quite like him, maybe it's the "great guy" part of him—his personality and character—that makes him seem so special, and the fact that he's a Christian is rather incidental. I don't know.*

I did know one thing for certain: My decision to ask Christ into my life had changed my heart. The anger and discouragement I'd felt for so long were gone.

Still, there was obviously more to being a Christian than that. What was it that made some Christians still go out partying—acting one way at church and another with their friends at school? I didn't get it.

I wanted something consistent. Something I could trust and count on when the rubber hit the road. So far, I had not seen many people who exhibited that kind of faith in God. If Mr. Kovats was right, there was more to this personal relationship with God stuff than I could understand.

As other areas of my life became less troublesome, I found I had even more energy to channel into sports. Mr. Kovats had talked me into playing basketball. I'd shot hoops on a goal in the driveway, but I'd never played on a real basketball team at any level. So I had a lot to learn about the finer points of the game.

My aggression was both my greatest strength and greatest weakness. I'd race up and down the court, diving headlong after loose balls, crashing the boards for rebounds. I played so hard that in my very first game I fouled out with five personal fouls in less than two minutes of playing time.

Despite eventually proving to be a good all-around athlete during my high school years, soccer remained my main game. My first love.

☺ ☺ ☺

Michelle had tried out for the varsity soccer team her freshman year, scared to death she wouldn't make it. But she did. The coach didn't actually start her the first game of the season—something about not wanting a ninth-grader to get too cocky. From then on, no coach in his right mind could have kept her on the bench. She started as center midfielder every game for the next four years for the Shorecrest High School Scots. Michelle's team won several metro championships, and her senior year they took the state championship despite the fact that a severely sprained ankle forced Michelle to play the entire final game one-legged. She made High School All-American her sophomore, junior, and senior years.

In the state of Washington, high school girls' teams played soccer in the fall. The boys played a spring season. In the spring of Michelle's sophomore year, Al Kovats invited her to work out and practice with his boys' team. He now admits that a big part of his motivation was that he thought it would occupy Michelle's time and reduce the opportunity and the temptation to resume that relationship she was then breaking off with her boyfriend. "But," he says, "I also thought the physical competition she would get playing regularly with high school boys would strengthen her and teach her to deal with the more physical style of play I knew she would eventually encounter on the college level."

☺ ☺ ☺

Mr. Kovats was right. I learned a lot about playing and surviving hard-nosed soccer. He also worked with me one-on-one to improve and perfect my heading technique. And he taught me the basic mentality and strategy for penalty kicks that I still use. He taught me to be consistent in my placement. "Before you kick," he always told me, "you need to pick a side and never change your mind in mid-approach." He also taught me to practice my PKs. A lot.

In addition to the soccer experience I got at school, I continued to play with my club team, the Flyers, most of the rest of the year. It was there that I honed my skills and began to gain notice on a national level.

Locally the Flyers' strongest competition came from our arch rivals, Team Adidas. It was easy not to like them, and not merely because they were a tough team. Because their team was sponsored (and therefore well-equipped) by Adidas, their players all walked out on the field wearing the latest Adidas warm-ups and carrying matching Adidas soccer bags. We nicknamed them La Machine because they always appeared so perfect.

The Flyers looked like a ragtag bunch of orphans in comparison. Team Adidas seemed so much more polished and confident it could be a little intimidating. We invariably lost most of the regular season games we played against them.

But being the underdogs usually motivated us come tournament time. Somehow we always managed to beat La Machine in the playoffs to advance to the regionals and, a couple of times, all the way to the national tournament. That felt especially satisfying the year we learned Team Adidas had already booked their flights to the regionals before we upset their plans in the state finals.

Over the years, the Union Bay Flyers earned a lot of publicity—especially the two times we captured the regional championship and traveled back east as one of four teams in the nationals. One year we actually made it to the national championship game before losing to a team from somewhere in Virginia.

Soccer played a huge role in my life during those teenage years. I invested countless hours and measureless energy in the sport. But it gave me so much more in return. It was on the soccer field, more than in any other part of my life, that I got hooked into lasting friendships.

Soccer left me with a wealth of rich memories. Sure I went to the prom—the fact that I actually wore a dress helped make that a newsworthy event. And I can still picture the school halls and a few teachers' faces in my mind's eye. But the most vivid and memorable moments from my high school years involve soccer.

Soccer even accorded me a new stepmother. Sue Separovich officiated some of the games my club teams played. The first time I ever said anything to her was a time she gave me a yellow card for mouthing off during a game. I got to know Sue better during high school when her daughter Shelley, who was a couple grades behind me, played with me on the Shorecrest varsity team.

After a while, I nicknamed Sue "the Rocket" for her goal-scoring abilities in the over-forty soccer league she played in. She seemed like such a cool, with-it lady. One time, in a bus on our way to an out-of-town tournament, I was talking to her when a thought hit me. "You know," I said. "I'd really like to see you and my dad get together."

Sue looked at me like I was crazy, because she and Dad were just casual friends. But I insisted, "I mean it. I think you guys would be great together."

Sue thanked me. "I think it's really nice you feel that way, Michelle. But I don't think it's ever going to happen."

Some of my teammates and I thought we might encourage things along. Throughout that weekend tournament we'd call Dad's hotel room to tell him where Sue was and suggest he go meet her in the lobby, the hotel restaurant, or wherever. He took the teasing well—laughing and basically ignoring our adolescent attempts at matchmaking. I still believe that was the beginning that got them thinking maybe there could be more than just a friendship there.

Of course, it took a little more encouragement before that happened. And another two years. They eventually began dating my senior year in high school and got married the following fall.

So in a way, I can say soccer gave me a whole new family, complete with a new sister and brother (Shelley and John), and a stepmother who became a very important person in my life as well as in my father's.

Soccer also offered me recognition and acclaim. The media coverage was a novelty at first. Seeing my name and picture in the papers seemed to mean more to family and friends than it did to me. The trophies and the attention were nice; people seemed especially impressed with the All-America honors. Still, I never understood the significance of any of that. Awards were okay, but another game was always coming up. I couldn't live off those accolades for long. I didn't play for awards or public praise; I played because I loved the game. I loved to compete.

Before long, I just wanted to play soccer whenever and wherever I could. I actually missed my own high school graduation to play in a tournament with the Flyers. It was a decision I never thought twice about.

I was already looking to the future. I wasn't a high school student any longer, but I was still, first and foremost, a soccer player.

Soccer had given me an identity.

Chapter Seven

FULL SPEED
AHEAD

There was one more thing soccer provided for me: a college education. From the end of my junior year through the fall of my senior year of high school, I received countless phone contacts and written correspondence from schools all over the country. I heard from so many college coaches that I began to dodge their calls. After a while, they all began to sound very much the same—like used car salesman offering me the educational deal of the century. Naturally they wanted to sign me up immediately, and when I told them I wasn't ready to do that because I hadn't made up my mind yet, most of them shifted into a hard-sell spiel aimed at convincing me on the spot.

Not many West Coast schools had strong soccer programs for women at that time, so it soon became clear that to get a full scholarship I would have to go somewhere out east.

Following the soccer season of my senior year I took some recruiting trips to explore what sounded like the best options. After campus visits to both the University of Connecticut and the University of North Carolina, however, I was no closer to making a decision. U. Conn. just seemed a little too "north-eastern" to ever feel like home.

I knew the University of North Carolina had *the* premier women's soccer program in the country at that time. Their coach, Anson Dorrance, was persuasive in his pitch and justifiably proud of UNC's well-earned reputation. I knew I would be challenged at North Carolina. But something didn't feel right for me there.

Perhaps what turned me off was that the Tar Heels reminded me of my Seattle club team's old nemesis, Team Adidas—very polished and almost, well . . .

perfect. They had so much of everything—a proud history, exceptional talent, proven coaching, top-of-the-line equipment, impressive facilities—that everyone, including most of their opponents, expected UNC to win.

I came home from my first two campus visits knowing where I *didn't* want to go, but without feeling any closer to a final decision. I knew my choice of colleges would certainly affect the rest of my life, and I also knew I had no idea in the world how I should go about making the decision.

The coach at George Mason University proved particularly persistent. And his hard-sell approach got through to me. When he actually threatened to withdraw his offer and give my money to someone else if I didn't sign within forty-eight hours, I finally agreed to go to his school. The next morning I realized I'd panicked under pressure and that the coach had taken advantage of my naïveté. Part of me felt like a jerk for going back on my word, but I also felt the guy had taken unfair advantage of a seventeen-year-old girl. So I swallowed my pride, gathered my courage, and called the GMU coach back to say I wouldn't be coming there after all.

Boy, was he mad! And I felt like I was making a real mess of what was turning out to be a trial-and-error recruitment process.

My family wanted to be supportive, but the recruitment game was just as new to them as it was to me. My mother talked to several of the coaches and helped sort through the financial details. My future stepmother, Sue, who'd only recently begun dating Dad at that time, had a lot of contacts in soccer circles. She had personally met a number of the top college coaches at soccer clinics over the years, so she proved a tremendous help gathering information and recommendations on various programs.

Dad encouraged me to consider my long-range goals. The prospects of a future in soccer beyond college didn't seem very realistic at the time. He wanted me to be thinking seriously about which schools could best prepare me for a career.

But no one tried to choose a school for me. That decision was going to be up to me. And in the end, it wasn't reason or logic any more than some coach's sales pitch that made up my mind. I simply made a gut-level decision based on a feeling I never could quite articulate.

My third campus visit—to the University of Central Florida—was almost an afterthought. Coach Jim Rudy had built up a women's soccer program that ranked among the best in the country. UCF was a moderate-sized school, but growing steadily. The intensity of the practice session I watched impressed me. And the team played a tough, physical brand of soccer I found appealing. All those factors added up. On the plane flying home after my weekend in Orlando I just knew. *UCF's the place for me!*

While I felt good about the decision, I wrestled with mixed emotions in August of 1984 when it came time to get on the airplane that would take me 3000 miles away from home to school. I cried saying good-bye to my family. I thought, *What am I doing? I don't know a soul in Florida! What if no one likes me? What if I stink as a soccer player? What makes me think I'm even smart enough for college? Do I really have what it takes?*

Walking through the door of the jetway I felt as if I were journeying alone into the great unknown. Yet an exciting sense of adventure and challenge enabled me to overcome my fears and board my flight.

No sooner did I arrive on campus than I discovered there was going to be even more adventure and challenge than I'd imagined. It started with a surprising dorm assignment.

I learned I would be rooming with another Seattle girl, Amy Allmann. The coach had mistakenly assumed since we both hailed from the same town, we must be friends. We weren't. We didn't even know each other personally—only as opponents. And that had been very personal—because Amy Allmann had played in goal for the dreaded and despised Team Adidas.

Now she was my roommate. *What rotten luck!*

❂ ❂ ❂

Amy says she was even more upset than Michelle when she walked into their dorm room. "There was Michelle Akers! I didn't even know she was going to UCF. We were enemies! Playing against her was terrible. The entire week leading up to the game everybody on my team would be saying, 'We have to play Michelle Akers!' It wasn't that we were going to play the Flyers. We were going to play 'Michelle Akers.'"

As an opposing goalkeeper, Amy Allmann had gotten tired of hearing Michelle's name. She says, "If the Flyers got a free kick my entire team would be warning me, 'Watch out! Akers is going to shoot it! Get ready!' I'd be like, 'No kidding! I'm doing the best I can back here!'

"So when I walked into that college dorm room and saw her I couldn't believe it. 'Oh great!' I thought. 'Now I've got to room with her!' I wanted to cry."

❂ ❂ ❂

Amy didn't confess until some time later that she had actually hated me and was even more upset than I'd been by our room assignments. But by that time we'd begun to forge a real friendship, based not so much on our past differences as on our shared challenge we now faced as college freshman living a long way from home.

One night, a week or two after school started, we were both awake in bed at what must have been 3 A.M. I said, "Amy, we're going to school in Orlando, Florida! We're 3000 miles from home. Do you ever stop and think, *What am I doing here?*"

Amy laughed and we talked about home, family, and our feelings about a lot of things. By the time dawn arrived, we'd begun laying the foundation for what would gradually become a meaningful friendship for both of us.

One of the things that bonded us was Coach Rudy's demands on his soccer players. We'd trained hard back home with our club teams, but neither of us was used to the grueling 6 A.M. preseason sessions of running, training, lifting, and sprinting for which our coach was famous.

As freshman we may have been a bit paranoid about meeting Coach's expectations, but we were scared enough to never want to be late to any team function. We always made it a point to set our alarm carefully so we'd have plenty of time to get dressed and out before six.

However, we awakened one morning to see the red LED numbers on our alarm clock flashing on and off in the predawn darkness. Realizing the power must have gone out during the night, we leapt out of bed in a panic, pulled shorts and shirts on, and sprinted across campus to the soccer building to meet the team for a three-mile run. There wasn't another soul in sight.

"We missed them," I said, my heart sinking. I had hoped we weren't that late. The rest of the team must have already taken off on a run. The question was, *Which way did they go?* Our training runs followed a lot of different routes around the backside of the campus.

"What do we do now?" Amy asked.

"I guess we start running on our own and hope we meet up with them," I replied.

So that's what we did—until we ran past a lighted clock and realized why everything seemed so quiet and we had yet to spot any of our teammates. It was only 4 o'clock in the morning. We laughed all the way back to our room.

⚽ ⚽ ⚽

Amy remembers another early morning. *"On the way to the fields for our session, Michelle kept saying she just knew she was going to get cut. I couldn't believe it. Here was this girl Soccer America magazine was calling 'a freshman sensation' and she wasn't sure she was even going to make the team. I thought that was kind of cool. A lot of people probably assumed she would act like she thought she was some superstar athlete. But she wasn't like that at all."*

On the very first day of practice, Jim Rudy had put his fastest veteran defender on Michelle. When Michelle beat her, he switched to his toughest, hard-hitting defensive player, who could kick an opponent into the stands. Michelle took her lumps, got up, and beat that player as well. Years later, Jim Rudy would say that when he realized no one on his nationally ranked team could even slow Michelle down, let alone prevent her from scoring, he knew she was going to be something special.

⚽ ⚽ ⚽

I only vaguely recall Coach Rudy throwing one defensive player after another at me. I rarely notice who marks me, even today. I just play. I do remember fighting and running my rear end off in those early practices, thinking, *I hope I'm doing okay against these monster chicks!* They were very big and very physical. Any success I had against them I attributed to the fact that I was playing in a frenzy of fear. I truly was afraid that if I didn't prove myself right away I wouldn't make the cut.

I was also afraid of getting yelled at by my teammates. If you weren't pulling your load, the older players on the team would scream at you and tell you to get off the field. "If you aren't going to play," they'd yell in your face, "then why don't you just go on home!" And they could back up their words because they were as tough as they were demanding.

From the beginning, I was very impressed by the physical, emotional, and mental intensity of the college game at UCF. So I didn't know quite what to think that first season when we played our biggest rival, number-one ranked North Carolina. Even the toughest of our veterans were visibly anxious in the locker room before the game. I'd never seen them like this. They kept trying to encourage and assure me everything would be all right. *Of course it would! What's the big deal?* I was too naive and clueless to feel nervous.

Apparently the UNC players had heard something about me, because, from the opening kickoff, they slammed and grabbed me whenever I got near the ball. One of the first times I went up for a head ball, a Tar Heel knocked me clear over the touch line. As I picked myself up off the Carolina-blue track and started back onto the field she snarled, "Welcome to college soccer!" A little later in the game another opponent seized me from behind and hurled me to the ground—breaking my bra in the process.

Though surprised by the physical competitiveness of college soccer, I was more fired up than intimidated. *If that's the way the game is played—great!* I thought to myself. I knew I had the fire in me, too.

Just like high school, I couldn't seem to get enough soccer. I'd go out early every afternoon from one to two o'clock for goalkeeper practice. That gave me extra time to work on my shooting. We'd have our regular team practice from two to four. Then, since Jim Rudy also coached the UCF men's soccer team, he sometimes let me stay and work out with the guys from four to six.

One reason I put in so much time was that at the college level I found I could no longer dominate a game solely on my own strength, speed, and ball-handling skills. Other teams had players just as physical, just as fast, and better skilled offensively and defensively than any opponents I'd ever faced before. If I wanted to succeed in college soccer, I very quickly realized it wasn't enough to physically beat an opponent. To win consistently I'd have to be, and play, smarter.

During and after my various workouts, Coach Rudy would try to help me better understand some of the same principles my club coach had drawn on his windshield after practice years before. How to play off my teammate in a two-forward lineup. How to position myself when I got the ball. When to check for the ball. How to support my teammate when she had the ball. What I should do after I passed the ball off. When and how to spin out. What kind of run to make when I wasn't the checking player. And how to play defense as a forward, a whole new concept for me. With time, practice, and repetition some of those lessons began to sink in.

The demands of soccer didn't leave a lot of time during the season for much of a social life, and the upperclassmen on our team didn't have anything to do with us off the field anyway, so Amy and I were left to entertain ourselves. Which we did.

I had asked my dad to ship my bicycle from Seattle. When it arrived safe and sound in a huge bike box big enough for two people to fit in, Amy and I got this brilliant idea. We pulled the box over our heads and cut small holes near the top so we could see out. Then we'd take the box out on campus at night. While no one was around we'd get in the box, lean it against some wall, and wait for people to come by. Once they weren't looking we'd stand up, move the box, and set it back down again. When they'd suddenly see it in a different place they'd think they were losing their minds. We called it SWAT-ing—for Seattle Washington Attack Team.

Or we'd lean the box with us inside up next to a pay phone and try not to crack up listening to some guy whispering lovey-dovey stuff to his girlfriend. That was a riot.

When we weren't out using it, we hid the box behind a giant wall-hanging in our room. We didn't tell anyone else about it.

One night we were out SWATing very late when we spotted one of our team-mates coming out of the library. We started stalking her. When she'd look back we'd stop, putting the box down. She'd start walking and we'd pick up the box and move again. Every time she looked over her shoulder we'd freeze. She walked faster and faster. Then we started chasing her. She took off running across cam-pus, screaming bloody murder with us in the box running after her, laughing so hard we could hardly stay on our feet.

She didn't tell anyone what had happened until one afternoon at practice a couple weeks later. "You guys are going to think this is weird," she told the whole team. "But one night when I was coming home from the library, this box started chasing me."

Sure enough, a bunch of players laughed at her. Amy and I never said a word.

Nobody suspected a thing until I gave a talk in speech class on the topic "How to SWAT in a Bike Box." I received an "F" for my effort, in part because I wasn't a very good public speaker, but mostly because the teacher thought I was mak-ing the whole thing up. The assignment had called for a true how-to speech and he insisted there was no way two people could fit in a bike box.

I brought Amy and the box to class to prove him wrong. The professor changed my grade, but we'd blown our cover. We would have to find other ways to get our kicks off the field.

My freshman year the UCF women's soccer team was pretty equally divided into two groups—conservative Christian girls on one side and the rowdier party girls on the other. Equally competitive and tough soccer players and teammates, their differences became apparent only off the field. And even then it took a while.

I had met a couple of the Christian crowd during my recruitment trip. When I told them that I too was a believer, those girls seemed especially pleased to have another Christian coming on the team.

When I arrived on campus that fall, I got to know and like all my teammates. Everyone hung out together and seemed to get along. The only real differences I noticed eventually showed up when it came to drinking, late-night partying, and guys.

It did seem the party crowd had more fun. By the end of my first collegiate soccer season, during which I'd become the team's leading scorer and earned All-America honors, I started hanging out more and more with the rowdy bunch.

This evidently bothered some of my Christian teammates. One of the girls actually left a note on my door informing me that I was "on the road to hell." That sort of judgmental, meet-our-expectations-or-else, holier-than-thou attitude was what I'd experienced and expected of religious people before I'd met Mr. Kovats. I began spending even more of my time with the rowdy bunch in the late-night scene.

Then I fell head over heels in love with a UCF football player. We met at a Halloween party, started going together by the end of soccer season, and got more and more serious throughout that winter. I'd never dated much in high school, so this seemed like new and exciting territory for me.

Early in our relationship, when we were still just getting to know each other, I told him I was a Christian. He told me he was too. And we actually went to church together a couple times when I went with him to Miami to visit his family for the weekend. But our relationship was in no significant way spiritual.

We did most of our socializing with the wild party crowd. We'd go out with his friends to local nightclubs that catered to the college community. He discouraged me from messing with any substances other than alcohol. (He got mad when he learned I'd smoked a little pot with some soccer buddies; I didn't like the way it made me feel either.) Neither of us did harder drugs, but we hung around a lot of people who did, which no doubt earned me even more harsh judgment in the eyes of some of my straight-laced teammates.

My fast-developing social and love life might have raised a caution flag or even created a little guilt, but I was enjoying the first seriously romantic relationship of my life. As far as I was concerned, this was the real thing. And since the man of my dreams was older and more mature than I was and had not only said he was a Christian but had grown up in a respected Christian family and gone to church all of his life (which was more than I could claim), I figured I could take my cue from him. If he did what he did, hung out with who he hung out with, and was still okay with the Christian stuff, then I figured it was okay for me as well.

Who cared what a few narrow-minded people might think or say? I was in love. And doing just fine on my own, thank you very much.

My approach to love (as with everything in life) was a lot like my style of soccer—whole-hearted, totally committed, full-speed ahead. I had yet to understand the risks associated with such an attitude. I was about to learn some painful lessons—both on and off the field.

Chapter Eight

NEW
SCHOOL
TIES

$\mathcal{I}$n the spring of my freshman year, I received a letter from the U.S. Soccer Federation officially inviting me to a tryout for a U.S. women's national soccer team that would be going to Europe for an international tournament later that summer.

Looking back, I realize I should have felt honored. That 1985 U.S. Women's National Team was a true first for American soccer. Never before had any women's soccer team officially represented our country in international competition. This was something the pioneers of the women's game had been working toward and dreaming about for years.

But in my youthful naïveté it didn't seem like a particularly big deal to me. As far as I was concerned, this was simply another chance to play soccer.

The coach of the team that first year was Mike Ryan, who'd coached the FC Lowenbrau women's team that used to scrimmage my Union Bay Flyers back in Seattle. The same Mike Ryan who'd yelled at his players, "Don't let that little girl beat you," when I was fourteen. I also knew a number of players Mike had recruited from club programs in the Northwest and that helped offset the fact that I was by far the youngest member of the squad and had very little in common with my teammates apart from soccer.

To be honest, the whole experience had the feel of an amateur all-star squad. We didn't even get together until early August for a four-day camp in upstate New York. That was our only experience playing as a team before we boarded a plane and flew to Italy for the tournament. We even looked like an amateur all-star team, wearing old hand-me-down men's uniforms.

The other countries' teams were so much more fit and soccer savvy that we seemed to play like amateurs in comparison, chasing them futilely all over the field. Plus, most of our opponents already had valuable international experience playing a much more physical style than any of us Americans had ever experienced before. The first time a defender flew into my knees with her cleats up, making no pretense of going for the ball, I realized I was in a battle. I remember thinking, *Whoa! I see how it is now! I gotta pick up my pace if I want to play with these chicks.* The other teams grabbed our shorts and yanked our hair on breakaways. They punched and stomped and kicked and actually spit in our faces. Inexperienced amateurs that we were, we angrily complained in vain to the referee, foolishly thinking we could expect a fair call from a referee when we were playing a team from his country. We eventually got mad and retaliated, only to earn ourselves a few yellow and red cards.

Despite our opponents' superior skill and our own glaring lack of international experience, our American team scrapped and fought and kept the scores respectable. Italy beat us in our very first game by a score of 1–0. Three days later we tied Denmark 2–2—the game in which I scored the first-ever U.S. Women's National Team goal.

Two days later, after traveling from Jesolo to Caorle, Italy, we lost a 3–1 match to England in which I scored the only U.S. goal and suffered a dislocated shoulder when I got taken down hard on a late-game tackle. I wanted to play despite the pain, but after the extent of my injury was diagnosed, I sat out our last game of that tournament—a 1–0 loss in a rematch with Denmark.

We all went home realizing we had a lot of work to do if we wanted to compete against the best of the world. No one ever said anything about getting together again. I didn't know that we ever would. And yet the entire experience, as painful as it had been, had whet my appetite for more world-class soccer.

I arrived back in Florida just a couple days before preseason training began that fall of my sophomore year. Our UCF trainers had to tape my arm tight to my side to prevent the shoulder from popping back out from the slightest blow. No sooner had I healed enough to dispense with the taping than I hyperextended my knee going into a tackle. I tried to ignore that injury as long as possible, but it got so bad I couldn't even kick the ball with that leg anymore. The doctors finally diagnosed torn cartilage, and I underwent my very first arthroscopic knee surgery.

When it looked as if I might be out long enough to miss most of our remaining fall schedule, the coach decided to "red shirt" me. While this required sitting out for the remainder of the season, it also meant I'd gain another year of college eligibility. The games I'd played at the beginning of that sophomore season wouldn't count against me. I could still play three more full seasons of NCAA soccer.

While I agreed that the "red shirt" decision made sense, it triggered a chain of events that made my sophomore year one of the most difficult periods of my life. First, this was the first injury of my life that sidelined me for an extended period of time, and that proved harder to deal with than I ever imagined. I hated being on the sidelines watching my teammates play. I even found it frustrating to sit and watch them train and run. I spent more time in the training room than I did out on the field with my friends. They'd go on trips and I'd stay home rehabbing my knee. It stunk!

But an even tougher blow came after the end of that soccer season, when my boyfriend dumped me. He explained that he was a senior and I was just "too young to get serious with." Funny, I had thought we already were serious. He was this handsome dude, nice, fun, from a great family; I'd figured it was true love for sure. I was devastated by the break-up.

And when he got back together with another girl on the soccer team he'd been dating before me, I couldn't help wondering, *What did he mean I wasn't old enough? What's wrong with me?*

In an attempt to mend my broken heart, soothe my bruised and battered ego, distract me from the pain, prove something to myself, and maybe even to my ex-love, I started going out with a bunch of different guys. Another football player here. A frat boy there. A soccer player or two as well. I determined to have fun, meet new people, find a replacement for my last boyfriend, and forget about how much I'd been hurt.

That strategy only compounded my problems and made things worse. Not only did I have to deal with my broken heart, but now I felt more empty and worthless than ever.

Drinking and partying dulled my disappointment with myself as well as the original pain. But it also created other problems. I was on the verge of flunking out of school from too many late nights. My performance in soccer practice suffered. I gained ten pounds over my playing weight. And my self-respect was in the toilet.

One day that spring when I showed up for practice obviously hungover, Coach Rudy decided to teach me a lesson. "We're gonna work today on headers. Michelle, you can start."

I spent the rest of practice heading goalkeeper punts as the pounding inside my skull increased to unbearable intensity. By the time the drill ended I sincerely wanted to die. But I got the point. I vowed never to come to soccer practice hungover again.

One day, after a practice when I'd struggled to maintain my focus and actually burst into tears at one point for no apparent reason, our assistant coach, Bill Barker, pulled me aside. He'd been watching me go downhill for weeks and must have figured it was time to step in. With obvious concern in his voice Barker asked, "Michelle, are you okay?"

"No," I honestly admitted, choking out the words. "I'm a mess. And I know I gotta get my act together."

It was soccer that finally motivated me to do that. My plummeting grades hadn't stopped me. My sinking self-esteem hadn't either. Only when I realized my self-destructive behavior was seriously impacting my soccer did I find the wherewithal to pull out of my emotional tailspin. And even then it was nearly too late.

My spring grades were so bad that I was academically ineligible to play soccer the next year. My last hope for maintaining my scholarship was summer school. Only if I earned enough credits during the summer session could I play again the following fall.

As my difficult sophomore year finally ended I took a hard look at myself. I decided no more late night partying. I would focus on soccer, school, and friendships that didn't revolve around the party scene.

I went home to Seattle for a very brief visit at the end of the spring semester before returning to enroll in summer school and trying to get my life turned around. Out of pride, I refused to ask my parents for any money for my added summer school expenses, which meant I survived those months crashing in some friends' apartment with nothing more than popcorn and Kool-Aid to sustain me a lot of days.

I was glad to see that summer end. By the time fall semester rolled around, I'd brought my grades up enough that I was excited about another great soccer season and a more committed school year.

Another reason I looked forward to that school year was because my brother Mike was enrolled at Central Florida as a freshman. I expected to see a lot of my little brother, since he would be playing defender for the UCF men's soccer team.

I enjoyed having my little brother around. I showed him the ropes and we hung around some together. But as fall began, soccer once again became my primary focus. *From now on,* I told myself, *anything that is going to negatively affect my soccer, I'm gonna have to change.* And I did.

The old intensity I'd had for the game was back. Nothing else mattered. At least not as much.

I remember a game against North Carolina, always a benchmark opponent by which to measure the caliber of our team and the potential success of our season. I went up for a header and crashed hard into another UCF player. Lying on the ground with my bleeding teammate, I realized the collision had knocked out two of my teeth. The referee called an injury time-out and all the officials and players got down on hands and knees to search the grass. When we couldn't find the teeth, we soon resumed play. I never once thought about coming out. Not even two lost teeth and a minor concussion hurt that bad.

Unfortunately, that just happened to be the very first college game my mom ever saw me play. When she realized what had happened, she got very upset. I guess she started thinking about all those years in braces and began to see dollar signs. Our game that day was the first of a UCF doubleheader. Since my brother played in the men's game which followed, I'd just taken my place along the sidelines with plans to watch the guys when Mom came rushing out of the stands to insist on taking me to an emergency oral surgeon immediately.

I was ticked. I couldn't understand why we couldn't at least wait until the end of Mike's game. But Mom insisted. The doctor performed surgery with the intention of implanting permanent posts after the swelling went down. I walked around campus for a couple of weeks afterward with a big, fat, split lip, ugly black-and-blue gums, and a two-tooth gap in my smile.

I couldn't understand why other people acted so surprised that I wasn't more upset by the loss of my teeth. No one could believe I'd kept playing after it happened. But it wasn't that big a sacrifice to me: I could get new teeth, but I couldn't replay a Carolina game.

☻ ☻ ☻

Central Florida tied North Carolina that year in Chapel Hill. Michelle earned All-America honors for the second time, leading her team to a 15–3–1 record that earned them a sixth-in-the-country ranking at the end of the season. Then she and the team received another devastating blow when they all gathered in the locker room to learn who they would be playing in the NCAA postseason tournament for the national championship.

"I don't know how to tell you this," a visibly upset Jim Rudy told his team. "We didn't make the tournament!"

Despite having tied North Carolina and defeating a couple of other teams that were included, the Golden Knights were not invited. Coach Rudy had called the selection committee to see if there had been a mistake. Anson Dorrance from UNC and another couple coaches whose teams UCF had beaten during the regular season called in support of Central Florida and to express their outrage at the injustice. But the decision was final.

"We had our bags packed and ready to go," recalls Lisa Gozley, one of Michelle's teammates. "It was just a matter of who we were going to play. When Coach made his announcement, it was a bad scene. People started throwing things around the locker room, screaming and crying.

"Michelle never showed any emotion. She simply sat there and boiled quietly. Some of the team decided we were going to a nearby bar to drown our sorrows and then go to the men's game that evening to just hang out together and feel miserable. Michelle said, 'I'll meet you there. I'm going to go for a run first.'

"It was almost two hours later before she finally caught up with us. When we asked where she had been, she somewhat sheepishly admitted she'd started running and when she finally looked around to realize where she was, she was in Winter Park someplace. She'd run more than ten miles. We couldn't believe it!"

⚽ ⚽ ⚽

I still hated losing every bit as much as I always had. I had just found a better way of masking my emotions. I was very angry and disappointed that some unexplained political considerations had cheated us out of a tournament berth, but I actually felt better after my run.

And I felt a whole lot better when the team put in such a good season the next year that there could be no denying us a place in the tournament. The year actually began badly with a 2–3 record for the first five games. But after Coach Rudy shuffled the lineup and started several younger players, we went on a twelve-game winning streak that carried through the regular season and into the playoffs. We breezed through the opening rounds to win our regional and reach the Final Four. I played well enough to be named offensive MVP of the tournament. But what I'll always remember best about the entire experience was playing the NCAA semifinals in the worst soccer conditions I have ever seen.

We'd arrived in Massachusetts to practice on a nice fall day. That night, however, a cold front blew through and temperatures plunged to all-time lows. We wore nylons, sweat pants, and three layers of shirts under our uniforms. We played in mittens and hats and one of our players still got a frostbitten ear. They set up gas jet blowers for heat along the sidelines by the benches. Another of our players actually melted a shoe trying to thaw her feet at half-time. There was just no way to keep warm when the game time windchill measured something like thirty below zero.

Our personal physical discomfort was only part of the problem. The surface of the field froze so solid it felt like we were playing on a concrete parking lot. I slide-tackled a girl in a patch of frozen mud that ripped a huge gash on my knee. Looking down at the blood soaking through the tear in my pants I remember thinking, *That should hurt!* But my legs were so numb with cold I didn't feel a thing.

When it hit you, the ball felt like a ten-pounder shot from a cannon. Moving it around the field was like kicking a cement block. The cold and wind got so bad that several of Amy Allmann's goalkeeper punts never crossed the eighteen-yard line. Needless to say, neither team could mount much of an attack.

The score was tied 1–1 when UMass finally managed a shot on goal with only a few minutes remaining; Amy couldn't react fast enough to do a thing. When we ended up losing the game by the score of 2–1, the disappointment over the loss was greatly overshadowed by the frustration of having had to play under such terrible conditions.

⚽ ⚽ ⚽

The Golden Knights didn't go quite as far in 1988 when Michelle was a fifth-year senior. UCF ended a 10–3–2 season with a tough 2–1 loss in the NCAA region final to North Carolina. Still her fifth season may have been her best season as a collegian. She led her team in scoring again, setting an all-time school career scoring record. She won All-America honors for the fourth time in her college career and received the 1988 Hermann Trophy as the national college player of the year. The Hermann Trophy had been awarded to the top male soccer player since 1967, but Michelle was the very first to win the new Hermann Trophy for women.

⚽ ⚽ ⚽

Today the Hermann Trophy awards ceremony is a major annual deal for both men's and women's soccer. The trophy itself is beautiful, and the impressive awards dinner is a big formal affair featuring some real bigwigs of the sport. But that first year was a different story.

Bill Barker, who had taken over as head coach my final year, and I received an official letter informing me that I'd won. I'd never heard of the Hermann Trophy, so I never gave it another thought for the next two months. That's when a shipping company delivered a cardboard box to the soccer office with my award inside. When the coach opened it, he found the trophy broken into so many pieces he had to screw the various parts together before he presented it to me.

The great soccer success I experienced in college was made all the sweeter because I was able to share some of it with my brother Michael, who earned his own soccer scholarship and played for the UCF men's team my last three years at Central Florida. But it wasn't always easy for Mike having to follow in my footsteps.

His first-year bio in the school's media guide began, "Freshman Mike Akers, younger brother of UCF All-America soccer player Michelle Akers . . ." Mike went straight to the athletic department to complain and said, "Please don't do that again." But wouldn't you know it, the next season his bio read, "Sophomore Mike Akers, younger brother of UCF All-American soccer player Michelle Akers . . ."

While he may have struggled for a while to establish his own identity outside the shadow of his big sister, I soon realized my 6'3" sibling was no longer my "little" brother. Indeed, he drove me crazy at times trying to play the protector role in our relationship. If we were out in a nightclub somewhere, he would interrupt me to warn whatever guy I might be talking to that he would have my brother to answer to if anything happened.

Mike also used to follow me home, knock on my door at all hours, even barge into my apartment from time to time just to make sure I was okay. He was only half joking when he told me he and some football player buddies were ready to pound anyone who wanted to mess with me or break my heart.

I could see that Mike's "help" was going to do wonders for my social life. Only after I convinced him that unless he wanted me interfering in his social life, he needed to give me a little more room, did we eventually come to a mutual understanding of our grown-up roles. From then on, the time we spent at college together in Orlando only strengthened and enriched the close relationship we'd had as kids.

There were other relationships which also played very crucial roles in my college experience. Lisa Gozley transferred from Long Island's Nassau Community College to play her last two years of soccer at UCF.

We met during her recruiting trip to Orlando the spring of my freshman year. She knocked on my dorm room at three in the morning saying she'd read about me in *Soccer America* and wanted to know what I was like. I would have slammed the door in her face except the coach had told me she was a player we wanted, so I let her in, hoping it would be a very short visit.

Fat chance! Goz definitely had an agenda. When I collapsed back into bed, Goz plopped down on my desk chair and began to grill me. I remember thinking, *She better be good. And she had better decide to come here!* I tried to answer as politely and succinctly as I could. *She's got some nerve showing up and* demanding to chat at three in the morning. Does she think she owns the world or what? When she announced that she didn't think I could possibly be as good a soccer player as people said I was, I laughed and told her I didn't much care what some cocky New York punk thought anyway. She laughed at that and kept right on asking me questions.

The whole time we'd talked Goz had been leaning back in my desk chair and holding onto the wall to keep her balance. Suddenly she lost her grip and tumbled over backwards into the closet behind her. I laughed my head off. So did she.

That's when I kicked her out of my dorm room so I could get back to sleep. I haven't been able to get her out of my life ever since.

☻ ☻ ☻

"We were such total opposites that people who knew us both acted shocked when we eventually became roommates," Lisa Gozley recalls. "Michelle was a native West-erner. I was an Easterner, a true New Yorker through and through. When I wanted to get psyched before a game, I'd crank up Led Zeppelin until the walls started to vibrate. Mish would slip into a corner, put her headphones on, and listen to Anne Murray. I could never understand how that motivated her to go out so aggressively and bang heads the way she did on the soccer field.

"I earned a reputation as something of a rebellious troublemaker. People thought Mish was apple pie and Chevrolet.

"I was a loud-mouthed New Yorker who never seemed at a loss for words. Michelle was so shy that if we were at a party and she saw some guy she liked, she'd go hide in the bathroom and say 'Oh my, gosh! He's here!'

"I'd tell her, 'Just go talk to him.' And she'd tell me, 'But I don't know what to say.'

"I remember when she was elected captain of the soccer team. She wanted no part of it. She wasn't comfortable talking to the team. She didn't want to be a leader. She just wanted to be left alone to do her job.

"Whether she wanted to be or not, she was a leader, if only by example. Her will to win and her commitment to do whatever it took to win was incredible. That's one thing we shared—we both despised losing. And we both put up a pretty tough exte-rior to keep people from knowing how we really felt.

"Michelle exhibited the same degree of discipline in her personal life that she showed every day in soccer when she'd be out shooting before anyone else got to prac-tice and then stay afterwards to run extra sprints. I'd never known anyone like her.

"I was an admitted partier. And while Mish was glad to do a little socializing with me, she had very definite limits. If someone stopped by at two in the morning to invite us to go out drinking, Michelle would say, 'No thanks. I've gotta get my rest.' And no matter how hard we tried to get her to go, once Mish made up her mind, you couldn't pry her out of bed with a crow bar."

Everyone who knew or played soccer with Michelle saw her intensity and her discipline; her well-earned reputation for commitment was practically legendary at UCF. So most people probably viewed her as a serious, no-nonsense kind of person.

"And they were wrong," Lisa Gozley insists. *"Only a few of us who knew Akes best realized that off the soccer field she could be light-hearted, laid back, sometimes silly, even a little goofy."*

✪ ✪ ✪

A little goofy? Sometimes I think I had to be absolutely insane to put up with friends like Goz and Laurie Hayden, a soccer team walk-on who also transferred in and hung around with us my last two years at Central Florida. Goz, Hades, and Akes. The three of us became so inseparable we dressed up for Halloween one year as Snap, Crackle, and Pop, the Rice Krispie elves.

There was always a special chemistry between us—a major element of which was laughter. And some of our best laughs came at each other's expense.

One day Goz and I timed things so we'd be taking our vitamin and mineral supplements just as Hayden walked up. "Hey, Hades," we said, "why don't you take some of these vitamins? They might help you play better."

She ignored the implication that she needed to improve her game and agreed that "It can't hurt."

We passed her a handful of tablets and capsules—including a couple niacin. What we knew but didn't tell her was what that large a dose of niacin did when people weren't used to taking it. Since it opens up capillaries and stimulates the blood flow throughout the body, it can make an unsuspecting person suddenly become flush and feel overheated. So we hung around waiting to see what would happen while Laurie took a shower.

Sure enough, hot water only enhanced the niacin's effect. Hades came hurrying out of the bathroom holding out two very bright red arms and demanding, "Look at this! I think maybe I'm having some kind of allergic reaction."

"Oh no, Hades!" we exclaimed, feigning alarm. "What's happening? Are you okay?"

"I feel a little feverish," she admitted, looking more worried by the moment.

"What do you think might have caused it?" we asked, acting as concerned as we could manage.

"I don't know," Hades insisted.

"Well, have you done anything different today from what you normally do?"

"Yeah," she told us. "I just used some new lotion. You think I'm having some sort of chemical reaction?"

"Could be . . ." We kept her going until she was insisting we drive her to the emergency room for immediate treatment. Only then did we break down laughing and tell her what was going on.

Another time when the three of us were eating out together at a Mexican restaurant Hades was, as usual, chewing a stick of Big Red gum while also drinking a bottle of Mexican beer. She'd downed only half the beer when she excused herself to go to the bathroom. While she was gone, Goz and I grabbed a habanera pepper and squeezed a very generous coating of fiery juice all over the mouth of Hades' beer bottle.

When she came back to the table and took another swallow of beer, she got this surprised look on her face and started running her tongue over her lips. "I think something in my gum is reacting with this beer," she told us.

"That's ridiculous," we told her. "Drink your beer and quit imagining things. What makes you think it's the beer? It couldn't be. Try another sip."

We kept her going that time until she jumped up from the table and ran to the waitress' station in the back of the restaurant to get ice to rub on her burning lips. When she came back to the table still holding an ice cube against her mouth, Goz and I were laughing so hard we couldn't talk. She knew then it must have been something we'd done. Once the blisters went down she was laughing with us and threatening to get us back.

Goz and Hades used to gang up on me too sometimes. They'd make fun of me for every reason you could think of. One time we needed to bake a cake for some party so we went to the grocery store to get everything we needed. As I started collecting flour, eggs, cocoa, oil, and other ingredients we needed, they were like, "*What* are you doing, Michelle?"

"Buying stuff to make the cake," I replied.

They practically laughed their heads off before they insisted, "Let's just buy a mix."

"Okay," I agreed reluctantly. Mom always cooked from scratch and I'd learned to bake from her. Then I started gathering ingredients for the frosting (powdered sugar, shortening, etc.) and they burst out laughing again.

"Let's just get canned frosting," they insisted.

"What?" I didn't even know you could buy frosting in a can. Goz and Hades thought that was the funniest thing yet and called me Betty Crocker for a long time after that.

They also nicknamed me "Grace" because I was always stumbling over stuff and banging into things. They made fun of me forever after I crashed my bicycle into a garbage dumpster. "How did you not see that huge green metal box right in front of you?" Goz demanded to know. She and Hades thought it absolutely hilarious that an All-America soccer player could be such an accident prone klutz off the field. But I was. I figured it was genetic; my dad is the same way. So I had to laugh with them.

They also teased me mercilessly for always being slow to get things—whether it was a new drill or an old joke. The coach would explain some play and then ask me if I understood it. "Huh? What?" was such a frequent response that it became a team punch line. Even the coach would mimic my "Huh? What?"

Sometimes when they thought I was acting more dense than usual, Hades or Goz would say, "Hey, Akes! Do we need to pump a little more air in your head?" And we'd all laugh.

Yet underneath the laughter, the constant ribbing, and the good-natured putdowns there was a deep, mostly unspoken commitment to one another. Goz was an instant memorizer. Where I could learn the gist of material quickly enough, I had real trouble remembering specifics like words and definitions. Goz would spend hours working to help me memorize body parts for an anatomy test when I was struggling big-time with that class. When I ended up with a *B* she was as thrilled as I was.

Of all the significant things my years at UCF afforded me—a good college education, numerous athletic awards, many wonderful memories on and off the field—what I will always treasure most from that exciting time in life is the friendships I shared with some very special teammates.

I knew Goz and Hades felt the same way. It wasn't anything we talked about, except once. Near the end of our senior year, Hades and I were eating at a place called the No Name Oyster Bar. She'd had enough beers that she became overly sentimental before suddenly excusing herself from the table. When she'd been gone awhile, I went looking and found her in the bathroom all by herself, crying.

"What's wrong?" I wanted to know.

She said, "I'm afraid you're going to become famous and forget me someday."

I burst out laughing and told her she was being ridiculous. "You and Goz are my best friends. We will always be friends!"

But then I didn't believe the part about becoming famous, either.

Part

THREE

Promise of Glory:
National Team
Beginnings

Chapter Nine
JUST KICKIN' AROUND THE WORLD

J graduated from the University of Central Florida following my final collegiate soccer season that fall semester of 1988. With my bachelor's degree in liberal studies and health, I still planned to eventually pursue my longtime dream of becoming a paramedic. But my immediate plan was to follow my heart, pursue my first love, and figure out some way I could afford to train and play soccer full-time.

There were no professional soccer teams for women. The U.S. Women's National Team didn't pay any of its players; we received ten dollars per diem (for meals and expenses) the few days a year we got together, fifteen dollars a day when traveling overseas. So money certainly wasn't the appeal. I just wanted to play soccer—to do what I loved doing most—for as long as I could. As a brand-new college graduate and a four-year veteran of the U.S. women's soccer program, I had already accumulated a wealth of memories.

After thinking that first team's trip to Italy in 1985 may have been my once-in-a-lifetime experience with international soccer, I'd gotten another letter from the U.S. Soccer Federation inviting me to play for the team again during July of 1986. Several players from the previous year were invited back, but North Carolina's Anson Dorrance, who'd been named to replace Mike Ryan as coach, also brought on more former and current East Coast college stars he'd known or coached.

That 1986 team assembled at a soccer complex in Blaine, Minnesota, for a three-game set of exhibition matches against a Canadian national team. We won two of these games and then flew to Jesolo, Italy, for the same tournament we'd played the prior year.

I went against the medical advice of my physical therapist in even making the trip. I played the entire tournament one-legged because I'd torn the MCL (medial collateral ligament) in my right knee and could kick only with my left. Yet we fared better as a team the second time around, downing China and Brazil by identical 2–1 scores, and then beating Japan 3–1 before losing our final match to host Italy 0–1. Our 5–2 record for 1986 reflected our gradual, but definite improvement as a national team.

Only in looking back at 1987 does that year's long-range significance for the U.S. Women's National Team become clear. We did play our most ambitious schedule in 1987. We hosted another four games in Blaine, Minnesota, that summer: beating Canada, losing to Sweden, and splitting two games against a team from Norway.

But instead of playing in Italy a third time that summer, the team made its first trip to China in August for a two-game set against their national team. We won one game and tied the other.

I missed that trip with another injured knee, but during the December break between semesters I rejoined the team on a memorable ten-day, five-game trip to Taipai, Taiwan. We beat Japan 1–0 before losing to New Zealand by the same score. I scored one goal in a 6–0 rout of Australia and two more in our team's 4–0 defeat of Canada prior to losing the final game of the series to Taiwan 1–2.

But far more vivid than any detailed memories I have from those games are the fascinating images I still recall from my very first exposure to the sights and sounds of the Orient. Everything seemed so new and different. I remember a number of us being especially intrigued by a dark, dirty, rather seedy street market section of Taipai known as Snake Alley. We didn't learn until later it was considered a very dangerous part of the city. That was after much of our team spent several evenings strolling in and out of colorful shops, purchasing unusual souvenirs, and gawking as people bought live snakes hanging in the sidewalk shops, chopped the reptiles' heads off, and drank the blood.

Having witnessed such customs on the streets, I guess it's not too surprising team officials were leery of local medical care. Which is also why another one of my most vivid memories from that trip took place in a Taipai hotel room. I'd gotten my noggin cracked in a head-to-head collision during the Australia game. Our trainers got the initial bleeding under control with a bandage that reminded me of Tonto's headband. But upon closer examination after the game, they decided the gash over my left ear definitely needed stitches. None of us wanted to risk going to a hospital, so the trainer and doctor decided they could do the job themselves.

Nobody had to go to Snake Alley for entertainment that night. There was standing room only as I lay on a hotel room couch feeling like a public spectacle, my entire team (and some of the Aussies) gathering around to watch the trainers shave the side of my head around the wound, numb me up, and then sew the two-inch gash closed with I don't know how many stitches. That was a treat. I played the remainder of the tournament and went home sporting my Tonto look, which showed up great in all the family Christmas pictures.

✪ ✪ ✪

A 6–4–1 finish gave that team one more win than they'd managed the previous year. But the most noteworthy change in 1987 wasn't the record, the more extensive schedule, or the team's first two trips to the Orient. The most significant development, measured by its impact on the future of the U.S. women's soccer program, was a decision Anson Dorrance made that summer. When the National Team played its invitational tournament in Minnesota in July, the U.S. Junior National Team was also there to play. Many of those under-nineteen players did so well that Anson told his squad that he was going to go with youth. He cut a number of veterans to make immediate room on the National Team for "the youngsters": eighteen-year-olds Linda Hamilton, Joy Biefeld (Fawcett), and Carla Werden (Overbeck); Julie Foudy and Kristine Lilly, who were all of sixteen; and fifteen-year-old Mia Hamm.

✪ ✪ ✪

Naturally, the move toward youth was controversial with the veterans—especially those who were cut in the middle of the year. But I trusted Anson's judgment. I didn't understand exactly what he was doing at the time, but it's obvious now that he already had his eyes on the future.

The decision did cause some major repercussions at the time. We eventually had to play an all-star team made up of players some of the higher-ups in the Federation felt were more deserving than the new players Anson had selected.

Anson told us before that game that some of our jobs were on the line and his might be as well. We ended up pounding the other team and quieting the critics, but not before I realized for the first time that politics were very real in sports at the national level and could have a significant impact on our team and my career.

While our new players all showed flashes of potential, I did think Foudy, Lil, and Mia in particular seemed pretty scrawny and a bit intimidated at first. They were just kids, young enough that they had to get parental permission to make those first overseas trips. And Lil still gets teased for taking along a raggedy stuffed tiger named Tamba because she couldn't sleep without him.

But if Anson wanted these changes and thought these kids could help the team, we'd go with them. As usual, my focus was playing soccer, not the team roster.

In June of 1988 I was injury-free and made my first trip with our national team in their return to China for the first-ever Women's World Tournament sanctioned by FIFA, the Federation of International Football Associations. What an experience that turned out to be!

Travel within China proved to be a real adventure. I remember waiting in some Chinese airport to board a flight to our next city when an airline official came out to inform us we could take only one bag with us on the plane. What a hassle! Like everyone else, I started separating out my luggage and sorting clothes and gear into my biggest bag. The official came back. No! We didn't understand. He meant we could take only one bag *for the entire team!* We opted for a large medical kit. The rest of our luggage had to catch up with us by train.

Another oddity of Chinese air travel occurred upon landing. Unlike the U.S., where everyone is instructed to remain seated until a plane reaches a complete stop at the gate, the moment our planes' wheels would touch the ground, all the Chinese passengers would leap to their feet and begin pushing their way toward the exits. What we'd do would be to get someone on the team with a big backpack to stand in the aisle and block people off (amid much complaining from the Chinese passengers) until the rest of us could file out. Even then, the adventure wasn't necessarily over. One time we got off a plane to find ourselves in the middle of the tarmac and had to dodge moving aircraft to reach the terminal. Crazy! I could see the headlines: "National Team Soccer Player Killed by Taxiing Plane."

Getting on and off elevators proved almost as hazardous. The moment the doors opened, people would elbow and shove their way in or out. We felt rude, but we finally adapted to Chinese elevator etiquette. It was either that or spend half the trip standing politely and patiently in hotel lobbies and hallways.

A lot of Chinese customs took getting used to. It seems that everyone in China spits. I remember lying on the bed of my room in a downtown hotel with my window open, listening to the steady stream of people hacking and spitting on the sidewalk as they passed by along the street below. Even more disconcerting to me were the little children wearing clothes with the crotches cut out, so they could just squat and relieve themselves whenever and wherever they felt the need. When in China, we very quickly learned, you don't want to walk in anything wet.

What bathroom facilities we did find, even in the hotels, left a lot to be desired. Many toilets were nothing more than a porcelain pot recessed in the floor with a couple footprints painted to guide those of us who weren't sure exactly how or where to squat. I vowed never to take an American toilet for granted again—or, for that matter, the toilet paper that goes with it.

Every meal was a culinary adventure. The head of our delegation told us that even though China was a poor country, they wanted to give us the best of everything they had. We begged for plain rice, but we were informed that rice was poor people's food; it wasn't good enough for special guests.

We didn't always know what we were eating, so we used veteran Lori Henry as our unofficial team taste-tester. When a dish looked or smelled suspicious, we always waited for Lori to take the first bite. If she liked it and said, "It tastes just like chicken," most of us would take a chance.

But no sooner would we take our first tentative bite than Lori or someone else would invariably give a little bark and we'd all groan in disgust. We probably did have dog at some point. I know we were served turtle soup, ox, snake, and, we suspected, cat. Sometimes the hardest things to eat were the ones we could identify all too easily. Like the time we had soup containing whole fish (including the heads), or the chicken dish served with the entire neck and head sticking out as garnish.

And then there was the vegetable we'd been served throughout the trip. It smelled okay and looked a little like chopped broccoli, so we had eaten a lot of it. Until the night it was served whole.

I cut into mine, took one look, and turned to Amy Allmann, my college freshman roommate who was now the starting goalkeeper for the National Team. "Amy," I said, "cut into your vegetable and tell me what you see."

She sliced hers open and, sure enough, just like mine, it was full of worms. None of us could eat any more that night.

Fortunately, we found the playing conditions in Punyu, China, much more agreeable than the food, travel conditions, and local customs. The stadiums and the playing fields were first-rate, and the enthusiastic crowds filling the modern arenas were the biggest we'd ever played for. But what I remember best about the Chinese fans on that trip was the sound they made. Not the cheering. In fact, the sound I'm referring to occurred when there would be a lull in the action and the cheering died down. Then, even from out on the field, you could distinctly hear the cracking sound of sunflower seeds being chewed all around the stadium. And if you walked up into the empty stands after the game, you would see sunflower seed husks heaped everywhere— under the seats and even out in the aisles.

We won only our tournament opener, downing Japan 5–2, before tying games with Sweden and Czechoslovakia, and losing our last game to Norway 0–1. I took a hard fall in the Sweden game, sustaining a head injury serious enough to land me in a Chinese hospital, where I spent several lonely nights while my teammates finished out the tournament. That would have been bad enough, but one of the team doctors speculated that my head injury might be more serious than "just a concussion" and that by continuing to play soccer I could be risking permanent damage.

When we returned to the States that summer of '88, I went to see a neurologist. Further tests confirmed that I had indeed suffered a severe concussion. But an MRI of my head and neck revealed no spinal cord or nerve damage. After a couple of weeks' recovery time from my concussion, the neurologist cleared me to play.

☻ ☻ ☻

However, in the meantime, some United States Soccer Federation officials had overreacted to the first doctor's opinion and decided Michelle was too much of a risk to have on the team anymore. She wasn't invited in for the next training camp or allowed to travel and play with the team on its four-game trip to Italy later that summer.

So she went in to see specialists recommended by the Federation. Those doctors also cleared her to play. Still she wasn't allowed to join her teammates. For months, Michelle and the USSF went back and forth, during which time she completed her final semester of college and tried to make plans for a future she could only hope would include an extended career with the U.S. Women's National Team.

☻ ☻ ☻

After graduation, to make ends meet and cover my very modest living expenses, I accepted an assistant coaching job with the women's soccer team at the University of Central Florida. A few months later, during the spring of 1989, I received an intriguing phone call.

The man on the other end of the line introduced himself and told me he was a sports agent out of Dallas. "I've got an idea," he said. "How would you like to become the first woman to ever play in the National Football League?"

Was this guy serious? Me? Kick in the NFL? Yeah, whatever, dude.

It turned out he was serious. He'd read or heard something about me and was convinced I could make it as an NFL placekicker. He wanted to know if I could come to Dallas to meet him for a tryout.

"Sure," I agreed. I didn't have anything better to do. While I'd given up my childhood dream of becoming the next Mean Joe Green, I was certainly open to the idea of getting on the football field as a kicker. *Who knows, maybe the coach would see how well I could catch a football and sign me up as a wide receiver.*

So I flew to Dallas where I met the agent and spent a few hours on a field giving him a kicking exhibition. I didn't know what to expect. I'd never kicked field goals before. *But how hard can it be?* I wondered. Turns out it wasn't tough at all without any linemen trying to squash me into the turf. And the agent acted pleasantly surprised by my accuracy and my distance. He seemed especially impressed when I kicked a fifty-two-yarder through the uprights.

Clearly the agent wanted publicity. He'd obviously put out word of our plans, because national newspapers picked up on the story. So did *People* magazine.

The agent told me he'd talked with Dallas Cowboy special teams' coach Ben Agajanian, who would be conducting a kicking clinic soon near his home in Santa Barbara, California. Would I be willing to take a trip to the West Coast for a tryout? I told him I would.

A few days later the agent and I flew to California. After seeing me kick a football, the coach told me he thought I definitely had the potential to play in the NFL. If I would be willing to spend the next year training full-time for football, working out to build up my strength and distance, he said, "You can make it!"

I thought about it. I figured he was probably right; I could do it. Kicking a football was fun. It seemed almost too easy. I might make history as the first woman to ever play in the NFL. But it would mean having to quit doing what I enjoyed doing more than anything else—playing *real football.*

I didn't have to think about the decision much longer. "I'm sorry, but I'm not going to do this," I told the agent as he drove me back to the hotel. "What I really want is to be a world-class soccer player."

He was so unhappy that he drove off and left me stranded at the hotel without a ride to the airport the next morning. That's the last I ever saw of the guy.

⚽ ⚽ ⚽

As determined as Michelle was to play soccer, the chance to rejoin the U.S. Women's National Team remained in doubt. No matter what she said about her health, and despite the medical clearance from the doctors they themselves had recommended, the U.S. Soccer Federation still wouldn't agree to let her play. Michelle's old friend Cliff McCrath, the Seattle Pacific University soccer coach whose camps she attended as a kid, called up the Federation officials he knew personally to argue her case. They wouldn't budge.

Michelle finally hired a lawyer who threatened to seek an injunction preventing the U.S. Soccer Federation from adding any new players to the team or from playing any games until they resolved the issue of her eligibility. That got the attention of a lot of folks within the Federation, including a boardmember by the name of Art Wahls. Just before a specially called board meeting to discuss the case, he phoned to ask, "Tell me, Michelle, what is going on?"

Michelle explained what had happened in China. She told him she'd been cleared to play by both her doctors and the Federation's doctors, who had all examined her MRIs and run all sorts of other tests. There was no medical reason for her not to play.

Mr. Wahls listened to everything she had to tell him. When she finished he said, "Okay, Michelle. I want you to know I'm going to stand up for you in this meeting. But you better be telling me the whole scoop, because if anything happens to you, this will fall on my head as well."

He was as good as his word. Michelle was soon informed that she was back on the team and would be invited to the next training camp, which wasn't scheduled until the following year.

⚽ ⚽ ⚽

While all this controversy had been going on, I'd missed several training camps along with the one and only game the U.S. Women's National Team played in 1989, a 0–0 tie with Poland in a game played in Sardinia, Italy.

With my collegiate career finished and no international competition at all, I spent 1989 trying to find ways to stay in training and keep fit for soccer. Assistant coaching at UCF gave me contacts there in the men's and women's programs. I could work out with those teams, and often found enough willing bodies for regular competitive pickup games. But once school let out and it got tougher to round up work-out partners, I had to do a lot more on my own.

Obviously, one way to stay involved with my sport for the long-term would be to consider coaching as a career. But coaching required teaching the sport, which I had no experience doing. I had only played the game. And I hadn't even been a very good listener when my coaches had tried to teach me. Too often, I had zoned out when they'd been explaining things; now I wished I'd paid more attention.

As a means of gaining some instructional experience and getting a feel for what coaching could be like, I explored the possibility of helping or just observing in a number of soccer camps that summer of '89. I went home to Washington and helped Cliff McCrath for a while with his Northwest Soccer Camp on Whidbey Island. And when I saw the name of Post to Post soccer camps in *Soccer America* magazine, I contacted the owner/director of Post to Post, Roby Stahl, to ask if I could meet with him to pick his brain and talk about the possibility of observing one or more of his camps.

We got together for the first time at a big amateur soccer tournament in Charleston, South Carolina. We seemed to hit it off from the start, and Roby invited me to work a couple camps with him as one of his instructors.

Roby was a former college and professional soccer player whose Post to Post clinics and camps were quickly earning a good reputation in soccer circles around the country. As I spent the next several months traveling and working with him all around the eastern United States, I understood why. Roby was a gifted soccer coach who not only showed me how to teach the sport, but who also began teaching me techniques I needed to be a more lethal finisher and goal scorer.

Up until then in my life as a soccer player, I had relied on the strength and power of my shots to score. Anson Dorrance, in his attempts to make me more of an offensive player, had encouraged me to refine my approach by understanding the important distinction between blasting and finishing. It's the same difference as that between a shotgun and a rifle: devastating short-range power, which becomes scattered and unpredictable the farther you are from the target, versus careful precision that can be deadly at longer distance.

Anson had already begun to work on my mentality by changing my idea of a goal scorer both technically and tactically. But it was Roby who helped me put my evolving philosophy into practice—through practice.

Working together, Roby and I designed and developed particular drills and overall practice routines aimed at improving certain skills and techniques to be used from specific points on the soccer field. I would spend hour upon hour working on basic technique. Sometimes with Roby watching and commenting, other times on the field all alone, I'd take a hundred and more shots a day, over a thousand shots a week, experimenting with the various surfaces of my foot so that instead of rocketing laser balls straight at the goal, I learned to bend my shots right or left, curving away from the keeper and into the upper or lower corners of the net.

When I'd get a specific shot down from one spot I'd move to another. Or we'd increase the intensity or the difficulty of the drill by giving me less time or a smaller target. My training became more and more methodical, with every exercise carefully thought out and focused on achieving perfect execution no matter how much pressure or how little time I had.

Spending so much time together on and off the soccer field during those months, it seemed almost inevitable that Roby and I became attracted to each other. He seemed like the perfect guy for me. To begin with, there was our mutual love of soccer. More than ten years older than I was, Roby also impressed me as a rock-steady, no-nonsense kind of man. He seemed so much more mature than the college-age boys I'd been dating—as if he already had life figured out. He was someone I hoped I could trust to love me and take care of me forever.

So after six months, when Roby proposed and we decided to get married in Seattle early in the spring of 1990, I felt it was destined to be. Just as I hoped we would live happily ever after.

Our first hurdle came just weeks after the wedding, when I left the country for three months to play for the Tyreso FF team in the Elite Division of a Swedish club league. I'd committed to play in Sweden months earlier and considered backing out when Roby and I had decided to get married. But we both agreed that more experience playing in Europe would benefit my soccer career. So I left my new husband, with his blessing, just weeks after our wedding, to embark on yet another soccer adventure.

I'd originally decided to play in Sweden because there were no comparable opportunities for ex-college players at the time in the United States, and because the Tyreso club promised to provide me with a place to stay and living expenses while I played. I foresaw the experience as an opportunity primarily to stay in soccer shape for the upcoming U.S. Women's National Team schedule and to put my new goal-scoring mentality to the test of real competition. My time with Tyreso also forced me to do something else Anson Dorrance had been encouraging me to do—assume more of a leadership role on my team.

I had to assume leadership on the Tyreso club for two main reasons. First, it was a struggling team in a very competitive league. I very quickly learned if I didn't score, no one would. Since I still hated to lose, I was forced to step up my game and develop a real on-the-field scorer's mentality over the course of that season.

The second factor that prompted me to assume team leadership was my teammates' laid-back style. Their nonaggressive attitude frustrated me no end, even after I concluded it was more a cultural mentality than a lack of competitive nature. It seemed that all of the Swedish players were so into the team concept that none of them wanted to step out and distinguish themselves by outperforming or in any other way "showing up" their teammates. Since I wasn't Swedish, that thinking didn't apply to me. I wasn't worried what my teammates thought of me. I didn't care if I was stepping on anyone's toes. After realizing no one else was about to step up, I quickly decided I had no other choice but to take the lead and become the dominant scoring force on the team. By the time I'd played two or three games a week for three months, I got used to assuming leadership on the field—not vocally, since my coach and teammates spoke mostly Swedish, but by simply taking charge of the play.

⚽ ⚽ ⚽

It was hard to know how much to attribute to that learning experience in Sweden or how much Roby Stahl had helped Michelle refine her goal-scoring abilities. Or whether her two years away from the U.S. women's team were a major factor. Whatever the explanation, there was no denying the fact that when she rejoined her teammates on the National Team at their Minnesota training camp in July of 1990, Michelle Akers had raised her game to a new level. She played not just with a vengeance—she'd always done that—but with a confidence no one had ever seen in her before.

She scored a goal in two of the three games played in Winnipeg, Canada, in which the U.S. defeated Norway 4–0, Canada 4–1, and Norway again 4–2. The next week, back in Blaine, Michelle had a break-out performance with seven goals in just three games against the USSR, England, and West Germany.

That was the entire 1990 schedule. Michelle had scored nine goals. The U.S. played only six games, winning them all. None of the games were even close.

✪ ✪ ✪

After our final game of the year, when we defeated West Germany, a team many considered the world's top women's soccer team, by the surprising score of 3–0, Anson gathered the team together in the locker room for one last speech.

He congratulated us on our best performance ever as a team and our most successful season. He thanked us for the effort we had made not only that summer, but over all the years leading up to that point. He reminded us of all we'd been through together. He told us he knew there had been rumors before about the possibility of a Women's World Cup tournament. The success of the big Women's World Tournament in China back in 1988 had created serious discussion, but any subsequent plans had fallen through. FIFA decided 1989 would be too soon, and 1990 had been a Men's World Cup year.

However, Anson now assured us he had it on good authority that plans were already in the works for the first Women's World Cup to be held in China sometime near the end of 1991. He told us such a tournament would be the culmination of a dream many people had worked for years to accomplish. He promised it would be unlike anything any of us had ever experienced. The pressure would be more intense, the competition stiffer, the challenge tougher than we had ever known before.

Even as Anson spoke, we all knew full well what he was doing. He was a master motivator. He had the entire team hooked and hanging on his every word.

He warned us that the coming task would be formidable. He challenged us to be prepared when the time came. And he insisted that the only way we could hope to be ready to survive the long road ahead of us was to commit ourselves to work not just to stay in shape but to improve our skills and our conditioning in the months before we all came together again as a team the following spring.

Anson raised our sights and our hopes by assuring us that the rewards would be worth everything it was going to cost us. And he finished his speech by declaring his vision and his goal. "I want this team to be the best in the world! Are you with me?"

Doggone right, we were with him! Are you kidding?

We were so fired up we could have whipped the entire world right then and there.

My teammates and I accepted Anson's challenge. From that day on, our goal was to be the best women's soccer team in the world.

But I also had a personal goal. I wanted to be the best woman player in the world. Nothing less would do.

Chapter Ten
LONG ROAD
TO CHINA

$\mathcal{S}$ometime during those next few months, FIFA made it official: The very first Women's World Cup would be hosted by China the following November. I could hardly wait to get back together with my teammates to begin our preparation.

Of course, I was already preparing on my own. I hadn't for a moment forgotten Anson's challenge. If he'd taught me and the rest of the team anything during his five-year tenure with the Women's National Team, it was the importance of being our own coach. We never played a very big schedule, and training camps were limited to a few days before each trip, so we got together as a team only a few weeks each year—at most. We never had enough time in camp to work ourselves into shape.

That was why Anson for years had focused on teaching us how to get fit, stay fit, and be playing on our own. It had been a tremendous learning process and required a huge commitment—because he expected us to arrive at each camp in condition and ready to play.

This meant that during the long months apart, each of us had to push ourselves to our physical limits—and beyond—to build and improve our fitness. We couldn't rely on a coach with a whistle and a clipboard to note whether or not we got up and out for our daily 6 A.M. runs. No one else timed our wind sprints, demanding we do one more when we reached the point of exhaustion. The discipline to train had to come from within.

We also had to organize our own playing environment. That meant we had to call people to train with and find players who would be better and could challenge us—mostly guys' teams at the college level. Then we'd have to find a field, sometimes find our own goals, and carry our own supply of soccer balls. We also needed to maintain a strength and conditioning program and make sure we were properly rehabbing any injuries as well. And we had to arrange and time our training program to peak at the right time so we could play our best whenever National Team games were scheduled.

But there was yet another dimension Anson taught us about being our own coach. We needed to learn to be objectively honest about ourselves as soccer players. That meant recognizing our weaknesses and working hardest to improve those areas of our game.

Every athlete's natural inclination is to want to practice what he or she is best at, because that's the most fun and brings the satisfaction of feeling most successful. A good coach insists that his or her athletes face their fears, shore up their shortcomings, and practice whatever parts of the game they like least, probably because they fail most often there. Being our own coach required doing that for ourselves.

These demands weeded out the big girls from the little girls and developed a team mentality and level of commitment that explain why the core group of players from that era has remained at the top of international soccer for so many years.

After Anson's "be the best" challenge, I'd spent better than half a year being my own coach and working on my own game and conditioning. Roby and I had decided to make our home in Orlando, where I had access to familiar work-out facilities and could continue to train with UCF athletes.

Roby kept working with me on fine-tuning my game, and I always enjoyed training with the oldest boys who attended our Post to Post camps and clinics. Those sessions invariably started out as a "prove it" kind of competition between us, with them challenging me to prove I could play with them. Only after I beat them a few times, or hung tough when they hammered me, would they just play. I loved changing guys' minds about the ability of a girl to play soccer.

Still, by the time our next training camp rolled around in March of 1991, I was more than ready to hit the field with my old teammates and begin our quest of the goal I knew we all shared: to be the best women's soccer team in the world.

Anson met with each of us individually once during every camp or tournament to assess our performance, discuss future goals, and determine a training emphasis. When he and I had our one-on-one sitdown we'd usually talk about the week of training, what he saw, what I saw, what we agreed I needed to improve on, and what he thought I needed to concentrate on to reach the potential he saw for me. We would talk about whatever I'd been doing that had made a noticeable difference in my game since the last camp or tour. Then we'd share those things that worked with the whole team so we could all keep improving on our own.

I remember in that spring of '91 Anson kept wanting to know how I'd improved so much when it came to finishing and how I had managed to improve my speed so dramatically. The answer was Roby, who had introduced me to a speed/sprint workout which took me from midrange on the squad to one of the six or so fastest players on the team. Several teammates soon implemented a similar program into their own training program with positive results.

Anson assembled a bunch of veterans for that 1991 squad. While I was one of only three members left, along with Lori Henry and Emily Pickering, from the original team in 1985, our roster boasted a wealth of international experience. Debbie Belkin and April Heinrichs had come on back in '86. Amy Allmann, Megan McCarthy, Wendy Gebauer and Carin Jennings joined the team in 1987. And those "youngsters" Anson had seen as the future of national women's soccer and snatched off the U.S. Junior National Team—Joy Biefeld (Fawcett), Julie Foudy, Mia Hamm, Kristine Lilly, Carla Werden (Overbeck), and Linda Hamilton—had all played regularly for three or four seasons already. Brandi Chastain, who was a forward in those days, and goalkeepers Mary Harvey and Kim Maslin-Kammerdeiner had also been around since '88 or '89.

We knew each other. We knew the National Team routine. We knew what our coaches expected. And we thought we knew what had to be done. But what we had yet to learn was just how different 1991 would be from any of the years that had come before. And the reason was the World Cup.

Being a take-charge goal scorer hadn't yet become first nature to me. Instinctively, I still looked to get the ball to others to start the scoring. But I did accept and thrive on the offensive leadership role Anson expected of me. And I immediately resumed the scoring pace I'd established in the 1990 season.

⊛ ⊛ ⊛

The 1991 U.S. Women's National Team began its year with a tune-up tour to Bulgaria, where in the first eight days of April they played and won five shutouts against five different European national teams—Yugoslavia, Bulgaria, Hungary, France, and the USSR. Only one of the games (2–0 against France) was even close.

By scoring an amazing eight goals in those five games—even though she came out of two games early—Michelle established herself as the go-to player on the U.S. team. And that reputation preceded her going into the World Cup qualifying tournament later that month.

Everyone knew it. Though Carin Jennings and April Heinrichs were just as big a threat to score, her teammates routinely looked to Michelle when the team needed a goal. Opponents targeted Michelle with their fiercest defenders. She was marked. But it didn't keep her from scoring.

FIFA, the international governing body for soccer around the world, is divided into six regional confederations or unions spanning the entire globe. Each regional body conducts its own preliminary qualifying tournament to determine its representative(s) who will compete in the actual World Cup. The U.S. Soccer Federation falls under the auspices of the CONCACAF region (Confederation of North, Central America and Caribbean Association Football), which scheduled its ten-day qualifying tournament for the 1991 Women's World Cup in Port-au-Prince, Haiti, starting on April 18.

Michelle easily won the CONCACAF tournament MVP award, scoring an astounding eleven goals in just five games. She tallied two goals apiece in the first four games, which turned into U.S. routs of Mexico (12–0), Martinique (12–0), Trinidad and Tobago (10–0), and Haiti (10–0). Then, to top it all off, she netted three balls in the 5–0 final against Canada to win the tournament and clinch a spot in the World Cup later in the year.

⊗ ⊗ ⊗

I don't have nearly as many lasting memories of the tournament game action as I do of that trip itself. Our team had already traveled some in the developing world, but we'd seen and experienced nothing like what we encountered in Haiti.

The hotel where we stayed shut off all power during the day to conserve energy. That meant we had no air-conditioning to counter the sweltering tropical heat. Likewise, there was no water to wash, shower, or flush the toilets. We'd go swimming in the pool after practice just to rinse off the sweat and dirt.

Even at night the electricity was sporadic at best. You never knew if, or when, your room and the entire hotel would be plunged into darkness. That was frightening enough. But then when the lights flickered back on, all manner of creepy crawly critters would go scurrying back to wherever they'd been during the day.

Julie Foudy, who was trying to prepare for her upcoming college finals while on the trip, spent so many hours studying by candlelight that her textbook pages stuck together with melted wax. One night she and Beef (Joy Biefeld) decided to go to someone else's room. Walking barefoot, feeling their way down the hotel hallway by flashlight, they heard a loud *crunch!*

"Oh, gosh!" Joy exclaimed. "What was that?" She pointed the beam of the flashlight down at her feet and practically screamed to see that she'd stepped on and crushed what looked like a six-inch long cockroach.

Those mega-roaches were everywhere. Any time the lights came back up, you'd see them skittering back into the walls and behind the furniture.

When we complained to Anson, he told us his own horror story. "You think that's bad," he said. "I was trying to get to sleep last night when a roach crawled over my face. I jumped out of bed and practically freaked out! I changed pillows and went to take the pillowcase off, and I found *more* cockroaches in my pillowcase."

Let me tell you, stories like that really made me want to crawl into bed and fall asleep at night!

On a more positive note, the stadium fields in Haiti were fine. The enthusiasm and the size of the crowds were great. But the poverty we witnessed away from the soccer venues was staggering. From the moment we landed at the airport we saw barbed wire and machine-gun toting security patrols wherever we looked. I watched hungry, half-naked children laughing and playing in open sewers. One day I even saw a man's dead body lying alongside the road. And I soon realized the complaints we had with our hotel accommodations paled in comparison to the daily plight of the poor people of Haiti, who begged us for money or food everywhere we went. It made it a little easier for me to keep soccer in perspective.

I needed that perspective because I had begun to notice a distinct difference starting during the tournament in Haiti. I noticed it during the games, among my teammates, and even in me. It wasn't so much what anyone did or said; it was more a feeling. We had played a lot of games in a lot of places since 1985. We had always wanted to win, but we were more concerned about improving. Whether we won a particular game or not had never really mattered to anyone but us. Now it did. The World Cup was still seven months away, but we were suddenly playing for higher stakes.

We had arrived in Haiti knowing only one team from the CONCACAF region would advance to the World Cup. That meant we had to win the tournament. If we lost one of those games, nothing else we could do the rest of year would matter because we wouldn't be able to play in China. If we didn't make the World Cup, everything we'd worked for—the blood, sweat, and tears we'd shed, the hundreds of thousands of miles we'd traveled in cargo planes, sooty trains, and rickety buses, the nightmare accommodations, the inedible food, the pain and the pride we'd invested in training—would have been for nothing. No telling how long it would be, if ever, before we had another chance at a world championship.

So we couldn't lose. It mattered too much. And there was something about feeling that kind of pressure that brought an added sense of intensity and focus to our play.

I'd never experienced anything that quite compared to that feeling, and I have to admit I liked it. So even though we'd known going in that Canada should have been our only real CONCACAF competition, it was gratifying to come out of Haiti knowing we'd lived up to expectations, handled the pressures, and taken that first big step on the road to reaching our ultimate goal.

While winning the qualifying tournament hardly made a huge splash in the pond of public awareness around America, our overpowering showing (outscoring our opponents 49–0) did create a few noticeable ripples within the portion of the sporting world that had connections in the soccer community.

While still in Haiti, I received an invitation to speak at a meeting of the Soccer Industry Council of America. I didn't know what in the world that was. It sounded like a real drag. I hated making speeches and certainly didn't want to go.

Anson told me that I had to accept. "You don't understand," he said. "This is a huge deal. No other woman has ever been invited to speak at this meeting before. You have to take advantage of this opportunity because there will be people there who will have the money and the power to change our game. You might be able to help alter the history of women's soccer."

No pressure there for someone who hates to stand up in front of people to speak and had never ever done anything like this before.

"What would I talk about?" I wondered.

"Just tell them about the team," Anson suggested.

So I went, not knowing what in the world would be expected of me.

It turned out that I was supposed to speak at a fancy dinner for all these bigwigs from throughout the sports world, the U.S. Soccer Federation, trade magazines, and the sporting goods industry. I started just the way Anson had suggested, by telling them about our team and our winning of the CONCACAF qualifying tournament.

I talked a little about the history of our team and some of the things we'd been through in the past six years. I talked about the dedication and commitment required of my teammates, some of whom had postponed careers and families, taken time out of their education, and resigned or been fired from jobs to play on the U.S. Women's National Team. I talked about how the U.S. Soccer Federation gave us pitifully little support. We didn't have training facilities of our own and still wore hand-me-down uniforms from the men's teams. I told them about the low-budget travel and accommodations we'd endured. I told them no one on the team received any financial assistance beyond our ten-dollar per diem expenses. And that our program needed more monetary support than we were getting at the time.

I assured my audience that my teammates and I had quit our jobs and put our lives on hold to play soccer for one reason—because we loved our sport. And I concluded by telling them we shared one, and only one, goal. We were on our way to the first Women's World Cup in history with the sole intention of coming home with a world championship. "This," I told them, "is your chance to jump on board and go with us."

Then I sat down.

I didn't find out until later that Alan Rothenberg, the newly-elected president of the U.S. Soccer Federation, was sitting right in front of me, probably squirming a little as I talked about the lack of consideration I felt we'd gotten from his organization. I had no idea who he was at the time. And I still don't know whether or not my speech had anything to do with the Federation's decision to award one thousand dollars a month in expenses to each team member from July through November of that year.

I guess my speech wasn't very tactful. It certainly was more impassioned than it was polished. I hoped people understood I was speaking straight from my heart. I said what I said because I believed the Women's National Team program needed more support, and the people in the audience that night were in the industry and had the bucks to do it.

I didn't exactly change the history of women's soccer at that dinner. But I did get the attention of at least one other listener. After the program a man who said he was with Umbro introduced himself as Mick Hoban, handed me his card, and said, "I'd like to call you later and discuss business."

Cool, I thought. Then I tucked his card in my pocket and promptly forgot about it over the next few days as I prepared for another soccer tour, this one back to Europe with the National Team.

If we thought things were going to change for us just because we were now guaranteed a spot in the World Cup, we were soon brought back to earth. Our first scheduled stop in Europe was a joint appearance with the U.S. Men's National Team at a tournament in France. A bus picked up both American teams at the airport and drove us to a bed and breakfast out in the countryside, which sounded promising but turned out to be a big, old, damp house with no functioning heat or air-conditioning and precious little hot water.

The men piled off the bus and disappeared inside. We stayed behind to unload our own luggage and gear. The bus driver not only refused to help us, he also demanded we unload the men's stuff immediately or he wouldn't come back to drive us to the game the next day. We needed that bus driver; we didn't want to jeopardize our chance to play in the tournament, so we hauled off the luggage and the equipment for the men as well.

All in a glamorous day's life of an athlete on the U.S. Women's National Team.

❂ ❂ ❂

The U.S. Women's National Team still may not have been getting the respect and consideration they deserved off the field, but their on-field performances earlier in the year continued to guarantee that the international soccer community, and especially their opponents, had to give the American women their due. And every team the U.S. played continued to target Michelle.

"I don't think people [today] appreciate how she intimidated and dominated everyone," says Anson Dorrance. "Teams set their entire defenses to stop her. She received more physical abuse than any player I ever coached. And she was less protected by officials than any player in the world. The referees never felt they had to protect Michelle because she was so strong and didn't complain. Plus we were naive. None of our players would get clipped and roll five or ten yards like a lot of players on other teams, who did it out of instinct for self-protection, hoping their opponent would get carded. When Michelle got fouled, she'd get up immediately, pretending nothing bothered her—which I thought was very noble. As a result, though, the referees had no compassion for her. The toll that sort of abuse took on her body was immense. I'm sure when she got up in the morning, every joint in her body creaked.

"I remember when I first started coaching her, I was so afraid she would get injured that I started lecturing her about tactical agility. I defined that for Michelle by saying that if her team was winning by six goals and there was a ball rolling out of bounds and the other team's sweeper was about to boot it out of the stadium, she

didn't need to go busting in there and try to keep the ball in play. Some plays just don't matter.

"But because Michelle never backed down, she would put her body at risk time after time, even for a meaningless ball in a meaningless game with the outcome already determined. I just couldn't get her to be more careful.

"However, as a coach it was one of those wonderful problems. It's great when a player you're coaching lists her biggest flaws as, 'I take too many physical risks and I'm too aggressive.' What a fantastic player you have on your hands, and that's what I had in Michelle."

Despite the abuse she took from opponents, Michelle scored a goal in each of the four games she started on that trip. The American women took three of the five games played against France, England, Holland, Germany, and Denmark.

✪ ✪ ✪

The more games we played that year the more I noticed another attitude shift. Not only were we playing for something—a world championship at the 1991 World Cup—but we had more of a shared identity as a team than I think we'd ever felt before.

I said earlier that when I started playing on the National Team in 1985 I didn't really feel as if I was representing my country. It truly had felt much more like a traveling all-star squad of select players who just happened to go play in Europe. As the years passed, we'd certainly begun to feel more like a team—we'd come to know and appreciate each other—I'm just not sure we ever really felt we were representing and playing for our country. Most of us simply loved soccer so much that we got as much satisfaction and enjoyment going head-to-head with our own teammates in practice as we did in games against teams from other countries. And a lot of times the competition was stiffer among ourselves.

So for a number of those years our greatest motivation both as individuals and as a team had been our love of the game more than patriotism. Not that we were in any sense un-American or selfish, playing solely for ourselves and our own gratification, but it's hard to get psyched up or even to feel like you're truly representing or playing for someone who doesn't know you exist. We remained so far below the radar screen of public awareness in America during those years that we felt we had no one to play for but each other.

That is probably one of the things that helped bond us so closely as a group. It didn't happen overnight, though. It took years of exposure to one another, experiencing shared hardship, training, and travel, and getting to know, learning to trust, and coming to depend on each other—on the field and off.

I'm basically a shy person with a naturally reserved personality. So during those early years I mostly hung out with two or three players I considered my closest friends on the team—Amy Allmann, Debbie Belkin, and eventually Carin Jennings. But as time went by, and team policies required the rotation of roommate assignments from trip to trip, I began to feel more comfortable around all of my teammates.

⚽ ⚽ ⚽

It also took several of Michelle's teammates some time to feel as if they knew her. Kristine Lilly, who has played alongside Michelle for thirteen years, remembers her early impressions: "The first National Team camp I came to, Michelle was just such an overwhelming force that I watched her play and thought, 'Holy Cow!' She could be dominant wherever she was on the field. She could take on any five players, get up, and still run and finish. She never stopped. She never sold herself short. She gave her all—every game, every practice, every drill we ran. I admired that. But it was intimidating."

Julie Foudy, or "Loudy Foudy" as Michelle calls her boisterous teammate, remembers much the same reaction when she began playing regularly in 1988. "I was in awe of her physically," Julie says. "She was such a presence on the field. That was back in the days before the National Team got any publicity or was ever on television. Yet people knew Michelle. She stood out.

"By 1991 she stood out even more. We were all among the best women soccer players in America. We played against more of the best players in the world. And then there was Michelle, who played on an entirely different, and higher, level.

"She could score all kinds of ways. She was better than anyone else at winning and heading balls in the air. Michelle had the most powerful shot in the world. Free kicks for her were always an offensive weapon. She could volley and half-volley with the best. And she could do it all with her left or her right foot, so she might score from anywhere at any time. Her skill as well as her intensity made her very intimidating—not just to opponents but to those of us who practiced with her."

Both Kristine and Julie admit it was a gradual process, but they eventually realized that the same person who could be such a dominating presence on the soccer field was very different from what they'd first assumed.

"She's so intensely focused playing soccer," says Kristine, "it took a while for me to realize she can be very laid-back and light-hearted in other situations. She is so gullible that she's the butt of a lot of jokes. We'll tell her the team is supposed to wear

*our gray shirts to dinner and she'll show up in gray only to find everyone else is wear-
ing red. And she'll laugh—she always takes it well."*

*"She's kind of the team's designated blonde," Julie laughs, "always getting direc-
tions wrong, often on a different page from everyone else. Someone will tell a joke
and Michelle will go, 'Huh? I don't get it.' One of us will try to explain it, but then
it's never as funny. Or Michelle will start laughing three minutes after everyone else
and when we look at her to try to figure out what's going on, she'll say, 'I just got it.'*

"That's when we tell her, 'You've taken one too many headers, Mish.'"

*Speaking of headers, Julie continues, "I'll never forget the time Mish came down
to breakfast with this huge black-and-blue bruise above one of her eyes. 'What happened to you?' I wanted to know.*

*"Mish looked a little sheepish, admitting, 'I had this real vivid dream. We were
playing this game. A ball went in the air and when I leaped for it I headed the night-
stand instead.' Then she began to demonstrate how she had actually headed a night-
stand in her sleep. She cracked everybody up."*

⊛ ⊛ ⊛

But only part of the growing closeness and camaraderie on our team was
the natural result of factors such as time, familiarity, and humor. The more
games we played against other national teams, the closer we got to that first
Women's World Cup in 1991, the longer we pursued our world championship
goal, the greater grew the sense that we weren't just playing soccer for ourselves, but for a greater purpose—a purpose we all shared. Whether or not
very many of our fellow citizens yet realized it, or cared, we were indeed representing friends, family, and country. We really were playing for the USA.

It was that knowledge that gave our team an unprecedented sense of mission, resolve, and unity. It was now *us* against the world!

Soon after we returned from that second European trip of the year, I got a
phone call from Mick Hoban, the Umbro executive who'd given me his card
after I spoke at the Soccer Industry Council meeting. He wanted to fly me to
the company's annual sales conference where I would sign a contract to represent his company and endorse their soccer shoes and apparel.

This was a big deal—not just for me but for the sport. Never before had
any company signed a woman soccer player to an endorsement contract.

There was one major problem. I was helping at a soccer camp at Evergreen
State College in Olympia, Washington, when I got the call from Umbro. They
wanted to fly me straight from there to appear at a big dress-up dinner at their

sales conference in the Smoky Mountains of North Carolina. All I had with me were blue jeans, T-shirts, and soccer shorts, and I couldn't get home to Florida before the meeting.

Fortunately, someone at the camp had a mail-order catalog of women's clothes. I phoned in an order for a classy-looking business suit and dress shoes in my size. My new outfit arrived the following day by overnight delivery, just in time for me to take off for the East Coast. That's how I showed up for the big Umbro shindig the next evening wearing my brand-new, orange Victoria's Secret dress suit—with Band-Aids on my feet because my new shoes were killing me.

The banquet itself turned out to be a very impressive affair, with a wonderful surprise in my honor. I sat up front, where I was introduced to all the Umbro folks and their guests. And then, after dinner, the lights went down and a voice boomed out over the speakers: "When Michelle Akers was still a little girl kicking a ball around her backyard in Santa Clara, California, Brazilian soccer superstar Pelé . . . the greatest soccer player in the history of the world . . . was leading his nation's teams to World Cup glory . . . then playing for the New York Cosmos in this country's first professional soccer league . . ."

At the same time, footage of Pelé playing and scoring and celebrating his many triumphs was being projected on a giant screen behind me. Then the film ended, the lights came back up, and there on the dais, smiling and waving in acknowledgment of the applause and cheers of our audience, stood Pelé himself. As a longtime company spokesperson, he welcomed me into the Umbro family and presented me with one of his Cosmos jerseys, which he autographed to me on the spot.

I was so overwhelmed it was all I could do to keep my bottom jaw from falling to the floor. Here I was sharing a platform and applause with the great Pelé. I couldn't believe it.

Someone asked if I had anything I wanted to say. I said, "No," and walked back to my seat. I didn't know what I could say.

I chatted a while that evening with Pelé, telling him about our team and asking him about his World Cup experience. What a warm, wonderful man.

And I did sign with Umbro. However, I had no idea at the time what that would entail. I remember being excited about the prospect of having enough income that I could afford to keep playing soccer and not have to borrow money or, as I'd done before, apply to sports foundations for grants to cover my expenses while I trained for the National Team.

I knew this was an important first not just for me, but for women's soccer. So I proudly signed my name to that endorsement contract thinking, *Good!*

People are starting to notice us. Now all the other players on the team will get sponsors of their own.

But that didn't happen right away. And in the meantime, I still had my own first World Cup for which to prepare.

In August of 1991 we took a pre-World Cup trip to China to play a three-game series of "friendlies" (non-tournament games) against their national team. I suppose the idea for the tour was to familiarize ourselves with the tournament setting ahead of time, but some of us began to wonder if this trip might also be one last attempt by Anson to further bond us together with yet another hearty dose of shared hardship. I'm pretty sure that was the trip we endured so many transportation snags and layover problems that it took us sixty-four straight hours of travel time to get to our first destination in China. And the hotel accommodations were little better than in Haiti. We had running water only one hour a day. Then our bathrooms flooded, leaving some of us to double up in other rooms and sleep two to a bed.

Playing without the leadership of our captain, April Heinrichs, who was recovering from recent knee surgery, we struggled a bit on the field as well, losing to the Chinese 1–2 in the first game and tying them 2–2 in the second. I scored one goal apiece in those games before finally breaking out for a "hat trick"—three goals in one game—in our 3–0 victory in the tour's final game.

Everything seemed to be back on track as we headed home—until disaster struck later that month.

During a short break in our National Team schedule, I worked another Post to Post soccer camp in California. I was out on the field doing a breakaway demonstration with a goalkeeper. On a long touch toward goal, as I tried to get past him, he dove, stuffing me and the ball. I went sailing over the top and when I hit the ground I heard a *clunk*. I had landed on a sprinkler head sticking out of the turf. I remember thinking, *Uh, oh! This could be bad.* I rolled over Bernie, the keeper, and got a good look at my right knee. The metal had torn a wicked-looking gash so deep and so long that it looked like I'd sliced my kneecap halfway off. I quickly pulled a chunk of loose sod out of the wound and covered it with my hand so no one else would freak out if they saw it. Bernie yelled for help. Thankfully, there was a trainer on site who helped carry me off the field and sat with me on the sideline applying pressure to control the bleeding until the session ended.

We then went to a local emergency room where a San Diego Chargers doctor used sixty-some stitches to sew everything back together and told me I was lucky I didn't do more damage.

He also told me I shouldn't be walking on that knee for a while. That it would be weeks, maybe months, before I should start playing on it again. That I might even have to miss the World Cup. I remember thinking, *We'll see about that!*

Then I had to place a very difficult call to Anson telling him what had happened. "I don't know how long it will be before I can play," I said. Then I had to hang up on him and run on my crutches to the bathroom and throw up because the pain medication was wreaking havoc on my stomach.

I missed the next couple of tune-up games the team played in New England against a Norwegian national team that promised to be some of our toughest competition at the World Cup. We lost both games, 0–1 and 1–2.

We hosted the Chinese team for our final two warm-up games during October. My knee still hadn't healed, and the suture scars were tender, so I played with a heavy sleeve over my knee to reduce the risk of the wound tearing open again during the game. We lost the first game of the set 1–2.

In the second game against China I got taken down on a hard foul. When the official didn't even blow his whistle, I was so ticked that I yelled at the ref, who gave me a red card for my choice of words. After Anson leaped up and voiced his own protest he was shown a red, too. We both had to leave the field and watch the rest of the game from the stands with my dad and Sue, who'd flown in on a red-eye flight from Seattle just in time to see me play an entire ten minutes of the first half.

They were less than happy. I didn't blame them. They did, however, get to see me score one goal before getting ejected—a free kick I'd been practicing with Tony DiCicco, our goalkeeper coach, for months. I netted it from almost thirty yards out, then sprinted to the bench and jumped on Tony to celebrate.

We ended up winning 2–0. Even so, that game was not exactly the kind of pre-tournament preparation I'd wanted or needed. My knee still wasn't right.

What bothered me even more was knowing I'd be facing the most important games of my life the following month. And it looked like I would be playing at less than a hundred percent.

Chapter Eleven
THE '91 WORLD CUP EXPERIENCE

In the last weeks before the World Cup I spent a lot of time trying to imagine what the experience would be like. In my mind, I had this recurring vision that always ended the same way: I would leap into the air with my arms extended in victory towards the heavens, and as my feet hit the ground, I sprinted in reckless abandon toward my teammates. Weak with exhaustion and emotion, I saw ecstatic, smiling faces. Some crying. Others laughing. Many doing both at the same time.

We hugged and tackled each other, rolling around on the ground. We were celebrating the first world championship of women's soccer. And when we regained our composure, we lined up to accept the trophy before our families and 60,000 applauding fans.

Every time an alternative ending to my World Cup dream entered my thoughts, I immediately dismissed it. In my mind only a fairy-tale ending would do.

I shared my vision with the millions of readers of *USA Today* in the first of a series of guest columns I was asked to write for that newspaper. I explained that our team's only goal was to come home with a world championship.

" . . . We are confident in our ability to compete at the international level. But we know," I acknowledged, "if we are not at our best on any given day, we can be beaten. There are no guarantees."

I wrote that in our last days of training in North Carolina, we were "focused and excited. But we are also apprehensive. After waiting six years to compete in a world championship, we're tired of waiting. Let the games begin!"

But first we had to get there. And let me tell you, whoever coined the saying "getting there is half the fun" never traveled from Chapel Hill, North Carolina, to Guangzhou (formerly Canton), China, for the FIFA Women's World Cup Championship.

Sunday morning the tenth of November we flew from Durham to New York City for the privilege of a six-hour layover at JFK. While in New York we received new sweats, T-shirts, shoes, and autograph cards. And knowing we wouldn't be on American soil again for almost a month, we took one last opportunity to stuff our faces with pizza, Taco Bell, frozen yogurt, and Diet Coke.

We flew directly from JFK to Zurich, Switzerland, where we met the plane FIFA had booked for us, along with four European national teams, to fly to China. The flight east seemed to last a lifetime, not only because of the distance but because we were forced to spend the time in such close quarters with our opponents from Sweden, Norway, Germany, and Denmark. It seemed such a strange, and strained, situation.

The Swedish coach, Gunilla Paijkull, and I greeted each other with big hugs. She had coached the club team I played for in Sweden and I hadn't seen her since the year before. We briefly brought each other up-to-date on our personal lives and exchanged tidbits of news about shared acquaintances. But out of deep respect for each other, we didn't talk about the World Cup at all. Neither of us even referred to the fact that we'd be opposing each other in the opening game that coming Sunday. Maybe after the tournament was over we would sit down and share our feelings, but there was just too much tension to discuss it right then on that crowded airplane.

It felt weird trying to be casual and friendly around people you knew you were going to compete against in the next few days. When we weren't sleeping, or at least trying to, we mostly kept to ourselves—playing cards, chatting, laughing, playing jokes on one another, and trying to pass the time the best we could. But looking around from time to time at our opponents, I couldn't help wondering which ones I'd match up against on the field, what made each one special, or who might score the goal which could put us out of the tournament. When I'd make eye contact with them, I realized these girls were very likely wondering the same thing. And they'd probably been dreaming the same dreams of victory for as long as I had. Yet I hoped my dream would be the one that came true.

What a relief to land in Guangzhou, China, at the end of our long journey. To escape our cramped quarters and just stretch our legs felt like heaven. Unfortunately, after not having slept for two days, our team went straight to the practice field. Feeling groggy, jet-lagged, even a little dizzy, we struggled through the last of our fitness training. "Let's just do this and get it over with," we told each other. Then we could check into our hotel and sleep.

In my next report I told *USA Today* readers, "Everybody is excited about being here. You'd expect people to be serious, but we are having fun. . . . It's a relief to know the hard part—fitness, the forty-hour trip, the player cuts—is over. Now comes the easy part. All we have to do is play."

But as thrilled as our team was to have finally arrived in China for the World Cup, our excitement actually intensified when the small but big-hearted contingent of family and friends arrived just before our opening game. Dad and Sue came, as well as Roby, along with a lot of other players' parents.

One of the most special aspects of that whole World Cup experience was having our families there to share it with us. To watch our parents look around in wide-eyed amazement at the World Cup excitement that gripped the entire nation—at the long, red World Cup banners hanging from all the downtown buildings, the front-page newspaper coverage, the television cameras following us everywhere, the crowds thronging around for autographs—was especially rewarding. After spending half their lives driving us to and from soccer practices, after investing a small fortune in select camps and uniform fees and soccer shoes, after years of lending us their emotional and financial support when we'd graduated from college and decided to pursue a soccer ball instead of a career—it must have felt like a validation of all our dreams. What we'd gradually begun to understand over the past few months, our families now suddenly realized: this was a *big* deal.

What made it feel even bigger was that this was the first time many parents had seen the U.S. National Team play real international competition. In the six years prior to 1991 we'd played a grand total of six games in the United States, all of them in Blaine, Minnesota.

We brought one other thing we couldn't get in China: some American nutrition. Carla Werden had lost ten pounds during our previous visit to China. On our trip to Bulgaria earlier in the year, Lil was so put off by the food that all she had eaten for days were cucumbers. We couldn't risk such dietary problems during a physically grueling tournament like the World Cup, so two North Carolina restauranteurs, Greg Overbeck (Carla's future husband) and Pete Dorrance (Anson's brother), came along to cook some of our meals for us in China. Rather than having us rely too heavily on our usual supplemental stash of Snickers and Combos, a little home cooking proved a great addition to our new game plan.

⚽ ⚽ ⚽

I proudly displayed my first trophy after a 1970 fishing expedition with my dad.

Dad, Mom, Mike, and me at my grandparents' for Christmas.

The only downside to my first day of school at Montague Elementary in Santa Clara, California, in the fall of 1972 was having to wear a dress.

Mike and I loved wearing Dad's old Marine Corps hats. (July, 1975)

I wanted to quit my first soccer team, the Cougars, because I hated losing every game even more than I hated the team colors. Mom (top right) made me stick it out. I'm second from the right in the first row, in braids and my sweet pink uniform.

I fouled out after only five minutes in my first game of varsity hoops at Shorecrest High School. Obviously not my game. Nice pose, huh?

I lettered in soccer all four years for the Shorecrest Scots. We won the state championship my senior year.

Here's a recent shot of me with Al Kovats, my fave high school teacher and a major influence on my life.

Soccer helped give me a new family when my dad remarried in 1984. From the left, that's my step-brother, John, my stepsis, Shelley, my stepmom, Sue (aka Sue-Sue, The Rocket, the step-monster, etc.), Pops, my brother Mike, and me.

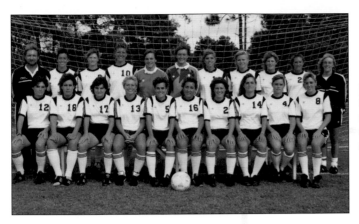

I played college soccer for the University of Central Florida in Orlando. That's me wearing #10, fourth from the left on the second row.

The intensity of college soccer surprised me my freshman year. But I loved it.

PERRY MCINTYRE

I had a lot to celebrate with my college team—winning seasons, high national rankings, regular appearances in the NCAA tournament, and All-American honors all four years.

None of us understood the significance of that very first U.S. Women's National Team when we went to Italy for four games in 1985.

A prize post-game portrait after a head-to-head collision versus Australia on a national team trip to Taiwan in 1987. My teammates and a few of the Aussies gathered to watch me get stitched up in a hotel room later that night.

My freshman college roommate and S.W.A.T. partner, Amy Allmann, also played with me on the Women's National Team. Here we are on a team trip to Bulgaria in 1991.

Dad flew clear across the country to watch me play a warm-up game against China prior to the 1991 World Cup. When I got booted (red carded) early in the match we had some unexpected together time in the stands.

I scored the first goal versus Norway in the 1991 World Cup final on a header.

PHIL STEPHENS

With only minutes remaining in the final match, I stole the ball en route to scoring the winning goal in the 2-1 U.S. victory over Norway.

Yeah, baby! We did it! The first ever Women's World Cup champs!

My step-mom, Sue, is not only one of my biggest fans, she's like a big sister and one of my closest friends.

Playing for Tyreso FF in a Swedish professional league in 1990 (and again in '92 and '94) helped elevate my game.

When I signed my very first endorsement deal in 1991, I was truly honored to have Pele there to welcome me into the Umbro family.

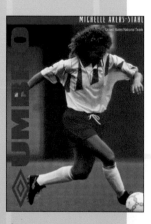

One of my first Umbro autograph cards from 1992.

I tried to hide it, but I was sick as a dog with CFIDS during this 1993 photo shoot with my two canine buddies, Keena and Ayra.

After our 1991 championship I spoke all over the world promoting women's soccer and crusading to get our game accepted as an official Olympic sport.

Hiking in the Cascades has always been my favorite getaway. Here I am with my brother, Mike, in 1993.

My college buddy Goz (Lisa Gozley) and I shared a lot of laughs and memories when she showed up at this Umbro appearance back in 1993.

After double knee surgery while playing pro in Sweden during 1994, the Swedish doctor told me my soccer playing days were over. I was too stubborn to listen.

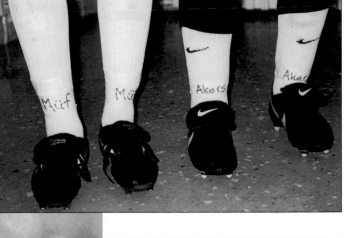

Inset left: Our team trainer, Patty Marchak, had to guide me off the field after a head-to-head collision with a Chinese player nearly ended my '95 World Cup experience in the opening minutes of the very first game.

Above top: After being knocked out of the tournament, my teammates honored me by writing my name on their socks for the following games.

Left: I made it back to play one-legged in our 1-0 semifinal loss to Norway. This Akers sandwich shot pretty accurately shows what kind of game it was for me.

Above center: I was back on the bench between Doc Brown and Patty for the 3rd place game. I may have been smiling on the outside, but in truth I was barely holding back the tears.

 My family's cabin in the mountains outside Seattle has always been a favorite place for retreat and renewal.

WORLDWIDE CHALLENGE

JUDY NELSON

↑
I board my horse Vinnie on a farm outside Orlando and ride him every chance I get.

↑
Showing kids a few speed movement drills during a clinic with Soccer Outreach International and Sports Specific Training group of Orlando, Florida.

WORLDWIDE CHALLENGE

My former WNT teammate Sal (Amanda Cromwell) regularly helps me conduct clinics and other Soccer Outreach International events. Here we are a couple of years ago at the Northwest Soccer Camp outside Seattle.

After speaking to an Orlando area high school soccer team, my good friend Steve Slain and I lead the girls in prayer.

Dealing with the media is a big part of our jobs as National Team players.

WORLDWIDE CHALLENGE

Longtime national team coach, Anson Dorrance, repeatedly reminded us that it was our job to "sell" our sport. Every game, every interview, every clinic we conducted, every person we met was "a chance to convert a skeptic into a new fan." That's one reason we now have so many wonderful fans.

WORLDWIDE CHALLENGE

I caught some perspective and restoration time hiking the North Cascades after the frustrating disappointment of the '95 World Cup. Dad took the photo.

My penalty kick in the '96 Olympics tied the semifinal against Norway and sent the game into overtime. We won 2-1.

Yes! Rock on! Putting the shot in the back of the net, knowing an Olympic medal was on the line, was one of the greatest feelings in the world!

Millie (Tiffeny Milbrett) tackled me after we took the Olympic Gold with a 2-1 victory over China. My strongest sensation was one of relief. Now I could finally rest.

During the medal ceremony I had to search the stands for Dad.

When I spotted him I showed and shared the Gold Medal moment with my Pops.

Getting a hug from coach Tony DiCicco in celebration of my 100th international goal against Portugal in January, 1999.

Looking a little black and blue after breaking my face in yet another head-to-head collision in the FIFA World All-Star game in February of 1999.

PERRY MCINTYRE

That's my trainer/buddy Steve Slain applying ice to a thrashed knee.

Millie is one team-mate I can always count on anytime to pick up some good java at Starbucks.

World Cup '99 action: 1. Challenging for the ball against Nigeria. 2. A tough tackle vs. China. 3. My extra special coffee brew helped raise my blood pressure enough to play. 4. Getting yellow carded for rough play during the final. 5. I wrote Joshua 1:9, my inspirational Bible verse, on my socks for the final. 6. My typical post-game IV treatment 7. Winning a header against Nigeria.

1. Got my bell rung again. 2. Doc Adams takes me to the trauma room after I collapsed in the 90th minute in the final. 3. A little later I made it back out to celebrate. Number one, baby! 4. Smashing through a Denmark player to win a headball. 5. Celebrating my PK against Brazil in the semifinal game. 6. One very short victory lap for the crowd; one very special moment for me.

Dad and I hiked the Cascades again after the '99 World Cup. But he got so sick we barely made it off the mountain. Doctors diagnosed colon cancer a few weeks later.

The Seattle Mariners invited me to throw out the first pitch at the second game ever played in Safeco Field.

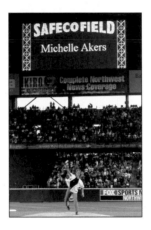

Cool, huh! Four of my teammates and I became the first soccer players ever to make it on the Wheaties box.

Jimmy DeYoung escorted me at the 1999 ESPN Arete Awards event.

After the World Cup '99 my college buddy Laurie Hayden (now Trevers) and I got together on her father's horse farm outside Atlanta. Despite the pre-graduation worries, Hades and I are still great friends.

Despite the U.S. Women's National Team's combined record from 1990 through 1991 of 21 victories, 6 losses, and 1 tie (including a string of fourteen consecutive shutouts), China, Germany, and Norway were the experts' picks to win the World Cup. Because the U.S. National Team's program was so new and because the U.S. had never been considered a true soccer power, the American women went into the tournament as real underdogs. And the recent spate of injuries also seemed to hurt their chances.

In addition to April Heinrich's having surgery on both knees, center midfielder Shannon Higgins was recovering from a stress fracture in her left foot. Marking back Linda Hamilton required surgery on her left knee. Goalkeeper Mary Harvey suffered recurring back problems as a result of surgery years earlier. Another midfielder, Tracey Bates, pulled a hamstring. Starter Megan McCarthy tore her ACL and didn't even make the tournament squad, though the players all pitched in so she could make the trip and be on the bench with the team. And Michelle's knee still hadn't fully healed from her August encounter with the sprinkler head.

How ready would the U.S. team be when the tournament began? Many question marks remained. The fact that their first opponent was a team they had never beaten only added to the suspense.

❂ ❂ ❂

Sixteen thousand fans packed the stadium in Punyu for our opening game against Sweden. Amazing. I don't know that we'd ever played in front of that many people in any one year, let alone one game. What a feeling!

Before the game, the national anthem brought tears to my eyes. It hit me like a wave. I realized, *This is it!* The anticipation of the unknown—victory or defeat—was almost too much for me.

No matter how much nervous energy and adrenaline is pumping before a game, usually once the action begins and my body gets a little tired, I lose the nervous edge and begin to feel more composed. Once I focus, it's as if everything shifts into slow motion and I can almost see things develop before they happen. But through the entire game against Sweden everything seemed to be racing at 100 miles an hour. And it never slowed down.

Carin Jennings tallied two goals early. And when Mia Hamm scored on a twenty-five-yarder during the sixty-first minute to give us a 3–0 lead, the game looked to be over. But Sweden scored twice in the next ten minutes and we staggered around in exhaustion the last twenty minutes of the game, fighting desperately to hang on. When the final gun sounded, we hadn't so much won as we had *survived*, 3–2.

On the field afterward, hugging my friend Gunilla, I could see the defeat and disappointment in her eyes. I felt a sense of genuine compassion. I knew that easily could have been me. But then, telling myself there could only be one winner, I quickly dismissed my sympathetic feelings. I wanted nothing to hinder us in our goal of becoming world champions.

Feeling relieved just to have a win under our belts, we talked at practice the next day about how we needed to play smarter with a lead. We couldn't afford to let a team we should have put away get back into a game. We chalked up the scary finish against the Swedes to first game World Cup jitters. We determined not to make the same mistake against Brazil on Tuesday.

We didn't. April scored two goals. Carin, Mia, and I each scored one in what turned out to be a much-easier-than-expected 5–0 win in our first-ever encounter with Brazil. Since the top two teams from each of three groupings and the two second-place teams with the best records all advanced, we knew going into our third and final first round game that we'd already qualified for the quarterfinals. Anson took the opportunity against Japan to rest five of our starters who were banged up with various dings and bruises. I scored early in the game to give us the lead. Then I scored again, and Wendy Gebauer slotted our third and final score just before the half in a game that never really seemed in doubt.

✪ ✪ ✪

After the 3–0 victory over Japan, Anson Dorrance told the press that his American team had gone into the game with the specific intention of getting more scoring opportunities for Michelle. He said he thought she'd played well the first two games of the tournament, but Michelle hadn't felt that good about her effort. "She's come off the field to ask me if she played well." Anson indicated what Michelle needed to understand: "She doesn't have to score to play well. She absolutely saved us against Sweden clearing balls out of the area with headers. But for her own confidence and well-being, she needed to stick a couple. We needed her to taste the back of the net. If we're going to win this tournament, we need her playing well."

In the opening-round games of the World Cup, after each of the three top scorers on the U.S. team had contributed two-goal games, the Chinese press dubbed the offensive line of Heinrichs, Jennings, and Akers the Americans' dangerous "three-edged sword." A fortunate opponent might avoid one, or two, but never all three.

What admiring press and fans didn't know was they hadn't seen anything yet. In the quarterfinals, Michelle did much better than "well." She set a World Cup record (which still stands) with an astounding five goals in her team's 7–0 trouncing of Taiwan.

"My shooting was on," she acknowledged to the press after the game. "But I didn't think I played particularly well except for my shooting. . . . I'm not the kind of player who dribbles through six people and gets a goal. I usually receive a pass from Carin, or Carin gets fouled and I get a free kick, or Mia gets fouled and I get a penalty kick. Those are the kinds of goals I get. It's a team effort."

The Americans were going to need a team effort in the semifinal game against Germany, probably the most skillful soccer team in the entire tournament. Like the U.S., they were 4–0 in the tournament. They had outscored their opponents 12–3; the United States had amassed an 18–2 scoring edge. The German's big offensive gun, Heidi Mohr, had already scored six World Cup goals, second only to Michelle's eight.

⚽ ⚽ ⚽

We knew we were in for a battle. You could feel the tension building over the next couple of days. Individually and as a team we realized we were going to have to sharpen our focus in order to compete, let alone win. Looking around at my teammates in practice I realized this was where we were going to learn who had it and who didn't. None of us had ever before played for these kind of stakes—never had there been so much on the line.

I remember thinking, *This is fun! This is what we've prepared for these past six years. This is what World Cup soccer is all about!*

After playing our first two games in Punyu, with games three and four in Foshan, we were back in Guangzhou for the remainder of the tournament. That too had been a major goal since our arrival in China, not only because it meant that we'd advanced to the final rounds, but because we were now finally staying in a first-class hotel.

"The goat city," Guangzhou, was China's *official* World Cup city. Bright, beautiful, yellow and red chrysanthemum beds had been planted throughout the city to provide festive tournament colors. Many of the downtown buildings were decorated with impressive strands of lights that twinkled at night.

Our hotel, the White Swan, was draped with colored lights depicting a flying soccer ball and the tournament mascot, "a luck-bringing thrush" the Chinese had named Ling-Ling. In the hotel lobby decorated with Chinese lanterns stood a case, guarded by two armed soldiers, containing the symbol of all our dreams: the golden World Cup trophy.

Of course, what excited our team most about the White Swan was that this hotel actually served American hamburgers.

We all had fire in our eyes when we paraded into Guangzhou's Tianhe Stadium for our match with Germany on Wednesday evening the twenty-seventh of November. For the first time in the tournament, the opening ceremonies included a full verse of "The Star-Spangled Banner" instead of a shortened thirty-second version. We all sang enthusiastically with the music as I searched the stands for my family. *There they are!* At 6'3" with long, blond hair, Dad stood out in a Chinese crowd. There was Sue. And Roby, watching through the lens of our ever-present video camera.

There too in the stands I spotted Pelé. The world's greatest soccer legend had come to watch the final matches of the first-ever Women's World Cup. *Wow!*

From the start of the game, it was clear the Germans had determined they were not going to let me beat them. Fortunately, I didn't have to. I'd never taken the kind of physical pounding I received in that game. Fouled repeatedly and absolutely hammered a number of times, I could only get back up and continue to distribute the ball to the other two edges of our "three-edged sword" attack. April scored twice, and Gumby (our team's name for Carin because she was pigeon-toed and so deceptive with her dribbling skills that her crazy legs whipped back and forth like rubber when she dribbled down the field) netted three balls.

By the time the final whistle blew for a final score of 5–2, I collapsed in exhaustion and cried in relief. We had made the finals!

The next day was Thanksgiving. There was so much for which we were grateful, not the least of which was a traditional American holiday feast, complete with turkey, dressing, and all the trimmings—which hadn't been that easy to come by in China.

It turns out that our team administrator, Heather Kashner, who arranged our special meal, had first asked our hosts if they could get us some turkeys for a holiday dinner. When she got back to our hotel the next night, she found a flock of live turkeys in her hotel room, like we were going to kill them, pluck them, clean them, and cook them ourselves! She had to graciously return the birds to our hosts, explaining that we preferred frozen Butterballs.

Once we sorted out that little cross-cultural misunderstanding, our Thanksgiving dinner turned out to be yet another incredible memory for us to share with our parents and families. By this time, the relationships that had begun to develop among the American contingent of families and friends were fun to watch. After years of developing our own friendships as teammates, most of us were meeting each others' families for the first time. To see our parents becoming friends gave our team a greater sense of unity than we'd ever before experienced. It was wonderful.

A special guest joined us for our Thanksgiving meal. I'll never forget the look on Dad's face when Pelé asked my permission to sit at our family's table, then thanked my father for having me. Pops got so flustered to meet Pelé that he actually knocked his own glasses off. (I come by my nickname "Grace" honestly.) Sue and I just about cracked up. And what a kick I got out of seeing the thrill Dad, Sue, and Roby experienced talking soccer over turkey dinner with the greatest to ever play the game.

Contrary to what most people might think, I felt surprisingly relaxed going into the final. The road to the final is always an uphill struggle in any big tournament. But when you finally get there at least you know you're at the top of the hill, and there's a real sense of relief.

We knew our opponent well. We'd played Norway more times over the years than any other international opponent. Though our record was only 3–4 in those matches, we knew what to expect from them. We knew what we had to do to win. And we knew we *would* win if we played up to our potential.

We were now only one step away from our dream. It was hard to think of anything else for the next two days.

We discovered there was plenty of anxiety left when Saturday evening rolled around. Our bus ride from the hotel to Tianhe Stadium seemed to last an eternity. We sat in our uniforms, cleats in hand, with Walkmans blasting. Waiting. As we inched our way through stop-and-go traffic, I stared out the window at the city, wishing I could fast-forward time to 9 P.M. so I could know the outcome and calm my nerves.

Walking into the stadium, I looked for my family. Even among 65,000 plus Chinese—the largest crowd ever to witness any women's sporting event up to that time—I spotted Dad right away. He waved wildly. I gave him a big thumbs-up gesture—which has been our personal tradition at soccer games ever since—and thought again how wonderful it was to have family behind us.

Sixty-five thousand people! Unbelievable! We'd played international games with crowds so small the fans couldn't have joined hands and stretched all the way around the field once. Now here we were playing in a packed-out stadium with our families present to enjoy the game and the glory.

After the usual pregame rituals, Pelé was introduced to the crowd before posing with both squads for the official team photos. He shook hands and offered a word of encouragement to each player. As he greeted me by name I wondered how he had felt before his first World Cup final.

When the game finally started, the Norwegians came out fired up. From the beginning, we had to withstand long-driven balls, hard tackles, and fierce attacks. They had come to play.

But so had we.

Twenty minutes into the contest the official awarded us a free kick just outside the penalty box, twenty-five to thirty yards from the goal on the right side. Shannon Higgins lofted a beauty, high toward the net. I leaped along with a Norwegian girl at the front edge of the six-yard keeper box, got my head on the ball, and sent it sailing back to the goalkeeper's left and into the right side of the net for our first score.

Unfortunately, that lead didn't last long. Norway scored minutes later off a free kick of their own. For the rest of the first half we ran up and down the field with neither team getting an advantage or capitalizing on any scoring chances.

We walked off the pitch with a 1–1 tie and into what quickly became a chaotic halftime locker room. People wanted to know who should mark up. What changes did we need to make? Everyone was really on edge. Anson was trying to give instructions and encourage people to calm down at the same time.

I remember sitting there, not listening to any of it, just wanting to get back out on the field and play.

Traipsing out of the tunnel for the second half, Tony DiCicco walked beside me. "Mish," he said, "you're going to be the one. You're going to have to take control of this game yourself."

I nodded. "Okay, Tony. Okay."

And that's what I set out to do. But the second half started much like the first. The Norwegians banged long balls into our half with our defenders trying to clear the balls out before they could press the advantage. Every time we'd work the ball forward they'd whack it downfield over our midfielders and we'd have to turn and sprint back on defense again.

We were slowly wearing each other down, yet neither team could score. Most observers, and a lot of people down on the field, were beginning to assume overtime or penalty kicks were inevitable. But I never quit feeling as if a chance would come.

With just minutes left in the game it happened. Shannon Higgins hit a long ball upfield. While it was a bit ahead of me, you never know what will happen if you apply a little pressure, so I sprinted after it. Two Norwegian defenders closed on the ball as it rolled toward their goal—but then they hesitated for a fraction of a second. Their mistake.

I picked up my speed and smashed into the girl closest to me, knocking her into her teammate. Before they could recover, the ball was mine.

I took a long touch a little to the left of the goal, and we had a footrace to see who would get to the ball first—the charging goalkeeper or me. I managed to touch the ball again to the left and still leap over the late-diving keeper. Suddenly, there was no one between me and a wide-open goal.

I was a little wide to the left, so a thousand thoughts raced through my mind in the next split-second. *Relax! This is my one chance. I've gotta make this. Don't kick it into the side netting. Don't kick it over. Whatever you do, don't miss the goal.* So I took one extra touch and passed it gently into the goal with the side of my right foot. USA 2, Norway 1.

My teammates told me later they died a thousand deaths as they watched and waited for what seemed like forever for me to carefully set up that last shot.

I know I pumped a fist in the air and shouted a loud "YES!" But I don't remember any other celebration. I think I was too tired to celebrate and wanted to conserve my energy for the remainder of the game.

I do recall that we spent the rest of the match just trying to clear the ball out of the stadium. And when the final whistle blew I thought it was a foul and began sprinting back into our box to defend. Only then did I see my teammates jumping up and down and realize the game was truly over.

The celebration was just as I had imagined. I jumped. We hugged. We laughed and we cried. My screaming teammates and I ran around in a wild frenzy, not knowing who to hug next or what to say. It was awesome. Even now, looking back, my memory of that celebration and the medal ceremony is one big crazy blur.

The American fans in the stands were going berserk at the same time. I spotted Dad waving wildly. My husband, Roby, found me out on the field just as the team started our victory lap. He abandoned his usually stoic demeanor as he embraced me, weeping openly. We stood there, crying like babies together, in front of all those photographers, television cameras, and a stadium full of 65,000 fans.

Many parents and families found their way into our locker room, where we shared more hugs and posed for laughing, teary photos, clinging to one another and our world championship trophy. But Tianhe Stadium wasn't even completely emptied when the team had to reboard our bus and rush back to the hotel for a special World Cup awards banquet held just for the teams and their official delegations.

Carin Jennings, who'd had such a fantastic tournament, won the Golden Ball Award as the tournament's Most Valuable Player. I was awarded the Golden Boot Award for scoring the most goals in the tournament—a total of ten in six games.

But what I remember most about that official banquet was how impatient I was for it to end. My teammates and I just wanted to get out of there so we could go really celebrate with each other and our families. I don't think we could possibly have been any happier.

"This is the best I've ever felt in my whole life," April Heinrichs told the press.

"It's the greatest thing that's ever happened to me," Carin Jennings said.

But Julie Foudy may have summed up all our sentiments best by saying, "When we first started this team, we never thought there would be a world championship for women. It was always this mystical thing—a World Cup. And now we're holding it in our hands!"

The fairy tale ending had come true. Just like I'd dreamed it would.

But if I thought that meant everyone was going to live happily ever after, I had never been more wrong.

 Part

FOUR

Broken Dreams:
The Valley Years

Chapter Twelve
DOWN FROM THE MOUNTAINTOP

*W*e had been focused on our goal for so long that I don't think many of my teammates had thought beyond November 30, 1991. I know I hadn't. I woke up on December 1 facing a future I hadn't prepared for and couldn't quite imagine.

Now that I'd achieved my dream, I expected life to be different.

Several members of the team planned to retire immediately. April Heinrichs, Shannon Higgins, and Tracey Bates were all planning to coach. Wendy Gebauer was undecided about her retirement plans. Others were thinking about getting married and starting a family or quitting the team to concentrate on finishing college.

We'd been together and shared so much for so long that the thought of anyone leaving the team felt like losing a family member. Yet I knew that people grow, priorities change, and there comes a time in life to move on to new challenges. We all realized that even though we couldn't stay together forever, there was a big part of each other we would always share. We had done something no one else would ever have the chance to do again. Together we were the first world champions of women's soccer. We figured the glow from that glorious experience would last us a lifetime.

We certainly basked in that glow as our team rode the train out of Guangzhou the next day. It's hard to say which we enjoyed more when we reached Hong Kong: eating at McDonalds or seeing our pictures and reading headlines about our victory in newspapers from all over the world.

Soccer people around the globe marveled that an American team had won the championship. Brazil, Germany, or one of the Scandinavian countries with a great soccer tradition such as Sweden or Norway would not have seemed so surprising. In fact, Anson spent a good bit of time explaining to disbelieving reporters that not only were we all born in America, we'd all grown up and developed our soccer skills not in European leagues but on American playgrounds and in American schools.

However, where the rest of the world had its eyes suddenly opened by our accomplishment, folks back in the U.S. barely blinked. I remember sitting by an American lady on one of the flights we took home. When she asked where I had been, I proudly told her, "I'm on my way home from China where I'd represented the United States in the first-ever women's world soccer championship."

"How did you do?" the woman asked.

"We won!" I told her.

"That's nice, dear," the woman said and returned to her reading.

The response was just about that excited once we reached the States. Four people met our plane at the gate when we landed at JFK: two reporters, the coach of the Men's National Team, and a friend of mine.

Julie Foudy later told the story of her first day back in school at Stanford University. When a number of classmates wondered where she'd been, she told them, "I was in China winning the world soccer championship."

"Great!" they replied. "Did you get to study for the chemistry final?"

So much for the fame and glory of women's soccer.

❀ ❀ ❀

After celebrating their ascension to the very top of the soccer world, some team members felt stung by the lack of recognition and appreciation they received in their own country. They very quickly concluded they were destined to toil in anonymity for as long as they planned to compete in their sport. Michelle, however, proved an exception to that rule.

Her amazing ten-goal World Cup scoring record and her even more astounding total of thirty-nine goals in the twenty-six international games she played during 1991 had earned Michelle superstar status throughout the soccer world. That international spotlight remained so bright that some of its glow continued to fall on Michelle even after her return to American soil.

The folks at Umbro, who'd signed her to an endorsement contract the previous summer, could hardly believe their good fortune. They had the hottest personality in soccer signed to promote their products. The day after Michelle returned to the States, they flew her to the Orange Bowl in Miami for a big Umbro photo shoot. And a week or so later, Michelle was invited to New York City for the pomp and ceremony surrounding the draw for the next Men's World Cup tournament, which was to be held in the United States in 1994. There again Pelé and other legends of the game such as Franz Beckenbauer and Fransie Mueller not only knew who she was, but sought Michelle out to offer their congratulations and talk soccer.

The following month, the growing intensity of the limelight grew uncomfortable when Michelle represented Umbro again, this time at the National Soccer Coaches Association of America convention.

⚽ ⚽ ⚽

Someone introduced me. Somebody else handed me a microphone and literally shoved me out onto the stage with instructions to "just talk to everyone." I was scared to death even before I reached the middle of the stage and looked out over an audience that seemed like a million people—including coaches, friends, players, soccer federation officials, company representatives and more. So I just talked.

I told the audience about our team. I shared some of the hardships we'd been through. I reported on our World Cup experience and described the incredible feeling of reaching our goal of a world championship. But I felt very uncomfortable standing up in front of people talking about soccer. *I'm just a player,* I remember thinking. *What do I know?*

I appreciated the respect being shown me in the soccer community. Being recognized for being good at what I did was gratifying. But it felt strange to see people standing in line for my autograph.

It all seemed to happen so fast. A little over a month after the World Cup ended I felt like I had been placed on a pedestal and was now expected to be this outgoing personality who smiles and poses with fans and shmoozes with half the soccer world. While I could do it, that wasn't really my personality.

What seemed even more terrifying was the expectation that I could stand on a stage in front of thousands of people to tell them how to be "great." Sure I played soccer and was good at it, but suddenly I was also considered a role model. I didn't ask for that job, had never thought about it before, and certainly didn't know how to do it.

Several things—but mostly three people—helped me change my attitude and see what was happening as an important opportunity.

The first person was Pelé. Umbro arranged for us to spend additional time together. The more I was around him, the more impressed I was—even more for the person he was than for the player he had once been. Wherever he went, whoever he encountered, he was a gracious, patient, and personable ambassador for our sport. He always had time for kids and for autographs. The endurance shown by his ability to maintain his positive public persona inspired me. He demonstrated to me by the incredible way he represented and promoted soccer that one person with a platform based on achievement and success really can make a difference that can be seen and felt around the world.

Another person who became instrumental at this point in my life was Umbro executive Mick Hoban. It was Mick who opened the doors and set the stage for me to interact with and learn from Pelé and other ambassadors of our sport. By positioning me in that company and then treating me as if I belonged there, he not only affirmed, but challenged me. And Mick also helped me see that these incredible opportunities I was given were opportunities for women's soccer and not just for me. He and other folks at Umbro convinced me I could make a difference in my sport. They gave me the means to realize that dream and to make it real.

What I learned from Pelé and Mick dovetailed perfectly with what Anson Dorrance, my third important influence, had already been telling me and my teammates since the beginning of the Women's National Team. He had repeatedly reminded us that it was our responsibility to "sell" the game. "Every time you play, or meet a new person, or conduct a clinic," Anson said, "is a chance for you to convert a skeptic into new fan." He always considered salesmanship an essential part of our player roles.

We had to be nice to people who thought we were invading their sacred turf by playing a game only men were supposed to play. There was often enough criticism and negative attitudes to wear the old patience pretty thin. But with the encouragement and examples I had, I determined to sell people on our game, to inspire kids to reach for their dreams if it killed me.

✪ ✪ ✪

"She was new to the business side of things," Mick Hoban acknowledges, "but the connection between young girls and Michelle was something I'd never seen before. They had an absolute adulation for her because they finally had a hero of their own.

"Michelle soon took it upon herself to fight for resources and recognition for the women's game. She became the point person, the crusader for women's soccer, and you could see her grow as a public person. Our promotions people helped with her public speaking until she even became pretty good at that.

"She quickly became singularly focused on her job as a spokesperson, and she did it without any sense of arrogance. Being the dominant player in the game, she fully understood what she represented and I never saw her use it for her own personal betterment. If she was going to get any recognition and attention, she was just going to drag the sport along with her. I had never been around anyone like that before."

⚽ ⚽ ⚽

It amazed and humbled me whenever I made an appearance, gave a presentation, or just signed autographs. I saw kids' eyes light up. I saw them dreaming. I saw people thinking twice about women's soccer. The media that never cared before suddenly swarmed around and asked questions. Every appearance I made I felt was helpful for the U.S. soccer program.

As I began to recognize and appreciate this unprecedented platform I'd been given, I also realized that with any platform comes a very real measure of power. And with power comes responsibility.

Using my new influence responsibly meant that I needed to be the best representative of women's soccer I could possibly be. Which was why I spent hours preparing quality handouts and videos I could use when I made appearances. I wrote my old camp director and mentor, Coach Cliff McCrath, for advice on how to do an effective talk. If being a spokesperson was going to be such a major part of my job, I wanted to feel as prepared and professional standing in front of a microphone as I did when I stepped across the touchline onto a soccer field.

To make that sort of commitment required some new and different goals. Since I'm such a goal-oriented person, I very quickly identified and developed several worthy objectives to pursue with the power of my new platform.

One objective was to benefit my team and my teammates by strengthening our American soccer program. But I felt very self-conscious at first about the individual recognition I received. No one else on the team had been thrust into the spotlight like that before. It's a team game, and I felt uncomfortable being singled out.

I didn't want my teammates feeling bad toward me, and I soon realized some of them seemed to misunderstand what I tried to do. Like my decision to come to team events wearing Umbro gear. I think some people assumed I was flaunting my contract, but that wasn't my intention at all. I did it to make a statement, and sure enough, that statement was heard.

At the time, the U.S. Soccer Federation required our team to wear Adidas apparel and shoes, but we were expected to purchase our own. When I showed up wearing Umbro gear, people noticed. When the team administrator pulled me aside to tell me I needed to change into Adidas, I agreed to do so, but only if and when they provided the gear for us. It wasn't long after that the Federation began supplying the whole team with new Adidas gear on a regular basis.

I'd made my point. But I was afraid that some teammates who misunderstood my motives would think I was a selfish jerk.

⚽ ⚽ ⚽

Julie Foudy says that for her and many other players, Michelle's endorsement contract caused no hard feelings at all. "Those of us still in college couldn't have signed a contract without losing our eligibility anyway. I think we were all basically happy about the attention Michelle received. Not only did she deserve it, but women's soccer had always received so little recognition I think we all realized any attention any of us got was good for our entire sport."

Kristine Lilly agrees. When Michelle first showed up wearing Umbro, she says, "I thought, 'Who does she think she is?' But I soon realized she was using her leverage and her position to benefit us all. The opportunity sort of fell into her hands and to her credit, she used it well."

⚽ ⚽ ⚽

In addition to benefiting the National Team and my teammates, I determined to use my new platform to build and promote women's soccer in general. Because my profile was even higher in the international soccer community and countries with a longer and richer soccer heritage than the United States, FIFA sent me around the world to meet with other national federations and promote the women's game.

Those experiences provided me with the contacts and the opportunities to work for yet another longtime personal goal. I joined what became a long and arduous crusade spearheaded by an Atlanta woman by the name of Marilyn Childress, who was trying to convince the International and U.S. Olympic Committees that women's soccer should be a medal sport in the 1996 Summer Games. I spoke out for the cause wherever I went, distributing petitions and encouraging participants and fans of women's soccer to make their voices heard.

Since childhood I'd dreamed of what it would be like to compete for and win an Olympic Gold medal. While that Olympic dream had lasted longer than my fantasy of playing for the Pittsburgh Steelers, for many years it hadn't seemed any more likely. Whenever I'd casually mention it to friends or teammates they would always say things like, "Dream on Michelle! Women's soccer isn't even an Olympic sport!"

However, once FIFA decided to hold a Women's World Cup, and especially after we achieved that dream of winning the tournament and becoming world champions, I began to seriously reconsider my Olympic dreams. In the last column I filed for *USA Today* from China after our victory over Norway, I actually put it in writing for millions of people to read when I said, "My goals in the next four years are to play in the Olympics and in another World Cup. . . . To continue to represent women's soccer." I wrote Cliff McCrath the same thing, telling him that my next big goal was to see women's soccer in the Olympics. Whatever power my new platform gave me, I intended to use it to help make that happen.

The third objective I had was to use my platform to inspire and challenge those who were now looking up to me. I wanted all the kids who came to my clinics, who read my regular column in *Soccer Junior* magazine, who lined up for my autograph, to learn what I believed: that if you want anything badly enough, and if you're willing to commit everything to work for that goal, you can succeed. I wanted to empower people to pursue and achieve their greatest dreams. In other words, I intended to change the world—through soccer.

While speaking for and promoting an entire sport seemed an overwhelming job at times, I determined to give it my all. However, as I tried to be everywhere and do everything for everyone else, I forgot about taking care of myself.

At the same time my soccer success brought all these exciting opportunities in my professional life, my personal life and my own physical health started on a steep and steady decline. I came home from the 1991 World Cup feeling absolutely exhausted. This was not much of a surprise considering the grueling year I'd had leading up to it. An emotional and physical letdown may have been inevitable after such a mountaintop experience.

Which is why the feeling of tiredness didn't bother me at first. I figured it would go away once life settled back to normal, the demand of all the public appearances slowed down, and I could finally get enough rest and sleep. But as time went by, I became increasingly listless and achey, like I was engaged in a never-ending battle with the flu.

Over time I felt noticeably worse, not better. I began to feel dizzy. I suffered frequent migraine headaches, nausea, and could never seem to get enough sleep.

Finally I went to the doctor.

"You need to take it easy," he said. "You've just come off a whirlwind couple of years. You had all that travel and buildup to the World Cup last year, then the tournament itself. Now all this travel and appearance business. You just need a vacation."

I figured he was probably right. I took things a little easier for a couple months before I jetted off to Sweden to play the 1992 soccer season with my old professional team. Roby went with me this time, to coach the Tyreso men's team. We lived for the season in an apartment in what was actually an ancient Swedish castle—picturesque accommodations which, though a bit cool and drafty, were generously provided by one of the board members of the Tyreso football club.

I still didn't feel right physically. Where I'd always been such a high-energy person, something inside me was definitely changing. I slept twelve hours a night and still needed a two-hour nap in the afternoons. Still, I pushed myself to keep playing soccer. And I performed well too, enough to win the Canon Shot Award, given to the top goal-scorer in Sweden's men's and women's club leagues, for the 1992 season. Yet I could feel my strength dissipating as the months rolled by. Every practice and game now seemed to require a monumental effort just to get going. I was having to push harder and harder mentally to do the same work I'd loved and thrived on only months before.

When we returned to the States, I continued to push myself to meet my other professional obligations. At one Umbro clinic in St. Louis I remember the company representative, Eva Ferara, had to dose me with Pepto-Bismol three different times just to get me through the day before driving me back to the hotel and pouring me into bed. I'd invested so much energy in my earlier appearances that the company representatives didn't understand why I was no longer living up to my previous standards. When I begged off, they would be disappointed, even angry.

I had much the same problem with Roby. Naturally, my post-World Cup notoriety helped our Post to Post soccer camps really take off. And since I was a major draw in bringing kids out to our camps and clinics, I needed to be at those clinics. In many cases, people came just to see me, so they were naturally disappointed and upset if I couldn't be there. I knew that disappointed and upset Roby as well. He expected me to suck it up and gut it out like I always had before. But even when I'd make the effort to show up for a clinic, and just didn't feel up to participating in all the demonstrations and drills I usually did, that also bothered him. He just didn't understand what was going on. In his defense, neither did I.

Fortunately for me, since I was struggling with my health, it just so happened that the National Team didn't have much of a schedule the year after our World Cup triumph. In all of 1992 we played just two games—both against Norway—up in New England during the middle of August. I would miss both games. The only veteran starters who did play in those international matches were Mia Hamm and goalkeeper Mary Harvey.

Unfortunately for me, time and rest didn't work to improve my physical condition at all. My doctor finally diagnosed me with a severe case of mononucleosis. That gave me hope. And something I could explain. The only cure for mono was time and more rest—which is what I tried.

By 1993, I would often sweat through two or three T-shirts a night and wake up the next morning feeling like I'd flown to Europe overnight without food or sleep, gotten right back on a return flight to the States, landed, and gone straight to soccer practice. Some days I felt so bad I couldn't sit up in a chair. The racking migraines stranded me at home alone, unable even to get up and brush my teeth or find something to eat. Just surviving through the day seemed like an accomplishment.

I pushed myself to make a trip with the National Team to Cyprus in March and even scored a goal in a 2–0 win over Denmark in our opener. But I struggled just to finish the game in 0–1 losses to Norway and Germany. I got sick with terrible congestion and a sore throat, and spent most of the trip in bed, blowing my nose, hacking away, trying in vain to get a good night's sleep.

I scored three goals as the team won five of six international games we played back in the States throughout the spring. But I remained so weak I couldn't even finish three of those matches. I skipped an entire five-game tournament held in Canada early that summer.

During this time I didn't tell the coaches or my teammates how I was really feeling or what was going on, in large part because I didn't know what to tell them. I also kept thinking that by pushing myself hard enough I would eventually break through. In the meantime, I figured if I could psych myself up enough to stay on my feet just long enough to practice or contribute something in a game, then I could go to bed and crash afterwards and no one needed to know.

The strategy worked until the Olympic Sports Festival in San Antonio, Texas, that July.

I became so delirious during a game that I wandered off the field in the wrong direction. My teammates had to come and get me. Since it was July in Texas with temperatures over 100 degrees, the trainers figured the heat had caused glycogen depletion—or sugar imbalance—and that's why I had no energy left in my muscles. They stuffed me with M&Ms and made me drink Coke with packets of sugar dissolved in it. When that didn't relieve my symptoms, they instructed me to try to eat well and get some rest to replenish my body before the next game.

I stayed sick with a pounding migraine, utter exhuastion, and nausea for two days before I tried to play again. I don't remember much at all from that game except feeling disoriented—like I was drunk or something—before I completely passed out on the field.

                               ✪ ✪ ✪

"I knew Michelle had been struggling all year," Julie Foudy says. "She just didn't play with the same energy as she had before—at least for an entire game. I thought the same thing Michelle had at first, that she was pushing herself so hard to meet the demands of her schedule that she was just worn out."

Tony DiCicco says, "Looking back, I think Michelle actually began to show symptoms back in 1991 during the World Cup preparation. She'd always played every game to the point of total exhaustion—never leaving anything on the field. While she had done that right to the final whistle in the past, she was now reaching the end of her rope before the game ended. I have to admit I wondered if the problem was one of conditioning. Perhaps she wasn't coming to camps in the kind of shape she had in the past."

"I saw her go down on the field in San Antonio," Anson Dorrance recalls. "No one hit her. She wasn't even in on a play. She seemed fine one second, then she passed out and had to be carried off the field.

"Michelle's dad and I were with her in the medical tent when she came to with a pained and confused look in her eyes. I remember holding a cool, wet cloth against her forehead and not knowing what to say when she asked, 'What happened?' Frankly I was scared."

No one knew what to say or think because no one knew what could be wrong. A lot of people were scared for her.

                               ✪ ✪ ✪

Including me.

Chapter Thirteen
LOOKING UP AGAIN

*H*aving missed the entire Canadian tournament in July, I thought I needed to join the National Team for a three-game series scheduled the next month in New York no matter how badly I felt. Though managing to play only part of the first two games—both easy victories—I did score a couple of goals in the second game before I had to pull myself out of the game.

The effort left me so disoriented and irrational afterward that our trainer took me to see some doctors he knew at Lenox Hill Hospital for further testing. They must have suspected some circulatory/heart problem because they gave me an echocardiogram and a bunch of other tests before concluding that my heart was just fine.

I took things easy again for a week or so, until I started to feel a little better and began training once more. *Bam!* I was sick again.

It wasn't like I rested and then felt fine. I was still exhausted and feeling awful, but the time off did allow me to gather the mental/emotional strength and stamina to go another round.

When I got back into training again, not only did my health plummet, but my will began to ebb as well. Throughout my life I'd tackled any problem I faced by coupling willpower and determination with a deep reservoir of personal strength. Now strength seemed to be the missing ingredient in my life. The reservoir was running dry, and I didn't know how or where to plug the leak.

I tried to take things as easy as I could that fall, but Umbro still wanted a chunk of my time to fly here and there for appearances. Because I still didn't understand the seriousness of my illness and had a hard time admitting my limitations, they never quite got the picture that I was often as sick as a dog.

When I would say I couldn't do something, some company officials thought I was being a prima donna. Though Eva tried to defend me to her company, the strain with Umbro continued and grew as I got sicker and could do less and less.

I felt the responsibility, though. As long as people were talking about me being the "best in the world" I realized I still had a unique position to represent and promote the game. And then there was Roby and our Post to Post camps. With my increased stature in the sport, there was so much I could, and maybe should, have done to expand our business.

But I already felt like I was staggering around carrying a truck on my back. How could I take on any more?

As frustrating as my health struggles had been over the two years since the '91 World Cup, they hadn't yet seriously hampered my soccer career, primarily because our national team hadn't played any significant games during that time. But I knew 1994 would be different. The U.S. Women's National Team once again had a slate of matches scheduled to begin gearing up for the next Women's World Cup to be held in Sweden in 1995. If I was going to help lead my team to another world championship, I needed to be healthy. I needed answers. And fast.

That's when I went back to my doctor, an internist in Orlando, and tested positive for chronic Epstein-Barr Virus (EBV)—which I understood as a more serious form of mono. I learned it was also referred to as Chronic Fatigue Dysfunction Syndrome.

I didn't know exactly what that meant, but the part about fatigue sounded accurate enough. Hopefully the doctor was right this time.

He made the diagnosis seem almost trivial, however. This doc told me to rest up, alter my schedule a bit, and that my body should bounce back and overcome the virus in six to eight months or so. I figured, as usual, that I was not the norm, so I mentally cut that time frame in half, decided to shorten my training a bit, and tried to maintain as much of my schedule as possible in the meantime.

I'd just have to walk that fine line I always had to walk coming back from injuries. I would begin training again, pushing myself just to the boundaries of the illness, and I should be fine. Just like recovering from knee surgery, slow, steady progress would be the key.

In March I joined the team for a training camp and a trip to Portugal to play in the Algarve Cup tournament. We won two games before losing to Norway in the final 0–1. I was sick, battling yet another chest cold, so I played only a few minutes in each of the three games and didn't score a goal the entire tournament. *But at least I played. Slow, steady progress.*

We played three more games in Trinidad and Tobago a few weeks later. I lasted only a few minutes in two of them, but I did score three goals. *More progress.*

Right after that, I went with Roby to Sweden for the beginning of Tyreso club season, for which he was coaching again. I figured my past success and familiarity with the Swedish league made that a good place to keep playing and making as much progress as I could.

❀ ❀ ❀

Three of Michelle's U.S. teammates joined her on the Tyreso club team that year. Julie Foudy, Kristine Lilly, and Mary Harvey all decided that a few weeks of competitive Swedish soccer would keep them tuned up until the National Team schedule resumed that summer.

Michelle enjoyed the camaraderie, and her friends' presence certainly made for a better Tyreso team. But being together every day for such a long stretch of time made it impossible for Michelle to keep hiding how much she was struggling.

"Obviously something was wrong," says Julie Foudy. "We would train and then Michelle would go back home and chill out for the rest of the day. All she did the whole time we were there was play soccer and sleep. She never seemed to have any energy to do anything else. And you could tell she just wasn't happy."

Her physical health wasn't the only problem. As the tension between Michelle and her husband had increased she had begun to sense their marriage was in need of some serious attention. When she thought about it, it didn't seem all that surprising. In four years of marriage, her commitment to playing soccer and his commitment to coaching had required them to spend a lot of time apart. The Umbro appearances and the celebrity demands brought added complications. Michelle's illness further strained their relationship. While it served to delay her facing their problems for a time, her deteriorating health eventually escalated things by stripping everything else away and exposing the hard reality of the relationship: she and Roby had little to hold them together except a love for soccer.

❀ ❀ ❀

Floundering in every other area of my life, I wanted to be able to hold on to something. The thought of losing not only my identity as a soccer player but also my marriage terrified me. I began going to counseling. Roby eventually went with me one time, but we didn't begin to scratch the surface before conflicting schedules and the ongoing pressures of life put an end to working on our relationship.

After I returned to the States that summer for National Team training, Roby stayed busy with camps and clinics for several months. Then he returned to Europe to coach the rest of the Swedish soccer season.

⚽ ⚽ ⚽

That was the same summer—1994—the United States hosted the Men's World Cup for the first time ever. Soccer was in the spotlight.

So was I. Parades. Umbro appearances. Travel. Receptions for soccer dignitaries. Parties. More appearances.

All the excitement and soccer atmosphere, as tiring as it was, inspired me. On June 27, I wrote in my personal journal:

> I'm now focusing on getting ready for the 1995 Women's World Cup in Sweden, where we will defend our world title. I had an awesome experience during the Men's World Cup game in Orlando, and it made me excited for our own tournament in Sweden. I got to run out on the field holding the men's trophy. I kissed it a couple of times, waved to the crowd, and pretended I was a world champion again . . .

My determination and renewed optimism was reflected again a few days later when my July 5 journal entry said:

> My training is good. Steve Slain is my new running partner and he really makes me work. It makes training a little more competitive and challenging for me. Steve also has been getting on me about strength-training my legs more, so I've started putting a little more emphasis on that. The Epstein-Barr is still there, but it seems to have leveled off. I just hope I can get through the next two months and not make things worse.

Steve Slain was a strength coach who had worked for the Orlando Magic for several years and had trained a lot of professional athletes. After someone recommended him to me, we quickly struck up a friendship. He reminded me a lot of Mr. Kovats—kind, gentle, and with that same inexplicable draw. Steve, too, acted excited about his relationship with God. He studied the Bible on his own and got fired up about going to church.

For the past few years I'd pretty much forgotten about being a Christian. Yet I think deep down I'd realized something was missing in my life spiritually. Being around Steve reminded me of that once again.

I clearly needed something to help me deal with all the problems in my life—including the constant up and down roller-coaster experience with my health. My July 15 journal entry reflects continued frustration and worry:

> I'm still feeling terrible. I just went through a couple really bad days. I'm getting back to fairly normal, but I still can't do my full workouts and I feel worse than I have in the past four months. I don't know why!
>
> I just pray that I get through the summer with the National Team and I'm able to play a whole match without killing myself. I am so sick of being sick and tired. Enough already. I learned my lesson. If only I could have some energy. It would be so great to play without this hanging over my head.

I did talk about Roby's and my relationship with Dad, who's an experienced counselor and has always been a great listener. He encouraged me to seek professional help—even if I had to go by myself, which I did. But my basic coping strategy was still to keep moving and try to ignore how bad things were—both on and off the field. Just getting through the day was the sum total of my life strategy for a while. It wasn't until later that I realized what a naive view of love and marriage I'd started out with. I'd thought marriage would somehow automatically enable me to live happily ever after. Now not only was my life and career coming apart, but who I was as a person was being called into question. On top of that, I realized my marriage had been based on superficial things and was a futile attempt on my part to make my life more complete. In other words, I had expected marriage to make me whole.

Yet here I was with my life falling to pieces.

I remember thinking, *I'm operating in survival mode here. I don't know if I can even play soccer or not. I don't know what's wrong with me. I don't know if I can even make it through this day.*

Maybe I could hang in there with the National Team. Maybe I could meet the obligation of my contract with Umbro. But I didn't even know where or how to begin to fix things in my personal life.

⚽ ⚽ ⚽

As if Michelle didn't have enough stress already, Anson Dorrance announced his retirement from international coaching. Fortunately, he was replaced by someone Michelle and the team already knew—their goalkeeper coach, Tony DiCicco. Even so, the transition required energy and time for adjustment.

"I remember my first talk to the team after the official announcement," says Tony DiCicco. "I wanted to set people at ease. To assure them that nothing would change; that we all still shared the same goal of winning another World Cup.

"But the longer I talked, the more I sensed I was losing Michelle. That she wasn't hearing what she wanted to hear. And I thought I understood why. She didn't want to be reassured so much as she wanted to be challenged. So I talked to her alone later and told her I was counting on her leading the team to another world championship, that we needed to be committed to do whatever that took, and that my first order of business was to gradually get her worked back into her role as a dominant scorer. That's what Michelle wanted, the challenge of a big goal to work toward."

❧ ❧ ❧

The first step was to work my way up to playing a full ninety-minute game. But that didn't happen right away.

I played only three partial games during the '94 Chiquita Cup tournament. But I did score two goals during the tournament in which we defeated Germany, China, and Norway—tough competition we expected to face the following year in World Cup action.

The very next week we flew to Montreal to begin the CONCACAF qualifying tournament to see who would represent our region in Sweden. I started every game and scored a total of six goals for the tournament. Any satisfaction I derived from that showing, however, was tempered by the fact that I didn't finish a single match. Fortunately, the team didn't need me since we outscored our regional opponents by an overwhelming margin of 36 goals to 1.

Surprisingly, I was named the Most Valuable Player of the qualifying tournament, but I felt I'd won more on reputation than on my actual performance. Several of my teammates had played better than I had—and for more minutes. Mia had also scored six goals. Kristine Lilly scored five times, as did Carin Jennings Gabarra. While I accepted my trophy with a gracious smile on my face, I couldn't help feeling I hadn't really earned MVP honors.

As far as I was concerned, the only redeeming factor of the tournament was that we'd won. We were now qualified for the '95 World Cup in Sweden the following June.

One other very significant thing happened during our time in Canada. It was personal and far more painful than anything I'd ever experienced or expected to experience on a soccer field: I finally lost all hope for my marriage. Being a child of divorce, this was the last thing I thought I'd ever consider.

I called Roby in Sweden and asked him to please meet me at the CON-CACAF tourney in Montreal. I told him we needed to talk.

It was probably the hardest thing I'd ever done in my life, but when he arrived in Montreal I told Roby that I just couldn't do this any longer. That I had tried, we had tried, but our marriage wasn't working, that I saw no hope, and that I was finally convinced our marriage was over. It was like I was some-how emotionally detached, almost outside myself, as we talked about break-ing up. Not until later, alone in the darkness of my room, did I allow myself to feel the pain and the loss of my lifelong dream to be in love, to love deeply, to be married, and to spend my life with one person forever.

On August 26, just five days after we routed Canada 6–0 in the final, I tried to reflect on everything that had happened by writing in my journal:

> It's late, or early, depending on the person. 1 A.M. I can't sleep again. Almost every night I wake up or can't get to sleep. This decision is taking its toll. I can't stop my mind from racing about the details of moving out, divorce, examining my feelings. It's driving me nuts.
>
> The act of breaking up this part of my life is painful and exhausting. I think I will rest easier once everyone knows. I *hope* so, anyway. I don't know how I'll tell my grandma and grandpa. They're about to celebrate their fiftieth wedding anniversary. I can't wait to talk to Dad more about it. He helps me, no matter how clouded my thinking may be.
>
> I feel weird thinking of myself as divorced. I think about the moment when I will take off my wedding ring, what I will do with my engagement ring, and how I will break it to the team. A lot to be strong for.
>
> My range of feelings is incredible. I am afraid. But I am excited to have a new future. I am sad. But I'm ready to move on. I feel lost and alone. I cry a lot. Yet I feel the love and support of my friends and family.
>
> I never imagined in a million years I would be getting a divorce. Live and learn. And never say never.

I didn't want to stay in Florida alone, so I decided to go out to my family's mountain cabin in the Cascades outside of Seattle. After all the pain I'd gone through over my decision, I needed a place near my family to sort out my feel-ings and figure out what was going on with my life, my health, my future.

I decided I couldn't afford *not* to feel. I needed to be sad—to experience the full range of my emotions and work through them. *If I don't handle this right,* I thought, *I may never be able to recover.*

Just arriving at the cabin, a place filled with peace and solitude, seemed to soothe my soul. Mountains, rivers, and nature had always had a way of humbling me and keeping me grounded. I needed that—now more than ever.

A forest fire had swept through the area earlier that summer, leaving a faint smell of ash and smoke like an old campfire. It hadn't touched our property, but you could trace its route through nearby woods and fields that were already lush with green vegetation and colorful wildflowers—symbolic of the forest's rebirth. My life needed a new start like that and I hoped this was the place to find it.

My second day at the cabin I set out on a short hike through the woods. I was feeling so good I'd walked sixteen miles through the mountains before I realized it and had to hurry—sprinting the last two hundred yards—to get back before dark.

I paid for that adventure the next day, and the day after that, when I felt so sick I could do nothing but lie on the couch and try to recover my strength. I realized then that a change of scenery alone wouldn't cure me.

I stayed so sick over the remainder of my stay that a five-minute walk wiped me out for the day. I was forced to spend most of my time at the cabin sitting and thinking about who I was.

I honestly didn't know. And that scared me.

Epstein-Barr, CFIDS, or whatever you wanted to call this illness I'd been fighting was a thief—yanking, grabbing, and systematically stealing everything that had been important to me. My health. My physical strength. My soccer career. My marriage. My independence. My identity.

All that was gone. I didn't know where. And I had no idea how to go about getting it back. There was this huge hole in my life and nothing to fill it with.

I couldn't have put it into words at the time, but I was reminded of the emptiness and despair I'd felt as a teenager. Then I remembered the incredible, indescribable peace that had come when I made my decision to give my life to God. *I want that again,* I thought. And in that instant I realized I needed to get things right with God.

Being around Steve Slain had reminded me I hadn't spent much time thinking about spiritual things since high school after Mr. Kovats introduced me to his faith in Christ. I'd gone to church a few times, mostly on Easter and Christmas, over the past few years. But my beliefs really didn't have anything to do with my daily life. God definitely hadn't been a part of my marriage or my soccer career. I'd thrown up a prayer now and again for help or strength or a team win, but I always made my own decisions and dealt with the consequences. All in all, I thought I'd done a pretty good job of keeping things under control.

Until now.

Now, as I sat in that cabin with nothing to do but examine my life, I didn't like what I saw. And I couldn't imagine where to go from here.

That was when I received a package Steve Slain sent me—tapes from a series of sermons his minister had recently preached. The first cassette I popped into my Walkman was a sermon about relationships, and how easy it is for Christians to let new experiences and relationships crowd out their first love. How they can lose a sense of passion and closeness they once felt toward God.

As I listened to that tape there in the Cascades, the words hit home. Alone in the mountains, examining my life and my heart, I realized that was exactly what had happened with me. I had forsaken God for years. I had let other relationships and other things come between us.

"You can have all this stuff," I finally told God. "You can have this body. You can have this life. You can have me. Because I've made a mess of everything."

I called Cliff McCrath to ask him how I could start learning about God and how to feel close to Him again. He suggested I begin by reading the Bible and praying. I tried doing what he said, but it all meant nothing to me. God still felt far away, and I still felt empty inside. No love. No peace. No change.

This God thing is not working! I felt frustrated and even more hopeless than before.

I listened to that tape over and over. I know it sounds odd, but I think that's what began to redirect me. The words and the music brought me peace. I remember sitting by a big river in the mountains and actually feeling joyful. Where I'd been so jumbled up and confused inside, I felt a ray of hope. Maybe God *could* help.

I finally came down out of the mountains to visit my family in Seattle. And on a Sunday I went to church with my grandparents.

In his sermon their minister told the story of a family God called to go to Africa as missionaries. He talked about what it means to be chosen and how God gives everyone special talents they can use to let others know about Him.

Once again I felt as if a preacher was speaking directly to me. I tried to ignore him, but I got this vision in my mind as clear as the vision I'd once had of us winning and celebrating the world championship in China. Instead of jumping up and down and running around a soccer field, this time I saw myself speaking to churches and soccer groups around the world—not just about soccer, but about Jesus.

I knew that up in the mountains a few days earlier I had told God He could have me. But I hadn't expected this. So right there in church I tried arguing with God. "Why me? Why do You have to pick me? I want to be a normal person in one area of my life and now You want to make me different in that area, too."

The idea upset me so badly I walked out before the minister even finished his sermon. I just whispered to my grandma that I had to leave, and would she see if she could get me a tape of the service. Then I stood up and almost ran out of that church. I found a pay phone a couple blocks away and immediately called Steve Slain in Orlando.

When he answered the phone, I practically shouted at him: "Slainer, you're not gonna believe what just happened to me!"

✪ ✪ ✪

Steve remembers that surprise phone call very well. "Michelle was practically freaking out. I said, 'What's the matter? Is someone chasing you or what?'

"She was talking so fast I could hardly follow her. 'Oh, my gosh! I was just in church with my grandparents and God was speaking to me and showing me this stuff and it scared the living daylights outta me!'

"She had my interest now. 'Well, what did He say? Let's make sure this was God.'

"She was convinced it was God all right. He wanted her to step out for Him, to share her faith, to get involved in Christian outreach, and in essence become some sort of missionary. The whole idea terrified Michelle.

"I tried to get her to calm down. 'Let's pray about this,' I told her, 'and talk again after you have a chance to settle down.'"

✪ ✪ ✪

So that's what we did. I called Steve again that evening. He assured me that if this was what God was calling me to do, then God would give me whatever it took to do it. I'd settled down enough by then to hear what he was saying. Maybe he was right. After all, I'd spent the last few years learning how to stand up in front of all kinds of audiences to talk about soccer. Maybe that was all preparation for this.

Maybe. But the thought of being some kind of missionary still scared me to death. *Me? A missionary for Jesus? This is just too much!*

Chapter Fourteen

UPHILL ROAD
TO SWEDEN

I returned to Florida from Seattle that fall with a renewed spirit. I still experienced up and down emotions. My health wavered as well. But my heart felt new.

I got my own apartment, hired Steve Slain as a personal trainer, and began working out with him five days a week.

Over time, I began to sense a little of that inner spiritual peace I'd felt as a teenager. But I still wasn't sure how to cultivate a relationship with God. Steve helped with my spiritual training as well, telling me that if I wanted to grow spiritually I needed to be fed. And if God did want to use me to reach out to others—a prospect I still wasn't so sure about—I first needed the kind of nourishment and strengthening that he had found through his church and a weekly program called Bible Study Fellowship. So I started attending Northland Community Church with Steve on Sundays and signed up for BSF during the week.

Northland Community Church wasn't like most churches I'd ever attended. It met in a remodeled roller rink—which seemed kinda cool. I also really liked feeling I didn't have to dress up. And the music was great.

At first I didn't know what to think about the minister, though. His name was Joel Hunter, and he talked a lot about the importance of including God in our lives—in all our plans and relationships. It was like he had an inside line to my heart and was preaching his sermons every week specifically for me. He even seemed to be staring right at me through the entire sermon which sometimes made me feel uncomfortable.

When I mentioned this to Steve, he laughed and told me he'd felt the same way when he'd first visited Northland, and that God still often used the words of the pastor's sermons to speak directly to him.

Whatever the explanation, I felt an inner strength and hope that wasn't there before. And I began to put my life back together.

Another encouraging development came along in December when the U.S. Women's National Team opened a residential training facility in Sanford, Florida, an Orlando suburb only miles from where I lived. Not only did this mean that I could live at home while I trained with my teammates for the coming World Cup, it also signified an unprecedented commitment to the women's game on the part of the U.S. Soccer Federation. The USSF had, also for the first time ever, offered contracts to a number of veteran players so that we could actually make a living while we trained. All this promised to make life a little easier for everyone as we prepared for the next summer's world championship. And it provided some of the reason for the optimism reflected in my journal entry on the first day of 1995.

> Happy New Year! Unbelievable. It's finally the World Cup year . . . this is the most excited I've been about January 1 in my life. The World Cup year and national training down here full-time. I'm very excited. I have been feeling miserable all week, and I'm just beginning to come out of it . . .
>
> Busy week. Busy month. So let's look at what I bring with me into the New Year. There's the final divorce hearing, but there is also my new apartment, new furniture on the way, a renegotiated Umbro contract or possibly a whole new sponsor, dreams to move to Seattle, a happy heart, a new commitment in Christ. I can't wait for it all to happen. If it's half as challenging and exciting as this past year, I'll be blessed.

Things didn't look so rosy, however, come the middle of that month when I went to the National Soccer Coaches Association of America's annual convention to make my usual appearances, speeches, and demonstrations. The weekend is always hectic, but this time it wore me down more than ever before. I was still feeling the effects a week later when I showed up in Phoenix for the first National Team training camp of the year. My journal entry reflected the uncertainty I was feeling at the time:

> I hope I'm okay today. I'm really excited about the World Cup, but nervous because of my health. I hope and pray I'll be able to compete and play without any physical restrictions. On the outside I will deal with it, but on the inside I will be heartbroken if I have to play sick or injured.

The camp went okay. I turned twenty-nine on February 1, and shortly thereafter headed home to Florida to rest up and wait for my teammates to join me at our new residential training facility in Sanford. By the fifth of February an almost equal measure of frustration and optimism prompted me to write:

> The team is moving down here again. I can't wait to train. I just wish I was healthy. I feel like I always have to ration myself to get through the week. I hate it. I cannot wait to do what I want, when I want to.
>
> My life is changing quickly, and God is leading me somewhere. I don't know where yet, but at least now I am trying to listen and do. We'll see where it takes me.

I did love to work out, which was a big part of the reason for the seemingly endless vicious cycle I'd been caught up in for three years now. Whenever I felt so sick and hurt so bad I couldn't train, I yearned for the chance to experience the joy and satisfaction I've always found in physical exertion. Whenever I would feel a little better, I would be so thrilled not to be going through debilitating pain and exhaustion that I would get out and push myself too far, suffering the consequences once again.

On one hand, working out made me feel better. On the other hand, it made me feel worse. When I could do it, I enjoyed being outside in the fresh air—playing soccer, being physical, challenging myself—and I was with the team, my friends, so I was not alone in my misery. At the same time, it was tough to deal with mentally because I realized I still couldn't train as hard as I wanted or needed to train. Neither my mind nor my body were responding the way they had in the past. Even at my best I felt sluggish, tired, slow. I was not the same player. I had no endurance. I wasn't fit. And that really frustrated me.

Now when my mind said "yes," my body was saying "no way!" The problem was, I refused to listen to my body.

Always before, my instinctive response to pain and injuries had been to summon up my determination, push harder, and refuse to quit until I came out on top. That strategy no longer worked, but I hadn't yet learned that lesson.

❂ ❂ ❂

Steve Slain had worked with a lot of top-flight athletes. But he'd never seen a case like Michelle's. He didn't understand it.

He had designed a soccer-specific training program for her, geared to strengthen the muscles and replicate the movements required by her sport. "I always chart the progress of the athletes I'm working with," Steve says, "but in Michelle's case there was no progress. Instead of improving from week to week, her marks actually went down after I first began working with her.

"My first thought was 'This gal's a slacker.' And I wasn't going to put up with that. I don't care whether you're Shaquille O'Neal or Michelle Akers, I expect the people I train to give me their best effort. So I confronted Michelle. I showed her the results on my charts and confessed I couldn't figure out what was going on. I told her if she was really giving me a hundred percent we should be seeing improvement in her performance, not a continuing decline.

"She didn't want me thinking she was slacking in any way so she finally admitted that after I worked her out good in the mornings, she'd been going back out in the afternoons and doing it all again on her own. Her problem wasn't that she was slacking at all. She was actually double-training."

Michelle mistakenly assumed that if two hours of pushing herself was going to help her recover, then four hours would enable her to come back even faster. But the human body doesn't work like that.

"Do you think you're some kind of wild mustang or something?" I asked her. I really chewed her out. I told her she needed to listen to me and follow the program we'd mapped out. She promised she would. But that was a tension we continued to battle for a long time because of the stubbornness and drive that was so much a part of her makeup.

"It was like she thought being the best in the world meant she not only could do more, but that she had to do more. That she had to carry her team because she was Michelle Akers and that was her job.

"As much as it frustrated me when I'd learn she worked out even on our days off, I soon came to understand and appreciate her commitment. I've never met another athlete, male or female, who could begin to match Michelle when it comes to passion and desire."

⚽ ⚽ ⚽

The work with Slainer and the time spent with my teammates in residency camp gradually began to pay off. When I played my first full, ninety-minute game in almost two years against Denmark in Orlando at the end of February, I was more excited over finishing the game than I was about scoring three goals.

Then came a fresh dose of realism, which I wrote about in my February 26 journal entry:

> I got a bunch of info from a fan about Epstein-Barr and Chronic Fatigue Syndrome. Scared the heck out of me. I didn't realize it was so debilitating and serious. . . . CFIDS is supposed to be the result of an over-active immune system. The system overworks, causing the fatigue and other symptoms. They say the headaches come from a lack of blood flow to the brain. It usually occurs after exercise and lasts up to 24 hours. It fits with what happens to me. I still can't believe I have this illness . . . of all people.

I talked to the guy who had sent me the information. His name was Robert Montgomery, and he said this was nothing to mess around with. That it can come back and hit you five times as hard as the initial infection. What really scared me was his warning not to exercise; that physical exertion only intensified the symptoms.

The only good news I read indicated that every person had his or her own level of tolerance and recovery rates. I figured as an athlete that I had a better chance. I wasn't going to quit and let this thing beat me. I'd just have to try to play within my limits and not worry about the limitations of other people who had the virus.

Throughout this time, my renewed faith was at the center of my recovery. Despite my physical ups and downs I was happier most of the time. I had begun to accept the idea that maybe God did have a specific plan for my life. I also felt he had put Robert Montgomery in my path for a reason.

I really did want to put my life in God's hands, but I was so used to doing things on my own, my own way, that it wasn't easy. Where some people need a tap on the shoulder from God to get their attention, I think it required a two-by-four over the head to get through to me. God sent Robert Montgomery along with that wake-up call—or more like a hammer to the head. The real message was "Pay attention here, Michelle. This is important. You can't beat this on your own the way you've always managed everything else. You're going to have to rely on Me and I will give you what you need."

There were plenty of setbacks that continued to try my faith. I wrote about some of them in my journal on March 2:

> Unbelievable how some things work out. The last couple of days I have been down in the dumps. I'm concerned about my health. Not the CFIDS especially, but my body. I pulled my soleus (calf) muscle and I'm out for a while with that. I have bruises up and down my left leg (it looks like a truck hit me), and now my shoulder is bothering me in a way that makes me nervous. I feel like I need to live in a room of pillows for a month so I can heal up and get back to training.

⚽ ⚽ ⚽

After a week of rehab Michelle joined the team just in time for their trip to Portugal to play in the Algarve Cup. But the illness and injuries had placed Michelle in an unfamiliar position; it seemed to her that everyone else on the team was in better shape. She needed to catch up, but not overdo it.

Though the team struggled in Portugal with two wins and two losses, Michelle was encouraged by her own progress. She played all ninety minutes in the last two games and scored once. Yet again she paid a steep price—not just with her illness, but as a target for opponents who knew her reputation and hacked her repeatedly to stop her. She returned to Florida from Portugal with a slight meniscus tear in her right knee, a shin hematoma, a deep thigh bruise, and a painful hip injury. Despite the battering, she was further encouraged when a visit to the doctor revealed her EBV numbers were way down.

⚽ ⚽ ⚽

After a quick three-game jaunt to France the middle of April, it was home again for final World Cup preparations. I couldn't wait. My April 20 journal entry reveals my mood:

> I looked at my photo albums yesterday. I decided to keep the 1991 World Cup one out to remind of where I want to be and how hard it was to get there. I want to be world champion again.

Spiritually as well as physically, I still had a ways to go. But some progress was noted in my journal a few days later when I wrote:

> There was a great service at church . . . on praying—when and how to do it. Joel Hunter, our preacher dude, was saying that God is not a "tooth fairy God," meaning you don't put your problems under your pillow and expect Him to magically take them away.
>
> Yet that's exactly what I do.
>
> I need to understand that God is giving me nothing I can't handle, and He gives me the means to get through it. He will bless me with something better (something a thousand times better than I can imagine if only I stay faithful). Just because He doesn't take my problems from me right now, it doesn't mean He's not listening. I can't give up. I have to keep praying and be thankful.

I had no idea how this lesson was about to be tested.

On April 28, 1995, the U.S. Women's National Team embarked on a "Road to Sweden" tour. It was a grueling, six-game, coast-to-coast road trip that started in Georgia and ended up in the Pacific Northwest. I played ninety minutes of the first game, but pulled myself out partway through the next four contests and did not play at all in the last game. I'd scored a total of six goals in the five games I played. But I was feeling so sluggish and EBVish that I feared making a mistake and pushing myself so hard that I might not be able to recover by the time the World Cup tournament started two weeks later.

So many uncertainties! How would I hold up to the intensity of World Cup competition? Could I even play six games in less than two weeks? Would I be able to help my team win? Would I be able to play like Michelle Akers?

I asked myself those questions every day. The only other person I voiced them to was Steve Slain. He and I had become even better friends, and spent a lot more time together, since he had become the Women's National Team's strength coach and massage therapist during our residency training in Orlando.

Steve knew when I was struggling—emotionally and physically. But he refused to hear my self-doubt. He told me he knew I was going to make it. I'd be fine. He knew that I was going to have an impact in the World Cup. That I'd play great. And he said that he had complete faith in me, which was more faith than I had in myself. I didn't think I'd have made it as far as I had if it hadn't been for Steve's training and his friendship.

I'd come to depend on Slainer's daily support and encouragement, especially on days I was dragging. On May 30, just two days before we were scheduled to fly to Sweden, I wrote in my journal:

> I don't know how I'll get through the World Cup. All I can do is pray. God will take me through it the way He wants. I just hope it's a fun World Cup and not a terrible struggle. I'm sick of fighting uphill. I am terrified and excited about it at the same time. I suppose these are the same feelings I had before '91. It will be tougher to put the same game plan into effect this time—I need to try to make the moment less important in my mind, play for fun, let go, and focus on the game. There are so many distractions. Gotta keep praying.

When we arrived in Sweden on June 1, I wrote in my journal:

> The team looks and feels ready. There's a quiet confidence. Less giddiness than in '91, more experience and calmness now. We'll just have to wait and see what comes up.

... This time when I try to envision the outcome it flashes between victory—sinking to my knees in relief and happiness, running crazy around the field, hugging everyone, and crying—or ... walking off the field with such an awful feeling in the pit of my stomach and wanting to punch each player on the other team as they celebrate what we wanted so badly.

I wonder which will happen ...

But before the tournament even began, I had two other unexpected crises to deal with.

Chapter Fifteen

CUP OF SUFFERING

Pre-Cup crisis number one came in the form of a phone call—from Steve Slain saying he wouldn't be joining the team in Sweden as planned. He'd injured his back and required immediate surgery.

It sounded serious. But when I expressed concern for him, Steve assured me he expected the surgery to be as routine as it was necessary. He obviously didn't want me to worry.

So we talked instead about the lousy timing. After working with the National Team for over a year, bonding with us during those months of residency camp in Orlando, and traveling to Europe and then back and forth across America, now he wouldn't be able to share with us what we'd all been working and training for. He was so disappointed that I couldn't help crying for my friend.

When I finally got off the phone with Steve, I also cried for myself. He had been the one person I had relied on most for emotional support and encouragement. In less than a year he'd become my best friend, someone I knew I could count on, who had teamed with me to help pull me through a lot of tough days. He had helped make me stronger by constantly rallying me—not just physically but also spiritually. I'd taken great comfort in knowing he was going to be with me in Sweden to help me cope with the whole World Cup ordeal.

I sat beside the phone crying and thinking, *How am I going to make it through this tournament now? I know I can't do it by myself.*

My teammate Amanda Cromwell was there in the room when I got the bad-news call from Slainer, so she was there to witness my reaction. As much as I hated to let anyone see me break down and bawl like a baby, at that moment I didn't really care. If any of my teammates had to see me like that, I was glad it was Amanda (or Sal as I usually called her—short for yet another crazy National Team nickname, Sally Mally Wally Jally).

I'd been pleased when I'd gotten my room assignment for Sweden and learned we would be roomies. A two-time All-American at the University of Virginia, Sal had begun playing with the National Team in 1991. For the first couple of years the extent of our relationship had been kicking the bejeebers out of each other on the practice field. Since she was a defender and I played up front, we often found ourselves going head-to-head—wrestling, kicking, grabbing, and tackling each other for the ball in practices—and had developed respect for each other but never really hung out.

We'd gotten a little closer when we'd roomed together on a couple trips. After I got sick and just didn't have the energy to do a lot of fun stuff the team always did together, I always appreciated the fact that Sal made a point of asking me if I wanted to go along and never took offense when I begged off. A couple times when I didn't have the energy to go out to a movie with everyone else, she'd say, "Why don't we rent a movie and bring it over to watch with you?"

One day during residency camp when I felt so low I didn't know how I was going to drive home, I guess she must have noticed the empty look in my eyes, gotten worried, and decided to follow me home. When I collapsed on the living room couch, she fixed me a bowl of soup for supper and made sure I was okay before she left me alone.

There would be other days after that when she'd sense I was struggling and volunteer to come help fix me a meal or just pick up some groceries for me to save me time and energy. I felt a little awkward about accepting her help at first, and about letting a teammate—someone I competed with and against— see me at my worst. But at the same time I gradually came to appreciate Sal's caring friendship and having one more person in my life with whom I could be completely open and honest.

I knew if anyone other than Steve Slain could help me through the World Cup, it was Sal. I was very grateful she was there even before I knew how much her presence was going to mean to me.

My second pre-World Cup crisis took even more emotional energy and time to deal with. But it seems petty in comparison. Because the issue was shoes.

⚽ ⚽ ⚽

Since Michelle's feet are wider than most female players, she always had trouble finding soccer shoes she felt comfortable in. When she wore shoes that felt too narrow she was always stopping to lace them tighter to get adequate support on the outside of her feet.

For a long time her favorite shoes were Adidas, in part because the company's triple-stripe trademark on the side of the shoe actually provided a feeling of extra stability. That presented a problem for Michelle because Umbro sponsored her personally and Nike sponsored the National Team. Both companies attempted to design a shoe that would give her the support her feet needed, but so far they hadn't come up with a shoe she felt good about. Which was why she had been allowed to wear Adidas—as long as the three white stripes and any other identifying marks were blacked out.

But months earlier, while working with Post to Post soccer camps, Michelle had picked up and tried on a pair of shoes Reebok had provided for Post to Post's staff. For some reason, no one asked her to black out the Reebok logo when she wore those shoes either in training or games, so for months she'd been wearing either blacked-out Adidas or non-blacked-out Reeboks when she played with the National Team. It was never a problem—until Sweden four days before the World Cup.

⚽ ⚽ ⚽

Suddenly the USSF had a beef with my Reeboks. The team administrator called me aside and asked if I had a pair of Adidas with me I could wear instead. I told her I did, but they were brand-new and would take time to break in. I preferred to stick with my Reeboks. I knew she wasn't happy with my response, but I didn't plan to change at the last minute.

Two days later I was summoned to an official meeting at our hotel and told I would only be allowed to wear blacked-out Adidas. I explained again that my Adidas weren't broken in, but that I would be glad to black out any identifying marks on my Reeboks. I figured blacked-out was blacked-out.

At a subsequent meeting I was informed if I wore anything but Nike, since they sponsored our team, I would need to be prepared for the consequences. I took that as a threat that if I didn't wear the team sponsor's shoes I would not be allowed to play. That threat was confirmed by phone calls to Federation officials back in the States. I couldn't believe it. If I was willing to black out all the identification, why couldn't I wear the shoes in which I was most comfortable? The whole thing made me mad.

If it didn't bother my personal sponsor, Umbro, why should it bother the Federation? Why make an issue just before the World Cup, of all times? Our player contract even stipulated that if the shoes provided to the team didn't fit right or caused medical problems we could wear our own shoes. I think some people thought I was just being stubborn, but I saw this as a matter of principle, a precedent-setting situation that could be a problem again for the team in the future. I thought the timing stunk, but I felt I needed to take a stand.

Finally, on opening game day, just hours before kickoff, I came to an agreement with the head of international soccer for Nike. He agreed to let me wear blacked-out Reeboks if I promised to try Nikes again in the Nike-sponsored U.S. Cup the following year. I said, "Whatever it takes." I just wanted shoes that worked. I didn't care who made them. Politics! What a mess!

It seemed such a minor thing to have made into a major controversy. And it ate up an enormous amount of emotional energy when I had so little to spare. But at least I could begin the tournament wearing shoes I felt comfortable in.

Through all these last-minute distractions I tried to keep my mind on our team's goal. Defending our title was our expectation. It was also the world's expectation. But my immediate focus wasn't so much on winning and dominating as it was on survival. *Can I get through this? How will I play being this sick?*

I'd been playing sick for years now. *Surely I can keep going for another two weeks.*

Warming up for our first game against China, I concentrated on preparing my body to play. Instead of feeling ready and light, I felt slow, off-balance, and as heavy as an elephant. Not a good sign!

Still, I felt the familiar spine-tingling excitement when we marched onto the field for the Opening Ceremonies. As usual, I looked for Dad, who was harder to find in a Swedish crowd than he had been in China. Fortunately, that challenge was made easier by the fact that he was surrounded by a dozen relatives and friends who'd spent a small fortune to make the trip to watch me play my second World Cup. The family experience had been such a highlight in China that a lot of other folks decided they wanted to share this one with me.

When we finally kicked off, I thought, *Thank God! I'm at the World Cup again. I made it. Here we go.*

I think I got a total of two or three touches in the first four minutes of the game before I dropped back to the edge of my own box to defend against a Chinese corner kick. The ball came in high. I jumped to head it away. I remembering making contact and . . . the lights went out.

❀ ❀ ❀

As Michelle leaped into the air, a Chinese player's head speared hers at the base of the skull. Michelle's head snapped forward and she crumpled to the ground with her leg twisted under her at an awkward angle.

Ironically, Amy Allmann, Michelle's college roommate and former teammate on the National Team, was doing color commentary on the game for ESPN2. "It was my job to describe the replays," Amy says. "When they showed the replay of Michelle's injury, I couldn't say a word. There was dead silence in the booth. J.P. Dellacamera, my broadcast partner, finally had to tap me on the shoulder to prompt me to say something. Everybody watching was probably thinking, 'I wonder how the U.S. is going to play without Michelle Akers.' I was thinking, 'I hope Mish isn't paralyzed.'"

For a long time Michelle didn't move. When she returned to consciousness and could answer a few basic questions from the doctors, she waved off a stretcher. As she hobbled off the field under her own power she gave her stepmom Sue the thumbs-up. But her eyes were crossed and nothing really registered. In fact, all she remembers of the next two days is what other people have since told her.

The team doctors took her to a nearby hospital where the diagnosis was a concussion and yet another knee injury. She awakened the next day in a haze from medication and the concussion to find messages and stuffed animals around her hotel room and even on her bed. Many of her teammates had written notes of encouragement and also expressed their feelings of admiration for her.

❀ ❀ ❀

I was overwhelmed. Later I told April Heinrichs, who was now one of our assistant coaches, about the encouraging and complimentary notes. I wondered why I never knew my teammates felt this way before.

April said, "Maybe it takes someone to be knocked down, or weak before others feel they can respond or tell them how they really feel."

Interesting. I was learning that people can relate to weakness better than they can to strength. All my life I'd tried so hard to be strong because I thought that was the way to win approval and achieve my goals. But the way to really impact people, to enable them to relate to me, was to let them share in my struggle. I'd started learning that truth in my relationship with Sal, but this experience really underscored the lesson in a way I hoped I would never forget. Maybe it's because you have to be strong to show weakness and people can connect to that.

⊛ ⊛ ⊛

Michelle slept for nearly twenty-four hours straight when she came back to the hotel from the hospital.

"I was devastated for her," says Amanda Cromwell. "I knew how much Michelle had suffered from her CFIDS. I'd seen how hard she worked to get to that World Cup. And now this! I tried to bring her food to our room, but she was just out of it. The second day Doc Brown and I took her on a twenty-minute walk. Later when I asked her about a guy we'd met and she'd spoken to, she couldn't even remember taking the walk. It was scary."

⊛ ⊛ ⊛

By the third day after the injury, I had recovered enough to write in my journal:

> So it's two games into the World Cup and I have played less than six minutes. Doc Garrett says I got over the Epstein-Barr only to get the Shanghai Shaft. Funny. Yeah, real funny. I had to go to the hospital for a CAT scan (yes, I have a brain) and poor Dad was there again, scared to death for me. I swear I will put him in an early grave. He's worse than I am, on the verge of crying, trying to be brave for me. Poor Pops, I know his heart is breaking. Even Sue was crying.
>
> Anyway, headwise I'm okay. But the knee is painful. A sprain to the right medial collateral ligament from the way I fell. The doctor says to push through the pain for a quicker rehab. Our motto is "Good pain is hard to find." Appropriate. I'm running already (straight) with lots of grunting and swearing. But at least I'm running. I'm hoping to be back in time for the quarterfinals next Tuesday. Please, God!
>
> I'm not as broken up about this as I would have expected. My EBV experience has made me so dang tough. I called home to pick up my messages and everyone was really worried about me. In the whole scheme of things, missing this World Cup would be a disappointment, but not the end of the world.

The hardest part was facing my family and convincing them I was okay with it. Dad and Sue were so disappointed and sad for me that it hurt to see them. They'd flown halfway around the world to share another great experience with me and they'd only gotten to see me play for six minutes. I wanted everything to be okay for their sakes. And I couldn't help thinking, *What else am I going to put them through?*

In the locker room before the first game after my injury something happened that I'll never forget. I was already struggling to remain composed for the team. I didn't want to be a distraction; I wanted to contribute. So I felt it was important that they saw me as okay, that I was taking my injury in stride. But when I walked in and all my teammates had my name or my number written on their sock tape to dedicate their play and honor me, I almost lost it.

In the pregame huddle, Carla Overbeck said, "If you get tired out there or feel like giving up, I want you to look at the bench and see Michelle. She never gives up, and we won't either. Let's play for each other from this moment forward." I nearly lost it again.

Even so, I struggled at first with my role on the bench. As a career starter, it was tough sitting on the sideline watching. Good thing I was wearing sunglasses when our team doctor came over and told me I was handling it like a champion; I teared up again. People may have thought I had it all under control, but my disappointment remained very close to the surface. Only God gave me the strength and grace to get through it.

I even managed to joke with Amy Allmann about the injury during an on-air interview before one of the next games. She asked me a question about the incident, something like, "What do you remember about the collision?"

I said, "Amy, I was knocked out. I don't remember a thing." After we laughed about that, she ran the videotape of the play and asked me to describe it. "Here's the kick. There I am going up for the header. Here comes the Chinese girl, and . . . Ouch! That must have hurt!"

We laughed again. But the truth was, just watching the replay made me sick to my stomach. I saw the Chinese player hit me and my head snap forward. I fell like a sack of flour and just lay there. If I had taken a blow like that to the face, I could have been killed. It was that violent. I felt lucky just to be alive.

Yet I still hoped to get back into action before the tournament ended.

⚽ ⚽ ⚽

Michelle rehabbed her knee furiously. She could run a little as long as she moved in a straight line. Cutting caused excruciating pain. Kicking remained a problem as well.

"She'd make me go with her to a little patch of grass across the street from our hotel," Amanda recalls. "And we'd kick a ball back and forth. Every time her foot made contact she'd wince or cry out. Still, she kept trying."

Without Michelle in the lineup, her team had tied China 3–3 in that first game and beaten Denmark 2–0 in the second. One more win and the U.S. would advance to the second round. Michelle hoped to come back by then.

A victory over Australia got the Americans to the quarterfinals against Japan. But when they jumped out to a quick lead and coasted to a 4–0 win, Tony DiCicco decided to save Michelle's fragile knee for the semifinal match against Norway.

The press hounded her the whole time. After every training session they surrounded her to ask, "Will you play?" "How's the head?" "What about your knee?" "Were you only kicking with your left foot?" It seemed she was getting more press than the people who were playing; she just wished they would leave her alone.

⚽ ⚽ ⚽

On June 15, the day of the semifinal match with Norway, this is what I wrote in my journal:

> I start tonight, and for the first time ever, I'm terrified to play. I don't know what I will be able to do. My knee is sore from only thirty minutes of light running yesterday. What will it be like after an intense forty-five? Tony says he doesn't expect me to "fly in and rescue the team," but I think a lot of people do. I just want to make a small difference. Actually, that's a lie. I want to make a huge difference. I want to score goals, to be a threat, to be the best player out on that field. And it's killing me knowing I won't be.

Norway scored a goal early and we spent the rest of the afternoon pounding shots at the Norwegian net, trying to fight back and tie. I limped around the field on one leg the entire game, unable to make anything good happen. I did what I could, but my best wasn't enough to make any difference that day.

When the final whistle blew I remember thinking three things. *This can't be real. I want another chance.* And *I refuse to let them see me cry.* The last thing in the world I wanted was to see my picture in some soccer magazine with tears streaming down my face.

So I just stood there, willing myself not to cry. I remember watching the Norwegians celebrating by forming a train and chugging happily around us on the field. It was awful shaking their hands. I felt more like punching them.

I headed toward the section of the stands where my family had been sitting. For some reason, I was the only player who did. When the whole U.S. contingent of families and friends saw me coming, they started cheering. I couldn't look at them. I kept my head down until I got to my dad. Then I hugged him and began to cry. He cried. Sue cried. My brother cried. My grandmother cried. Everybody cried.

This was more than just another lost soccer match. They'd been through so much with me just to get there, and now we'd come up short.

Two days later we defeated China for third place. But consolation games are never any real consolation. I just wanted to get the whole nightmare over with and go home.

The next day we did. That was the same day I wrote this report about the end of the tournament in my journal:

> The final between Norway and Germany was horrendous to watch, and the banquet was even worse. It seemed each was meant to rub our face in the disappointment of losing. The Norwegians won every award, and came into the banquet singing. Gumby and I had to give our '91 awards (the Golden Ball and the Golden Boot) to the winners, both Norwegians. Gumby came back to the table crying.
>
> Tony said some good stuff on the bus ride back to our hotel. He told us, "Never forget the feeling we have this night. The margin of victory on the field is so small. But the margin off the field is huge."
>
> The Norwegians were in the limelight, receiving awards, holding the trophy. The U.S. team members were in the back of the room, unnoticed and forgotten. Hopefully, Tony's message will stick with everyone and will propel us to the winner's platform at the Olympics next year. We now look toward the Olympics. This team will be ready. I will be ready.

Whatever it takes!

Part

FIVE

Going for the Gold:
Atlanta 1996

Chapter Sixteen

ONE MORE
ROCKY ROAD

I absolutely crashed when I got back to Florida. I couldn't even make myself journal my feelings until I'd been home two whole weeks. By then I'd spent so much time reflecting on the experience that I was beginning to gain some perspective, as shown in my July 5 journal entry:

> I came home from Sweden upset. But I worked through it, began rehabbing the knee, got checked and okayed by the neurologist, and got on with my life. I went back to church and began to understand the purpose, or part of the purpose, of my World Cup experience. I realized it can be a blessing and an incredible witness to the strength and trustworthiness of Christ. I've started to see my life—my disappointments as well as my victories—in a new light.
>
> I have struggled to put into words the testimony or praise of what God has done with my life in the past three or four years. I kept thinking, *Who cares about this stuff? Who really wants to know?* But I kept getting this little nudge to write it down. So here . . .
>
> Having CFIDS has been the most frustrating, depressing experience of my life. By far, this is the toughest thing I have ever fought. The recovery process is long and tedious and requires positive thinking and the utmost patience—which is not a strong trait for me. There have been days when I wanted to die or just give up because of the headaches, fatigue, and fevers.
>
> But recently I've learned to view CFIDS as a blessing. Being so sick has made me rethink my life, and as a consequence . . . I started going back to church. Slowly, ever so slowly, I began to make a comeback in my health and my soccer . . .

It's been tough, the last year and more. I feel like I'm constantly being thrown huge challenges. I overcome one thing and another is thrown in, seemingly out of nowhere. At times I get tired of having to overcome. I wish life would be easy and run smoothly for a change.

But as I look back at how far I've come, I realize God has blessed me. And is still blessing me. I am the kind of person who has to literally be knocked over the head to get the point. So through these hard times— CFIDS, injuries, divorce—God has forced me to open my eyes, examine my life, and find the "narrow road" again. To listen, love, and follow Him. And to trust.

I now know that my successes and struggles in soccer are to be used. I understand that the frustrating, disappointing, and tough experiences are for a reason. It's all been to prepare me to do something down the line, to give me experience to share, and to test and strengthen my faith.

So that brings me to where I am right now. I heard my preacher, Joel Hunter, give a sermon last weekend and I'm excited to start in earnest. I swear he still looks right at me sometimes when he talks. His message to me was, "Forget what others think. Forget about the logistics of how or why. Put your eyes on God. Listen and learn. Trust. Then just go out and do it."

I found a lot more time to examine my life in the wake of the 1995 World Cup, because after I rehabbed my knee enough to play only portions of three August games, I underwent my eleventh knee operation. Recovery time always gives me both reason and opportunity to think.

I realized winning the world championship back in 1991 had been a defining moment in my life. I had struggled, our team had struggled, to overcome all obstacles—lack of support, injuries, inexperience. We had struggled to win. We wound up with the trophy, but the mountain we had to climb to get there was long and grueling, covered with sacrifice and hardship. In that World Cup I discovered my own capabilities and that I had the talent to be the best in the world. Winning the championship hadn't been easy, but I had been rewarded for my efforts with a fantasy moment on the winner's podium, a fairy tale kind of ending I now know doesn't always come true.

The 1995 World Cup had been a very different kind of experience—but clearly another defining moment, because Sweden didn't show me what I could do, but who I was, and what God could do in me. I still hated to lose as much as I ever did, but I found victory despite defeat. And defeat, disappointment, heartache, and frustration are more real in this world than the fairy tale ending of 1991.

When I found myself knocked out of the World Cup after so much pain and sacrifice to get there, God enabled me to handle the whole horrible experience with grace, dignity, and maturity. I knew I couldn't have done that myself. The key to shining in all circumstances is experiencing Christ's victory instead of our own failure or defeat.

Coming to this conclusion marked the point at which I really began trusting my life to God. I say that because, before when I was trying to follow God, I hadn't fully, completely, given Him everything. I was still hanging on to soccer—for my own sake, not His. And there were many other areas of my life that I held on to as well. Now that I'd learned I could trust God in the very worst of circumstances, I realized I was a lot better off letting Him have complete control.

Of course, that was not an easy lesson for me to put into practice every day. Especially when things didn't look like they were going my way.

I hit the first big bump in my road to the Olympics before the end of 1995 when the U.S. Soccer Federation sent out player contracts for the coming year. The problem revolved around USSF's proposal for Olympic compensation. They wanted to only give us a bonus if we won a gold medal. My teammates and I felt there should also be some consideration for winning a silver or bronze. When we proposed that, the USSF said the contract offer was final and we could "take it or leave it." We said "no way" and first thing we knew, nine of us—all veteran starters—were considered "on strike" and "locked out." We weren't even invited to the first training camp of the new year. The whole mess lasted almost two months before the Federation realized we were serious and finally conceded.

Fortunately the contract dispute ended just in time for most of the veterans to make the National Team's first road trip of the year—to play four games against three different international teams in Brazil in mid-January. It was while we were there that coach Tony DiCicco introduced what I first considered another huge challenge.

✪ ✪ ✪

"After World Cup '95, when I reflected on our loss in Sweden," says DiCicco, *"I didn't feel we had the quality of distribution out of our midfield that we needed. I also felt Michelle could give us that distribution and controlling presence at midfield, and at the same time not get hammered as much and have to take the physical beating she did as a front-runner."*

"So after the first game of that Brazil trip I had a one-on-one meeting with Michelle to say, 'I'd like to try something. I've been thinking about using you as a midfielder.' But as soon as I got the words out I could see the fire in her eyes. She wanted to know what was going on; to her this sounded like a demotion.

"I told her, 'No, my reason for doing this is that we need your ability to distribute the ball and control the game for us.' But as I went on to explain my thinking I could see she was not buying into it at all. She saw it as being less involved, less of a scoring threat, and playing less of a central role on the team.

"Finally I added the rationale: 'Plus, I think I can extend your career.' All of a sudden, I could see in her eyes that I'd said something she wanted to hear. That made sense to her. So I went on, 'As a front-runner you're getting hammered from behind game after game by two defensive backs every time you receive the ball anywhere near the goal. In the midfield you're not going to have your back to the pressure as often, you won't always have two players marking you, and you're going to be able to dish out as much physical contact as you receive.'

"She liked that. The idea of extending her career was the trump card. She was willing to give the plan a try. So we began experimenting with it. After we came home from South America we had a home game in Tampa against Norway. We played Michelle in midfield, where she had an awesome game. The Norwegians simply didn't know how to deal with her. She would take the ball, escape pressure, and change the point of attack more quickly than we'd ever been able to do against Norway before.

"The Norwegians love to play a scrappy, destructive style—a kick and run game. And they have a method to their madness: the less structured the game, the better they like it. But with Michelle winning all their long balls in the air and controlling things in the middle, they were forced to chase the ball and play a style they didn't like.

"We won that game against the reigning world champions 3–2. And I knew right then that if and when we faced Norway in the Olympic Games, we would definitely play Michelle in the middle. Since I didn't want to give away our strategy, however, I planned to alternate her at forward and midfield in the games leading up to Atlanta."

⊛ ⊛ ⊛

What neither Tony nor I realized was that there would soon be serious questions as to whether I'd even make it to Atlanta. I injured my knee just five minutes into that Norway game in Tampa. When it still didn't feel right during pregame warm-ups at our next game a couple nights later in Jacksonville, I asked one of the team doctors to take a look. His diagnosis devastated me. He told me my MCL was "shot"—torn almost all the way through. I needed major reconstructive surgery right away.

But if I did that, I would never make the Olympics, which were just five months and seventeen days away. *That's it,* I thought. *No Olympics. What now?*

I left the locker room in tears, searching for a pay phone to call my good friend, previously with Umbro and now my business manager, Eva Ferara. Fans streaming into the stadium kept stopping me and asking for autographs. I finally found a phone outside, talked to Eva, and settled down enough to go back to the team. But when I tried to reenter the stadium, the ticket takers wouldn't let me in.

I stood outside the gate, in full uniform, crying, my Olympic dream shattered, arguing with security and unable to even get inside the stadium. Finally I walked a little ways away, scaled the fence, and rejoined my team on the bench.

The next day I went to my own orthopedist in Orlando who had operated on me several times and was more familiar with my knee's history. He told me, "It's ripped pretty bad, but I think you can rehabilitate it."

So that's what my longtime physical therapist and good buddy, Rodney Negrete, and I decided to do. We would spend two or three hours a day over the next few months trying to get my knee ready. I would come from practice (whether I was watching or participating) in the middle of the day to work my rear end off with Rodney. Then I'd go back to practice in the afternoon and finally home to collapse in bed.

I would have been a lot more discouraged that spring if I hadn't had some great company to share my misery. My friend Sal, who'd already had some tough times of her own over the previous few months, blew out her own knee during a training camp scrimmage game against a team from Denmark.

Despite having been with the team more than five years, she'd gotten word last fall that she wasn't being invited back to National Team training camp in January. She'd called me upset and we'd talked a while. Then she got invited after all during the contract dispute when the nine of us veterans weren't going to camp. Sal had called me then too, afraid that she'd just be cut again if and when the bonus issues were settled. I told her she should come anyway, she could stay in my apartment, we'd work out together, and hopefully she would play herself back on the team. And that's what she'd done. She played well enough on the Brazil trip that she was asked to stay in camp with the team. She'd gotten her hopes up about making the Olympic team, and now this.

When she went home to Virginia to try to rehab her knee, we continued to keep each other updated on our progress by phone.

❀ ❀ ❀

"It meant so much to have someone I knew understood what I was going through to talk with," Sal says. "We could be honest about our pain and discouragement. In doing that we could encourage each other.

"When she invited me back down to Florida to live with her so we could continue our rehab together, that really meant a lot to me. I knew how much Mish valued her own space and sense of privacy. She had devised her own daily routines to conserve energy and get the rest needed to protect her health. So I was reluctant to accept her offer until she insisted.

"Over the next weeks and months we became a lot closer. While I was just hoping for a chance to make the team, Michelle was intent on once again being her old Michelle Akers self and taking on the world. But for a while there we were both in the same place, sharing the same pain, even the same physical therapist. And our friendship grew through the experience."

Since Sal lived in Michelle's apartment, sleeping on a futon in Michelle's home office, she was there to see her friend's daily struggles with pain and discouragement, not just with her knee, but also when her CFIDS acted up. *"I could tell by looking at her when she needed help,"* Amanda says. *"So I would volunteer to do the grocery shopping, cook meals, and just take care of her. As she realized I truly did want to help, I think she reached a turning point in understanding that it's okay to be vulnerable."*

❀ ❀ ❀

After the '95 World Cup in Sweden I'd thought a lot about my teammates' response to my injuries and disappointment. How making yourself vulnerable lets others in. While being strong is good, rarely do people share with those who appear to have everything together and under control. I was beginning to loosen up, to not keep such a tight rein on my emotions. I had come to the realization that it was okay to let people see me cry.

Sal had seen me cry in Sweden. So when she'd been hurting, first by getting cut from the team, then after fighting her way back on it only to rip up her knee, I wanted to be there to help her.

It was about this same time that I read a wonderful book called *The Power of the Powerless* in which Christopher DeVinck tells the story of his profoundly handicapped brother Oliver who lived his entire life in a bed in an upstairs bedroom, unable to feed himself, to see, to speak, to interact with other family members, or even to straighten his shriveled and twisted limbs. Yet DeVinck writes not only about the tremendous impact Oliver had on his own life, but how God had used Oliver's story to touch hundreds of thousands of people around the world.

Reading that little book reinforced the lessons I'd been learning. I knew that if God could use someone like Oliver to make an impact on the world, He was certainly capable of using CFIDS or any other personal limitations I had to help demonstrate His power and ability to work through my weakness. My growing relationship with Sal and her regular attendance with me at Bible Study Fellowship was added, convincing proof.

That's not to say my physical problems were no longer a struggle. The emotional and physical roller-coaster ride continued through the spring. On March 30 I wrote in my journal:

> The last few days I have been intently studying CFIDS and its emotional/personal effects on its victims. I have realized on a deeper level that this disease is not only physically debilitating and emotionally gut-wrenching, but as the days and months pass by, it gradually steals away who you are—or better yet—how you define yourself.
>
> CFIDS cuts you to the core. It takes away all of what the world—and you—determine as successful and useful in a person—independence, work ethic, personality, energy. That is why this illness is so devastating. It not only makes you sick, taking away your lifestyle, career, and friends. It also kills your identity.
>
> It cruelly grinds down everything you have been able to rely on and trust implicitly: *You*. No longer can you rely on your ability to perform, think, plan, or hope. For example, due to the physical effects of CFIDS, I am limited in my duties as a soccer player and company spokesperson. At times my thinking is profoundly affected; my brain is foggy and I can't concentrate. I am reluctant to plan appearances or group activities ahead of time because I don't know when I might crash and have to beg off at the last minute. And on the very bad days I teeter on the edge of utter hopelessness in my battle to overcome this dogged disease. Will I ever be *me* again?

Four days later I added more thoughts on how CFIDS was affecting my life:

> I was once what you call a low-maintenance person. No special attention or needs. Independent. Strong. But now I need all these special considerations, excuses, rules to live or do the things I want to do. I am high-maintenance. Fragile. For example, to play for the National Team is tough. Sometimes I can practice and sometimes not. That's not very reliable. I hate getting sympathy for feeling awful, yet I want people to understand how badly I feel and that I'm not just copping out. I *want* to train, I just don't have the gas to get the job done and still be able to function at the end of the day. I dread having to tell the coaches I can't practice . . . and the thing is, I can practice, but if I do, I'll feel awful and then tomorrow I'll feel even worse. So technically, I can, but I won't. I hate that.
>
> I am starting to realize that just as I've had to adapt my "person" to this disease, so will I have to adapt Michelle the soccer player to CFIDS. I can no longer be the fittest, strongest, quickest all the time. I have to choose my moments. I pray for those moments to be there when I need them. If CFIDS is running its course that day or that week, I can't think right. There may be times I have nothing to offer my team except maybe my presence. Will that be enough?
>
> In the meantime, I can try to change the kind of player I am when I am healthy and conserve the explosiveness and energy for the days and games to come. Be smart. Be savvy. Skillful. Let the ball do the work, as they say. Be a veteran and orchestrate the game. Take it over mentally. Can I do that?

Two days later I was feeling more encouraged again:

> Well, things have certainly gotten better health-wise. I took a couple of days off and, *voila!* I feel better. It's just getting through those tough days that's the tricky part.

Each day I had to assess which "me" would show up. I had to figure out how to compete and play as an impact player. *What kind of work will I be able to do? Bust or save? Quick thinking or a bit slow tactically? Strong or weak? Can I take defenders one-on-one, or is it just dishing off today? How do I prepare myself in warm-up? How much should I conserve? Do I tell Tony or not?*

And then there was my mental preparation. *What is my role today? Healthy or sick?* And when the role changed because I didn't have the energy or the mental sharpness to handle it, I had to make the transition to a lesser Michelle

Akers. And that meant accepting the disappointment of not being who I wanted to be. *So, who am I today?*

Some days I cried in the shower and prayed, "Lord, I can't make it through this day. Please give me the strength because I just can't do it."

I played my first complete game in over two months on April 20 and was so excited I wrote in my journal:

> Phew! I'm back! I am back! Semi, anyway. We played Holland and I lasted the full ninety minutes . . . barely. I scored a goal on a header and played okay.

I played only part of the two remaining games scheduled in April, scoring one goal in each contest. During that time I picked up a rather controversial book about CFIDS titled *Osler's Web*. What I read really scared me. No one knew the risk of a person with CFIDS trying to compete physically at my level. There could be permanent damage to my body. How much risk was too much?

For the first time, I seriously considered and surprisingly accepted that fact that I might need to give up the game I loved after the Olympics. And I wondered, *What would God want me to do?*

Colleen Hacker, our team psychologist, told me, "God can't direct your steps unless you're taking some." So I decided to start by trying to E-mail Dr. Paul Cheney, a world-reknowned specialist in the treatment of CFIDS, to ask his advice. To my surprise, he responded immediately. We set up a phone consultation the next week. When we talked, he did express real concern that I might be risking my ongoing health. He told me I had two choices to reduce that risk—quit playing soccer or try a ten-week elimination diet.

That would mean cutting dairy, caffeine, red meat, gluten, and sugar out of my diet. In other words, I could forget anything that tasted good. No more TCBY, no Cinnabons, pizza, or my beloved Starbuck's.

I opted for the diet. I took it as an encouraging sign that the last day of the tenth week would fall on July 21—the day of our first game in the Olympics. I began living on gluten-free cereal, Powerbars, dried gluten-free soups, gluten-free bread, rice milk, popcorn, gluten-free pancake mix, corn or rice pastas, peanut butter, and carrots . . . lots of carrots. I juiced more than two pounds of carrots a day.

Some time earlier I had been invited to testify before Congress on May 11 for CFIDS Awareness Day. I had more than enough travel with the team, though, and didn't feel up to an extra flight to Washington and back. So I sent my testimony to be read into the record.

It was the most I'd revealed publicly about my ordeal, and I think it marked a turning point in my acceptance of the disease. Here's what I said in my Congressional testimony:

In 1991, I was named the best women's soccer player on this planet, and my team, the United States of America, became the first ever FIFA women's world champions. We went undefeated in the tournament and I scored an unprecedented ten goals in five games.

It wasn't long after the World Cup that I began to notice a change in my energy. Over a two-year period, almost imperceptibly at first, I began to fade. Finally, I collapsed and became delirious on the field during the 1993 Olympic Sports Festival. The doctors thought at first that it might be muscle glycogen depletion, then a heart dysfunction, and finally, after collapsing yet again, I was tested for the Epstein-Barr Virus. My numbers were sky high. Bingo. We had found the culprit. Or so I thought. I was diagnosed with Chronic Fatigue and Immune Dysfunction Syndrome (CFIDS). In 1994, three years later, I finally had a name to the thing I had to fight to regain my health.

My name is Michelle Akers. I am 5'10" and weigh 150 pounds. I am muscular. I am tan. I have wild, sun-bleached curly hair. My teammates call me "Mufasa" from *The Lion King*. I love to laugh. On vacations, I love to hike in the Cascade Mountains near Seattle with my dad and brother. I am the starting center forward for the world-class American women's soccer team . . . and soon to be a 1996 Olympian.

If you saw me today, you would see a healthy, physically fit, elite athlete. But I'm not. I am sick. And I am hanging on by the very will and courage that helped me attain my status as an athlete. Some days it is all I can do to get through the day, let alone be an elite athlete. On those days, the only way to step on the field is to stop, close my eyes, take a deep breath and gather every ounce of strength and will, focusing solely on surviving the hour and a half of practice ahead of me. Most days, I survive the practice—sometimes, I do even better than survive and actually see glimpses of the player I used to be. Those days are glorious. To feel good. To have energy. To be light and strong. This is what it's supposed to be like. Fun. And carefree. I revel in the feeling and the gift of good health.

On the very bad days, it is all I can do to survive. I walk off—drag myself off the field, my legs and body like lead. They seem to weigh so much. My breathing is labored. It is all I can do to get to the locker room, change my clothes, and keep from crying from utter exhaustion and weariness. I am light-headed and shaky. My vision is blurred. My teammates ask me if I am okay, and I nod yes. But my eyes tell the truth. They are hollow, empty. Dull and lifeless. It scares me to look in the mirror when I get like this. I have crossed that invisible line between functioning and being very, very sick. How long will it take to recover from this one?

I slowly get to my truck and concentrate on the road, willing myself to keep moving, not to pull over and rest. *Almost there,* I tell myself. *Just a few more minutes.* By the time I arrive home, I leave my bags in a pile by the door and collapse on the couch. I have no energy to eat. To shower. To call someone for help.

I tell you these things not to gain sympathy, but so you too can experience a day in the illness. The pounding migraine headaches that can incapacitate me for days. The insomnia that plagues me even though I am exhausted. The overwhelming fatigue that keeps me from going to a movie or dinner with a friend because I don't have the energy to talk, sit up, or eat. The GI upset has caused me to go on a extreme gluten-free diet, dairy-free, caffeine-free, sugar-free, and alcohol-free diet in hope of finding relief or possibly a cure for the fogginess that causes me to lose concentration and forget where I am, or how to get someplace that I've been a thousand times before.

This illness demands attention in every detail of my life, and if I don't pay attention, it punishes me. Without remorse. It is a difficult experience to explain because it encompasses so much of my being—of who I am. There is grief in realizing that you will never be the person you were before the illness. CFIDS becomes who you are at times, leaving you—the old you—a mere shadow.

I have always believed that you can accomplish anything through hard work and perseverance, through dedication and commitment. This is how I became a world champion and an Olympic athlete. That is the irony of the illness. The harder you work, the more it drags you down. The more it disables you. It is the first time in my life I have been beaten. It is the first time in my life I may have to quit before I accomplish my goal. I cannot defeat this illness through hard work, or pure drive and desire. It is the first time I cannot overcome on my own terms, in my own strength.

I am a fortunate CFIDS sufferer. Because I am an elite athlete, I have access to the best doctors, the best care in the United States and, therefore, the world. I have an incredible support system through my team and family. For example, my team is going to join me in my new gluten-free diet one evening. They help me with my bags when traveling. They force me off the field when I am pushing too hard. They drive me home when I can't make it myself. My friends pray for me daily and lift me up when I am at the end of myself.

My family, friends, coaches, and employers (the U.S. Soccer Federation and Reebok) are sympathetic and flexible in regards to my health and limitations. They have never doubted that I am sick and not just depressed, mentally unstable, or, God forbid, faking it.

Yes, I have lost a lot. Yes, CFIDS is a devastating disease. And no, I am not the same person before I was stricken with CFIDS and probably will never be. But this is not a message of hopelessness or defeat. It is a story about courage, growth, and a challenge. It is a story about overcoming. I have gained a lot from this illness. Nothing that can be touched or measured, but through the suffering and heartache, I have gained a strength and purpose that carries me when I cannot do it myself. I have seen and experienced God's grace and peace only because I have been in the valley. I now know it took this long visit in the depths of this illness to open myself to a more meaningful and purposeful life.

I live by the verse in 2 Corinthians which says, "My grace is sufficient for you, for my power is made perfect in weakness . . . that is why, for Christ's sake, I delight in hardship . . . in difficulties. For when I am weak, then I am strong." Through God, through this weakness—this illness—God's power rests in me, and I am strong. His power is made perfect in me. I will overcome, but not through any effort of my own. That is the final irony. The more I struggle to save myself from this disease, the more it takes my life away. The moment I rest in the strength of God's perfect grace is the moment I begin to overcome.

I have learned to accept CFIDS as an opportunity to make a difference. I have turned this weakness into a strength. And even though it is still raging inside me, I refuse to be beaten by it.

I will overcome. And I will show others how to overcome also. Thank you.

In attendance during the reading of my testimony was Dr. Peter Rowe of Johns Hopkins University, who contacted me the very next day to tell me he would "bet his house" that I had a blood pressure disorder called Neurally Mediated Hypotension (NMH) common to CFIDS sufferers. He offered to test me as soon as I could get to Baltimore. He had hopes of finding a treatment that might relieve some of my most debilitating symptoms.

Wow! I couldn't believe what was happening. First Dr. Cheney, and now Dr. Rowe. Things were beginning to look up again. I'd been on the diet a week and already was feeling noticeably better. I had enough energy to play soccer again.

☺ ☺ ☺

In May the Women's National Team hosted the 1996 U.S. Women's Cup—a three-game tournament with Canada, Japan, and China played in three different American cities. In the first game Michelle played ninety minutes in a 6–0 win over Canada. She also made a difference in her team's 4–0 win over Japan. The USA then met China in the final in Washington's RFK Stadium in front of 6,081 fans. Michelle pounced on a loose ball thirty yards from the goal and drilled a shot to the corner late in the match to give the U.S. a 1–0 victory and earn herself tournament MVP honors.

☺ ☺ ☺

On May 20, I wrote in my journal:

> The USSF brought Pops and Sue in to see the China game in D.C., and I played well. I got the winning goal on a cracker of a shot. What a boost! It was a nice day. I felt like I had a small taste of what winning the Olympics will be like—so much relief, pride, and justification that it was all worth it. Finally something positive has come of this mess.

But before I could begin to get too optimistic, yet another obstacle of Olympic proportions popped up out of nowhere. Part of a diagnostic procedure—called the Tilt Table Test—which Dr. Rowe conducted on me at Johns Hopkins required that he inject me with a stimulant called Isuprel. I never gave it a thought at the time, but on the plane flight home it hit me that I had my pre-Olympic drug screening in just two days. Isuprel was on the banned substance list.

I called the team's general manager, our trainer, and Doc Adams for advice. We all agreed I needed to confess what had happened in a letter to the U.S. Olympic Committee. Dr. Rowe wrote a second letter. The plan was for me to take the drug test and be prepared for the worst. Meantime I would stop taking all supplements which were part of my elimination diet and hope my body would get rid of everything within two days.

On May 23, just fifty-eight days before our first Olympic game, I went in for the urine test. I brought all the supplements the testers had asked to see and learned that one of them—ENADA—also included a banned substance. Now I was furious. I'd called the U.S. Olympic Committee's drug hotline twice before I'd started the diet two weeks earlier. At that time they'd said everything was okay; now they said there was a problem. I possibly had two different banned substances in me. And I'd have to wait two weeks for the results of the test.

I couldn't believe it. After everything I'd been through, now this! *What else, Lord?*

Chapter Seventeen
OLYMPIC EFFORT

$\mathscr{M}$y teammates would often see the strange stuff I was now eating and ask, "Can I taste some?" Then they'd go, "Yuck! How do you eat that?"

"If it's going to make me better," I shrugged, "then it's what I have to do."

Truth was, my new diet was working wonders. I had increased energy and stamina, balance, peripheral vision, and strength. I was feeling healthier by the week.

My June 5 journal entry read:

> Another day in the life . . . Sheesh! I hurt my stupid big toe! Can you believe that? I can't get one day's respite from controversy or injury. Nothing goes smoothly in my life. Can I just do something without complications? Just once?
>
> I was shooting. Jolly (Michelle Jollicoeur) blocked it and *ouch!* I played a little longer on it, but it hurt pretty bad. As the day went on, it got worse. I'm going in for x-rays . . .

I had suffered a grade-two sprain of the joint that attaches the big toe to the foot. It swelled up like a balloon. I couldn't walk on it, let alone run or kick a soccer ball. In fact, I couldn't even wear a shoe on that foot for almost two weeks.

In the meantime I waited and sweated the outcome of my drug test. When it finally came, I couldn't believe it! I was clean! Nothing showed up! I was officially cleared for the Olympics!

When I was able to practice again, my injured toe had to be carefully taped (like a growing number of my body parts). Even then, I couldn't play without being constantly aware of it. But I wasn't about to let a little pain stop me.

After living with a chronic illness, suffering numerous concussions, enduring eleven knee operations, and surviving a drug test, I couldn't imagine announcing to the team that I wouldn't be able to play in the Olympics because my big toe hurt.

We had two remaining tune-up games before the Olympic opener on July 21 in Orlando. We won both matches against Australia, and I played just long and well enough in each contest to gain a little confidence going down the home stretch. The day after game two against the Aussies, July 7, I wrote:

> It's amazing how much clearer my head is after being on this diet. And what's really amazing is how I've been functioning in a complete fog the past few years. Tunnel vision I call it. It's scary. How did I survive without completely ruining my life?
>
> God can be the only answer. Thank God He was there showing me a glimpse of light to follow in this crazy path.
>
> I tried to practice today with a migraine and decided to quit. No more of that, unless I absolutely have to. No wonder I got injured so often.
>
> The team is looking good—fit, fast, and focused. We are going to win. All the ingredients are there. I read my article in *USA Today* from '91 and discovered I feel exactly the same way for this one—confident, peaceful, prepared to win.
>
> I can imagine the feeling when we do it—awesome. A champion at last. Victorious at last. Personally and professionally. What an exciting journey!

The last weeks and days leading into any big tournament is a time for me to narrow my focus. To withdraw sometimes. My daily routine becomes even more significant. If I can concentrate on the things I normally do, it helps me avoid growing excitement and any last-minute controversy that might sap my energy and keep me from being fully prepared to compete.

But the sense of anticipation of the coming Olympics held in America, with women's soccer as a medal sport for the first time ever, was just too exciting, too huge to ignore. This could be a springboard for women's soccer, the culmination of what so many of us had been working so hard and for so long to see.

I remembered when I'd met one of the head honchos from the USOC at the Olympic Sports Festival back in '93 and thanking him for their decision to include women's soccer in the Atlanta Games. He'd laughed and told me the committee didn't feel like it had any choice after all the letters and petitions they got as a result of our grass roots campaign.

I also remembered back in 1994 when Brian Glanville, a leading soccer journalist, wrote a column in *World Soccer* magazine protesting the Olympic

Committee's decision. He evidently didn't feel the level of play in the women's game was worthy of the Olympic tradition. His article also demeaned the U.S. Women's National Team by referring to us as "Amazons."

At the time I had responded to Glanville's column with one of my own. "Let's go one-on-one, Brian," I had suggested, so we could settle the dispute on the field. He never responded.

I'd been personally slammed by the press again a few months earlier when a writer in *Soccer America* suggested I should be cut from the team because of my ongoing health struggles. Fortunately, Tony gave no more credence to press opinion than I did.

Because of attitudes like that, there was still a part of me that saw the fast-approaching games as a chance for me to prove something to the experts and to the world, as well as to myself. But that was the old Michelle Akers. There was another, newer part of me that was learning to say, "You're in charge, Lord. I'll do what I can. But whatever happens, I'm with You."

☯ ☯ ☯

On July 18 the team traveled by chartered bus from their training center in Sanford, Florida, to the Olympic village at Michelle's alma mater, the University of Central Florida, escorted by motorcycle cops and police cruisers with sirens wailing and lights flashing. Traffic parted like the Red Sea. The city of Orlando, an Olympic venue for soccer only, had adopted the U.S. Women's National Team as their own.

Michelle's teammates then flew to Atlanta for the Opening Ceremonies. Michelle had decided to stay behind, afraid the travel and the late night would zap the energy she needed for the tournament. She tried to stay up and watch her friends march in the opening procession wearing their snazzy red, white, and blue garb, but she fell asleep by 10 P.M.

☯ ☯ ☯

When we paraded into the Citrus Bowl for our opening game against Denmark, 25,303 people screamed and cheered and waved flags and banners. That was 16,000 more than the largest American crowd to have ever seen us play before. I spotted my dad in the stands and gave him and the rest of my family—Sue, my brother Mike, my mom, my Aunt Gini, my grandparents—my usual thumbs-up and a wave. I had to choke back tears because it meant so much for all of us to be there together as a family. *Pretty doggone cool,* I thought.

The crowd was not only huge but enthusiastic. The Citrus Bowl rocked. Add to all that the Olympic theme and the national anthem . . . and *Whoa!* We're talking goosebumps and a major lump in the throat. Then the game started and it was all business.

We may have been too keyed up at the start; a number of early shots sailed high. But we steadily wore the Danes down in the 102-degree heat. With ten minutes to go in the first half, Tisha Venturini scored the first Olympic goal in the history of the U.S. Women's National Team. With her back to the goal, she let a Brandi Chastain throw-in bounce past her chest, pivoted, and knocked a perfect, right-footed rocket to the far corner from twenty yards out. The goalkeeper got a hand on it before it ricocheted off of the post and into the net.

Five minutes later I saw another chance.

⊛ ⊛ ⊛

As Denmark got set for their goal kick Michelle told Mia Hamm if the ball came anywhere near her, she was going to head it as hard as she could toward the Denmark goal. "She kept telling me, 'Mia, pinch in,' Hamm remembers, "because I was too wide. As soon as I moved in, she headed it back in and I had a clear path to the goal. If she hadn't told me to move, I never would have scored that goal. If it's a header, I'm putting all my money, and all the other team's money, on Michelle." Mia, who had learned to trust Michelle over the years, gave the U.S. a 2–0 lead.

⊛ ⊛ ⊛

We ended up beating Denmark easily by a 3–0 score. And when Tony subbed me out in the seventy-sixth minute so I could conserve energy for the next game, my hometown crowd gave me a standing ovation. It felt absolutely overwhelming and incredibly satisfying to be there with so many people who had supported me over the years, who had helped put me back together and had cheered for me. Medical people, church friends, college acquaintances— now they were able to see firsthand the impact of their time and encouragement: an Olympic athlete. Maybe a gold medalist.

I made it through the postgame press conference where I told the international media that I "had a blast out there." But then I just collapsed in the locker room. However, this time the team's medical staff and I had a new strategy.

As I'd learned more about CFIDS in recent months, I'd started talking to Doc Adams more about the disease and how I was feeling. He did some research on his own and helped come up with a new strategy he thought might help me recover faster after games. He wanted to try IVs to help restore my body fluids and raise my blood pressure faster.

⊕ ⊕ ⊕

"Our plan for the Olympics was this," strength coach Steve Slain recalls. "I would help her off the field and into the locker room, where Mark Adams would take over. The IVs really helped. Michelle would always have a migraine after games. In general, she'd be a mess. But with the IVs she bounced back a lot quicker. She'd be okay the next day . . . at least she could eat, anyway."

⊕ ⊕ ⊕

I needed to recover as quickly as possible because we had our second game just two days later. We would face a Swedish team that had lost their opener with China and were desperate for a win to have any chance of advancing out of our group to the semifinal round.

Game two was also a scorching day. We scored early on another beautiful goal by Tish Venturini. But the Swedes fought hard—grabbing arms, shirts, shorts, necks, and anything else they could, to slow down our faster players. The official called them for eighteen fouls and still lots of rough stuff went unchecked.

With sixteen minutes remaining in the game, Mac (Shannon MacMillan) scored to give us a 2–0 lead and it looked like Tony was about to give me another rest when the Swedes came back two minutes later to make it 2–1. So I had to keep playing till the final whistle.

⊕ ⊕ ⊕

"Michelle was dying at the end," says Julie Foudy. "When she hit the wall you could see it. It was so loud on the field that you couldn't really talk to anyone. But because of my position, I was the closest one to her, so at every opportunity I would get in her face."

"Hang in there! You can do it, Mish!" Foudy would yell. "It's almost over. We need you!"

Mia Hamm was carried off the field with a badly sprained ankle late in the game. Michelle trudged off the field bruised and battered.

Kristine Lilly remembers walking into the training room after the game. "And there's Michelle with an ice bag on her head, an ice bag on her thigh, two more ice bags on her knee and ankle, her hand and toe all taped, hooked up to an IV. I took her picture. She just looked at me and we both burst out laughing."

❀ ❀ ❀

The next day we flew to Miami, and the day after that we played China in the Orange Bowl in front of 43,525 loud and supportive American fans. What an experience! And what a game.

We missed Mia's scoring punch; she sat out the game with her bad ankle. Despite outshooting the Chinese 19–7, the game ended in a 0–0 tie. And despite all my personal energy conservation strategies, for the first time in the tournament, I felt as if I'd pushed myself too far.

Near the end of the game my brother, Michael, came down near the field and yelled at me to "dig deep!" He says I just looked at him, no animation or recognition in my eyes whatsoever. I do remember him doing that, though. I also recall looking at him and thinking, *I'm already giving it everything I have . . . there is nothing more.* And then I thought, *Maybe I do need to dig deeper. There's got to be more in there somewhere.*

When I get empty like that, I begin to draw into myself. I try to find something inside and grab onto it so I can continue to play. It's like if I can condense myself somehow and focus so keenly on whatever there is left, I can make it. But I often find myself so intent on the struggle to keep going step by step that I will look at the clock and find fifteen minutes have passed. Then I say to myself, *All right! Just hang on another five minutes!*

I've also learned to play within myself and make field decisions based on my energy level versus the price of those decisions. For instance, in a flash I determine how much energy a certain play is going cost me. Then I ask myself, *Can I afford to spend that much of my reserves? Do we need me to do this or can someone else make the play?* If the answer is *No, I can't afford it. This isn't the time,* then I play conservatively. But if I'm the only one who can make the play or if it is time to risk it all, I go for it no matter what the consequences. *If I drop, I drop.*

After that game against China I dropped.

❀ ❀ ❀

"Michelle looked awful," Carla Overbeck says. "She was sitting in the locker room in a heap. Every game she gave every ounce of energy she had, and you could tell it just by looking at her. I just can't imagine a human being going through that. We were concerned about it, but then we realized she'd been through this before. She knew what to do, and we understood that. We just let her do it. And then we'd help her gather up all her things and take her back to the training room."

⚽ ⚽ ⚽

The tie against China didn't matter. We both advanced to the next round where we would have to play our old nemesis—Norway.

Since the semis and the medal rounds were all scheduled to be played in Athens, Georgia, we flew to Atlanta the next day and checked into the Olympic Village. Fortunately, we had an extra day's rest, with two days off instead of just one like we'd had during the first round in Florida. I needed all the time I could get.

I felt like I'd reached the beginning of the end. I could barely shower. My symptoms and weariness grew more severe after every game. I was running out of gas earlier during the matches and finding it harder to recover afterwards. Injuries were taking a toll as well.

My right knee had to be drained the day before the Norway game, the result of more torn cartilage in the China game. My big toe still needed to be taped. My hand was taped because of a sprained thumb and finger. And I had a bad quad bruise from a charley horse suffered in the Sweden game. Our trainer, Patty Marshak, joked that half the U.S. Soccer Federation budget was being spent on tape just to hold me together. I laughed, but I was worried. It was going to take everything I had just to finish a game against Norway, let alone be an impact player. And I wanted very badly to do well.

All the way through the Olympics, Tony had been starting me at forward, so as not to tip off the Norwegians to his new strategy. But he'd told me all along that I would play midfield against Norway, and that he was counting on me to do two things: win head balls and start the attack by distributing the ball quickly to my teammates. I just hoped I'd be able to execute Tony's plan.

⚽ ⚽ ⚽

More than 64,000 fans showed up at Sanford Stadium on the University of Georgia campus to see that semifinal match between the United States and Norway. And Tony DiCicco could not have been happier about Michelle's performance.

"She really surprised Norway," he remembers. "They had no answer for her. She won every headball that came near her."

Tisha Venturini, who started beside Michelle in midfield and is a world-class header in her own right, laughs at the memory. "It was hilarious. At first we'd both go after the air balls but I finally gave up and told her, 'I'll just let you take them, Mish. You're gonna get them all anyway.'"

Michelle's dominance in the air robbed Norway of their main offensive weapon— long, accurate passes from their backs to their front-runners. Virtually every pass Norway flew in her direction went off Michelle's head back toward Norway's goal. They couldn't get their offense started.

But that wasn't Michelle's only contribution. "We got twenty-eight shots against Norway in that game, which is unheard of, because they are such a great defensive team," says DiCicco. "We did that because Michelle was spraying the ball around very much like a great quarterback hitting receivers all over the field. Her technical speed—the ability to receive a ball, prepare it, and play it somewhere—was so fast. And her skill at serving balls with the inside or the outside of either foot is the best I've ever seen from any player, man or woman. She proved that to me again in that game."

◈ ◈ ◈

Not quite halfway through the first half, Norway intercepted a clearance pass and chipped the ball over two of our defenders to their top striker, Linda Medalen. She took it in stride and shot it just under the right hand of a hard-charging Brianna Scurry into the net. We went into the half trailing 1–0.

I stumbled into the locker room and sank to the floor. I told Steve Slain, "I can't keep going. I can't do it. I'm outta gas!"

And he kept telling me, "You will finish! You've got to finish! They need you!"

The second half began much like the first. Lilly pushed up the side time after time to create good shots. But we couldn't get the ball in the net. Time was running out.

With just ten minutes left in the game, and our hopes for an Olympic gold fading fast, the official whistled a Norwegian defender for a handball in her own penalty area.

I was sprinting for the corner when the whistle sounded and at first didn't realize what had happened. I could barely stay on my feet and was just grateful for a chance to stop and catch my breath. But the second I realized we were being awarded a penalty kick, I wanted it.

I looked around to see who else wanted it. Carla was off getting water. Brandi was standing in the back; she was out. I looked at Tony, and he pointed at me. *Rock on!* I thought.

Stepping up to the mark, I took the ball from the official. I thought to myself, *This is the moment I've been waiting for all my life.* I was calm. I was confident. And very aware of the importance of this kick. *If I miss, we'll probably lose and there will be no gold medal.* I decided to go to the left and drive it so hard that if the keeper did get a hand on the ball, it would take her right into the net. I looked to the right and then focused only on the ball during my approach. I felt no doubt.

The goalkeeper guessed right. The ball went left. And the score was tied 1–1. What an incredible feeling! I leaped high into the air, both arms pumping in delight, again and again. Foudy was the first American to get to me before we were mobbed by the rest of the team.

⚽ ⚽ ⚽

Tony DiCicco has his own take on that goal. He says, "I always list two or three names on the board, players I'll use to take PKs during a game. You never know who's going to be in there when a penalty is called. The first person on my list for the Norway game was Brandi Chastain because she'd become our best penalty kicker during that year. And then I'd written Michelle's name, and probably that of Carla Overbeck as well.

"But when that foul was called, only one person turned and looked at me. And the assertiveness with which Michelle stared toward the bench communicated loud and clear. She was asking 'Who do you want to take this?' But her body language said, 'It had better be me!'

"So I just pointed to her. Because that's exactly what I like to see as a coach. Somebody who wants to take that critical shot in such a pressure situation. We're down 1–0. They had eliminated us in the World Cup the year before by the same score. We've got maybe ten minutes left in the game. If we don't score, the Olympics are over for us. Who knows what happens after that. Maybe a big rebuilding going into the '99 World Cup. So everything was on the line.

"And when she made it and I saw her exhilaration, jumping up and down and waving both arms ... Wow! What a contrast from what had happened to her in Sweden the year before!"

☙ ☙ ☙

The celebration was short-lived, but it pumped me full of just enough adrenaline to get me to the end of regulation time. Then I crashed again. Hard.

Walking off the field I told Slainer, "That's it. There's nothing left." No one else heard me because I didn't want them to know how bad it was. Steve practically threw me to the ground, onto my back, and started working on me, shaking my legs, shoving a Powerbar and Gatorade down my throat, and insisting, "You can do this!"

Everyone gathered around Tony for instructions prior to overtime. I lay flat on my back in the middle of the huddle. And as I looked up at my teammates stacking hands above me, I prayed for the strength to hold on another few minutes. Steve pulled me to my feet, smacked me on the butt, and told me to get out there and do it.

Some of my teammates waved their arms to exhort the crowd to cheer. I just walked to my position telling myself, "Hang in there. Just a little longer."

In the sixth minute of the first overtime Tony sent Shannon MacMillan in for Millie (Tiffeny Milbrett) at striker. Four minutes later, on just her second touch of the game, Mac took a perfect pass from Foudy and slotted it.

When I saw the ball go in I remember thinking, *We did it!* And then, *I did it!* I had lasted the entire game and I didn't know how. Well, I did know how. It was only God's strength that had carried me through.

Doc Adams confirmed that opinion in the locker room afterwards when he said, "I don't know how you did it, Mish. It had to be a miracle. There is no other explanation."

There was no on-field celebration for me after that Norway game. Steve Slain whisked me off the turf. I couldn't say anything to the reporters gathered at the mouth of the tunnel. I didn't even look up and wave at the fans calling my name. It was all I could do to stagger to the locker room.

Then I got word that my presence was required at the postgame press conference in a room that was up four flights of stairs. I wouldn't have made it if Slainer hadn't grabbed me by the shirt collar and the waistband of my pants and practically lifted me up those steps.

Afterwards, he and Doc Adams carried me to the bus and finally into the training room at the University of Georgia dorm, got me comfortable on the training table and hooked up the IV. Only then did the thought hit me. *We still have to face China for the gold medal!*

Four days later, August 1, 1996, we played the gold medal match at Sanford Stadium in front of 76,481 people—at the time, the largest crowd ever to witness a women's sporting event anywhere in the world. Tony threw a new wrinkle at the Chinese by playing three speed demons at forward—MacMillan, Milbrett, and Hamm—with me at midfield again. I probably had no business being out there at all. Fifteen minutes into the game I knew I had nothing left. But I didn't want to leave because this was the gold medal game.

I guess I was doing okay because Tony didn't yank me.

⚽ ⚽ ⚽

Michelle was doing better than okay.

As in the Norway game, her assignment against China was to win balls in the midfield and distribute them quickly and accurately. That's just what she did in the eighteenth minute of the game. Tiffeny Milbrett came up with the ball in a crowd and dropped it back to Michelle, who led Kristine Lilly perfectly on the left flank. Lilly took the pass, sprinted to the box, and crossed the ball right in front of the goal to Mia Hamm, who volleyed a screamer that hit the keeper's hand and bounced off the left post. And there was Shannon Mac to finish off the rebound. USA 1, China 0.

It wasn't long before China came back to tie. The game remained 1–1 at the half. Again Michelle went through her usual halftime routine, trying to rally for the second half.

She later said she felt twenty-five times worse than she did after the Norway game. But she still didn't want to come out.

"All through the Olympics Tony had given me a special assignment," Steve Slain says. "It was my job to tell him when I thought Michelle had reached the end of her rope. And in that second half against China he checked with me over and over again. So on the one hand I had Tony saying, 'Whatever you do, you better tell me when she has to come out. Don't wait till it's too late. You gotta tell me.'

"And on the other hand I was thinking, 'I know Michelle, and she is going to want to rip my head off if I tell Tony to pull her out of an Olympic gold medal match.'

"So every time Tony turned and with those big eyes glaring at me over that great big mustache of his asked, 'What do you think?' I told him, 'She's looking great. She's doing fine!' And then I'd try to hand her a Powerbar next time she ran by and hoped it was true."

⚽ ⚽ ⚽

The truth is, very little even registered on my brain that second half. I could hear Loudy Foudy occasionally above the dull roar from the crowd. But that was it.

My dad and Sue have home video of me holding a half-eaten Powerbar while stripping the ball from a Chinese girl. And you can hear Sue screaming, "Yes, Mish! Just like Popeye and his spinach!" I watched the whole video later and as the clock ran down you could hear Sue saying, as she followed me in the viewfinder, "C'mon, Mee-Mee, hang in there. You can do it."

Such a contrast from the '91 World Cup when she was saying, "C'mon, Mish, score another goal." Now it was just, "Hang in there!" For my family, as for me, the primary goal was to make it through the match without having to pay too steep a price. Whatever the outcome, the victory was in being on the field.

I was beginning to dread the prospect of yet another overtime as the game passed the seventy-minute mark. Then Mia got the ball on the right sideline and passed it right between two Chinese defenders to a sprinting Joy Fawcett, who carried the ball all the way to the penalty box. And when the keeper charged, Joy slipped the ball left to Millie, who poked it in for a 2–1 lead. The stadium went berserk.

But we still had eighteen minutes to play. It seemed like forever before the referee's whistle blew one, twice, and the crowd's roar drowned out the third. The game was over.

My initial feeling was more relief and gratefulness than anything else. *It's over! Now I can rest!*

Of course there was still the little matter of a gold medal ceremony. The team had to change and go back out to the tunnel to wait for the ceremony to begin. I felt so dazed and dizzy I had to sit down. Mia leaned over and told me, "Just a little longer. You can do it." I wasn't so sure.

But when I walked out into that stadium and realized not one of those 76, 481 people had left, it all seemed worth it. I found my family in the crowd and raised both arms in a triumphant salute. And then I climbed onto the medal platform for a moment so many people dream about.

Let me tell you, it's everything you could imagine. Almost surreal. Extremely emotional. Tears. Laughter. Disbelief. Joy. All at once. And all very overwhelming.

When the Olympic official hung my gold medal around my neck, my first thought was, *Wow! That's heavy!*

A few minutes later NBC—dubbed "No Bloody Coverage" by irate fans because they hadn't shown the gold medal game live—staged a group interview with our entire team. I was still so excited that I held up the medal and told Bob Costas, "You see this? It's the gold medal, baby!"

The next day, August 2, I wrote in my journal:

> My thoughts are scattered and disjointed, but the sentiment and unforgettable memories will forever be embedded in my heart. My mind keeps returning to the past few years when I thought I was so alone, so isolated in my struggles and pain.
>
> God is so good. Through it all, He was preparing me for this moment, this experience. He's so faithful. He took it all away, but He gave me back so much more. I go to bed tonight an Olympic champion.

Chapter Eighteen

BEYOND
THE GAMES

*W*hen we came out on top in China back in '91 I had felt like a character in a fairy tale. After playing the best tournament of my life, I thought I was ready to take on the world. When we won the Olympics, I felt more like an old warhorse who had fought the final battle on its knees and arrived on the podium victorious, but wounded.

There was perhaps an even deeper sense of satisfaction and accomplishment, but I also knew I needed time to heal.

After major reconstructive surgery on my knee (my twelfth knee operation) I told Tony I had to take some time off to recuperate from all I'd been through the past few years. And to think about my future.

I could imagine the incredible experience of playing World Cup '99 at home in the United States. But I knew all too well the personal cost required to prepare and train for another world championship run. Was it worth the cost? Could I pay that price again? I needed time to consider those questions.

More than a year passed before I knew the answer. It wasn't until October 30 and November 1 of 1997 that I rejoined the National Team to play against Sweden in my only two soccer games of the entire year. I eased back into more of the routine in 1998, playing in fifteen of the National Team's twenty-five-game schedule.

The time away from soccer brought exciting new opportunities. My church sent me to Egypt in 1997 to meet with representatives and leaders of Christian congregations from throughout the Mideast to discuss the potential use of sports ministries as evangelistic and outreach tools.

My reduced soccer schedule also gave me some unaccustomed, but much needed, time for reading, learning, thinking, and planning. During the summer of 1997, as I read Billy Graham's autobiography, *Just as I Am,* and journeyed through his amazing life, I thought to myself, *I need to write and ask him if I can share my testimony at one of his crusades.* I dropped the letter into the mail daydreaming about the opportunity, but figuring it was next to impossible. I promptly forgot all about it until I got a phone call from Cliff Barrows, Dr. Graham's right-hand man, saying they had been praying for a female athlete they could use when—*voila!*—my letter arrived.

That's how I got invited to speak at the Billy Graham Crusade in Tampa a year later. My little part was sandwiched between two singers. A short video introduced me and then I had exactly three minutes and twenty seconds to talk about my whole life.

I had practiced incessantly for three days in front of my roomie Sal's stopwatch—cutting, rewriting, and rearranging my talk in order to fit the time limit. When the moment came I was ready to rock. No nerves. No fear. Only calm and confidence as I stood backstage looking out at the 60,000 people in Raymond James Stadium waiting for the guy to push me out to the podium. All of a sudden, it was my turn. I ran out there, (yes, literally ran) and began talking:

> Helloooooooooo, Tampa!
>
> Many of you know me as an athlete, as a great soccer player, but tonight I want you to know there is more to me than what you see on the soccer field. Tonight, I am going to share my heart . . .
>
> Basically, we all search for three things: security, significance, and success—and I am no exception. All of us spend our lives trying to arrange circumstances, build possessions, acquire wealth, and gather people around us to ensure our sense of security and well-being . . .
>
> It wasn't until the age of twenty-eight that I realized I had based my self-worth on World Cup trophies, media acclaim, and the number of goals I could score in a year. Somehow as I grew up, I equated my personal value with performance. After I got sick and I was stripped of my view of personal worth, I felt useless and worthless. It was in this circumstance that I started asking myself some tough questions, and that is where I came face to face with God.
>
> Here's what God showed me. Number one, God created me as an original. He intentionally put me together in every detail—including the hair—just like I am, on purpose. In Ephesians 2:10, God says we are His masterpiece. We are his highest work of art. Number two, God loves me just as I am today. He knows all my junk. He knows all my inadequacies

and lack of faith, and He loves me anyway. However, He loves me too much to leave me the way I am. Number three, God bought me at a high price. Christ paid for me with the highest price of all, and that was with His life.

It was acknowledging and internalizing these truths that I realized I am significant simply because I am God's masterpiece.

My whole perspective on success has changed over the years. The world taught me success is stature, position, money, power, and popularity. I had all these things, yet none of them filled me up, restored me, gave me hope when things got tough. Jesus says success is to serve, to love, and to follow God at all costs. Now my whole focus is not to win World Cup trophies or gold medals, but to be faithful and obedient to my God.

Listen, tonight is a hugely exciting event. We get to hear and meet Billy Graham. It would be easy to walk away excited about that alone. However, if you do that you've missed the most important thing. And that is who Jesus is, what He's done for you, and the necessity for you to have Him in your life. Make your decision. Step over the line. Become a follower of Christ. Make heaven your goal. God bless you.

After months of thinking and preparing, now in three minutes and twenty seconds I was done. As I high-fived everyone backstage and even got a hug from Billy Graham himself, I couldn't help remembering that vision planted in my mind at my grandparents' church three years before of me speaking to soccer and church groups about God. The idea had seemed so unimaginable, so terrifying, at the time. *Me? Standing up and talking to people about Jesus? No way!*

Now here I was speaking at a Billy Graham Crusade to huge crowds of people and flying halfway around the world to talk to churches and other Christian groups about using soccer to open doors for sharing the gospel message. *Who would have thought?*

My experience in Egypt and then at the Graham Crusade helped give further impetus to an idea I'd been thinking about for a while. In 1998, with the help, support, and prayers of many wonderful friends and volunteers, I actually founded a ministry of my own called Soccer Outreach International. The whole idea behind SOI is to work with groups, churches, and individuals to help challenge, inspire, and equip people, especially kids, to reach their potential and achieve their goals and make a difference in the world. We want to impart character and leadership and faith.

Sport, but especially soccer, provides a unique common denominator which links diverse cultures and peoples with a shared passion and respect for the game. The SOI dream is that this sport, along with the influence of a growing number of athletes in the game, will enable us to reach millions of people around the world—one person at a time. Simply put: soccer serves as the platform from which we can share a powerful message of hope, personal purpose, and faith.

⚽ ⚽ ⚽

Michelle's own soccer platform actually grew bigger and stronger during this time of personal reflection and rejuvenation. The sport she'd loved and promoted for so many years honored and recognized the significant role she has played in the history and development of women's soccer.

In 1998 she was named the CONCACAF Women's Player of the Century. And the international governing body of soccer granted Michelle its highest honor, the FIFA Order of Merit, which is bestowed on individuals who have made outstanding contributions to the international game, on or off the field. They cited many of her on-field accomplishments from a distinguished career as a player as well as her contribution to the successes of the U.S. women's soccer program. They also recognized her successful efforts in persuading the International Olympic Committee to, make women's soccer a medal sport in the 1996 Olympic Games and her other charitable work off the field, including the establishment of Soccer Outreach International.

Michelle was the first woman ever to receive the award, whose former recipients include people like Pelé and Henry Kissinger. When she learned she was to honored in a Paris ceremony along with Nelson Mandela and other high-profile members of soccer's elite, Michelle says her first reaction was, "Me, Kissinger, Mandela? Get outta town!" But after it sank in a bit, she realized what an overwhelming honor and opportunity it was.

But that wasn't all. In November 1998 Michelle was one of twenty renown figures from the international soccer world to be named to the newly created FIFA Football Committee. Made up of players, coaches, officials, and others directly associated with the sport of soccer, this group was the brainchild of FIFA President Sepp Blatter, who charged the group with "acting as guardians of the game" and "concentrating on the future welfare of the sport." This working committee would meet several times a year to address important issues and help shape and guide the future growth of soccer worldwide.

Michelle's platform grew even bigger.

⚽ ⚽ ⚽

As excited as I was about all these opportunities and their implications for my personal life and ministry after soccer, I came to the conclusion during 1997 and 1998 that my own immediate future included the pursuit of another World Cup with the U.S. Women's National Team. After taking more than a year off, much of '98 was spent just working back into playing shape. But by the time our team began its five-month pre-Cup residency camp back in Orlando again in January 1999, I was feeling fitter, stronger, healthier, and readier to play soccer than I had in years.

I was excited by the prospect of Women's World Cup '99. But I also knew from experience that the road to another possible world championship would be a grueling one, filled with unexpected obstacles and marked by memorable milestones.

The first milestone came early—on Saturday, January 30—in a game against Portugal in Fort Lauderdale, Florida. My good buddy Millie (Tiffeny Milbrett) sent a beauty of a corner kick into the box where I turned and launched a left-footed volley past a paralyzed keeper for the one hundredth international goal of my career. Since I was only the fourth soccer player in history to do that, my teammates mobbed me, the crowd gave me a nice standing ovation, and the officials stopped the game to present me with the ball.

Another 1999 milestone for our team, and for women's soccer, promised to be an exhibition game featuring the U.S. women versus a team of international all-stars. The idea was to bring the greatest female players in the world together for one game, during halftime of which FIFA would generate publicity and excitement by staging the official drawing to determine the opening round match-ups for the coming Women's World Cup tournament in June.

This U.S. vs. World All-Stars game in San Jose, California, was also the first women's soccer game in history to be broadcast live to a worldwide audience— the perfect time and place for me to make a spectacle of myself encountering the first of those unexpected obstacles on the road to Pasadena. It happened as I was leaping for a ball off a corner kick in just the nineteenth minute of the match. My face collided with the back of my Norwegian buddy Linda Mendalen's head and I went down hard. When I came to, a mob of people had surrounded me and Lil was yelling, "She's bleeding! She's bleeding!"

"Who's bleeding?" I asked, trying to sit up and check to see if the other girl might be hurt.

"You're bleeding!" Lil yelled at me. "Stay down!"

I finally noticed the blood gushing everywhere from my head and nose. Doc and our trainer took me to the locker room, and when Dad and Sue walked in a few minutes later I knew it must be serious.

I was rushed to a nearby hospital where the emergency room folks sewed up the gash over my left eye with twenty-five stitches, found three broken bones around my eye socket, and diagnosed a concussion. I wouldn't have considered that a good day, except the doc told me it was miraculous I hadn't done more damage, especially to the eyeball, considering the blow and the location of the injuries.

When I finally looked at myself in the mirror two days later, I couldn't pry my left eyelid open far enough to see daylight. The whole side of my face was purple and swollen, and I still couldn't stand up for long without throwing up. As usual, Dad was totally freaked out and kept waking me up to get me to eat, but I would have none of that.

I had to spend three days in California, then another three days in Seattle at my dad's before the doctors would okay me for a cross-country flight back home. I flew first-class to Orlando, and no one (and I mean no one) asked me what happened or even looked at me all the way to Florida.

The ER doctors told me I'd be sidelined for six to eight weeks. Of course, they also said they didn't think my injury would require surgery. I proved them wrong on both counts. Back in Florida on March 3, I underwent out-patient surgery to have the knot on my cheekbone removed and what's called a *closed reduction,* meaning the doctor pulled the crushed bones out to their normal position without opening me up.

Though I still looked like I'd tried to kiss a freight train, the plastic surgeon told me I should heal up as good as new. The doc even cleared me to go to Portugal with the team to play in the annual Algrave Cup just ten days later. He assured me the odds of getting hit again with that same kind of force in the exact same spot would be astronomical.

I figured, *If I get hit, I get hit. I might as well get back in the saddle. Giddyup.*

In all the years we'd played in the Algrave Cup, we'd never won the Portuguese tournament. This year we flew to Lisbon determined to change that. We played well, and made it all the way to the final of the eight-team tourney before losing to China 2–1. I ran out of gas and Tony pulled me midway through the second half of that final. While I was mad about having to come out, I breathed a big sigh of relief knowing I'd made it through a tough tournament with no further injuries.

We all knew even then that China was going to be tough competition come World Cup time. We got another good gut-check and a chance for payback when China came to the States for two friendlies the next month. In the first game at Hershey, Pennsylvania, I had to pull myself out at the half when we had a 1–0 lead. The Chinese tied the game and after Tony subbed in Tish Venturini with two minutes left to go, Vench scored on her very first touch in the final seconds of the game. We won 2–1.

However, that was a costly win for me. I felt sick as a dog the next morning, slept the entire three-hour bus ride to New Jersey, and spent the rest of the day and night in bed. I didn't train with the team that next day either, but my batteries began to recharge and I could feel my body returning to strength.

The day after that we played the second match against China in Giants Stadium, the same venue where we were scheduled to open World Cup play on June 19, less than two months away. China started the game in a frenzy that made it seem like they had five extra players on the field. They scored early, controlled the play, and took a 1–0 lead into the half.

Something clicked and we played much better in the second half. We got our USA mentality back, surged forward, crunched tackles, won headballs, and created scoring chances until Julie Foudy finally slotted one to tie the score 1–1. Then it was back and forth until the final minute of play—just like last game. Only this time it was a Chinese girl who scored. And everyone in Giants Stadium heard the final whistle, because the stunned crowd was absolutely silent.

That loss ended our team's streak of more than three years and fifty games without a loss to international competition on American soil, so it hurt even more than most last-second defeats. Combined with the fact that the Chinese had beaten us two out of three times since the beginning of the year, it provided a sobering reminder that we couldn't afford to take anything for granted going into the World Cup.

A few days later I reflected on that lesson in my journal:

> Playing against China this past week may be just what the doctor ordered. We were reminded firsthand how narrow the margin is between winning and losing on the field and how huge that margin is once the game is finished. The winners get the gold and the losers get nothing. This reminder of how close things actually are at this level is something we needed to mentally prepare us for the World Cup competition. Rock on, USA.

In spite of feeling so physically fit when the year started, the intensity of our training combined with the draining demands of our team's pre–World Cup travel schedule took its usual toll on my health. Instead of gradually building my strength as training is supposed to do, the CFIDS symptoms seemed their worst in May, only a month before the tournament was to begin.

I hit what felt like absolute bottom when I pulled myself in the middle of a game against Holland up in Milwaukee, Wisconsin. I went into the locker room totally discouraged and exhausted from the mental battle and the physical struggle and cried in utter weariness.

Colleen Hacker, our team shrink, eventually found me and the two of us had a long and fruitful talk. Hacker suggested that I needed to find a new strategy for dealing with the constant and drastic up and down swings of emotion that went with my CFIDS. I'd learned to cope with the physical fluctuations pretty well, but always attempting to keep a positive face on everything while trying to ignore the emotional ramifications—my usual tough-it-out strategy—was no longer working. Hack understood that I didn't want to burden or distract my teammates with my personal emotional baggage, but we agreed I needed to make myself more vulnerable to one or two people who were close to me, individuals I knew could understand something of what I faced, who cared about me, and who would be strong enough to listen, support me, and help carry my emotional load.

I chose two. Because my good buddy Sal and I had already shared so much, she was an easy choice for someone with whom I could be even more vulnerable. The other was a guy I affectionately referred to as "Sweet Jimmy."

I'd met Jimmy DeYoung just a few months earlier during the making of a video documentary about my soccer career and life testimony. I soon found that Jimmy and I share a love of soccer (he was an All-America keeper in college) and horses (he is a cowboy, too). More importantly, we both had real commitment and passion for our faith as Christians (in addition to film and video production, Jimmy works for an international Christian ministry his parents founded). But what most impressed me about Jimmy was his desire for a close relationship with God and his sensitive way with people.

From day one, we hit it off and found ourselves able to share about deep things of the heart. We also committed ourselves to carry out our relationship with God's blessing and in God's timing—which is not always an easy thing to do. Through many hours on the phone (we should own stock in the phone company by now) and a few brief face-to-face rendezvous here and there, Sweet Jimmy one of my closest friends and strongest encouragers.

Just telling Sal and Jimmy what I'd decided has become and hearing their willingness to take part in this new strategy Hack and I had devised encouraged me. Their care and support gave me renewed hope.

⚽ ⚽ ⚽

The week after she pulled herself from that Holland game in Milwaukee, the New York Times *ran a nice feature on Michelle's past contributions to women's soccer and her current status on the team. It acknowledged that, "At 33 she is struggling to find a measure of durability for the 1999 Women's World Cup, which begins on June 19. Somehow Akers finds a way to keep going, and even when she is running on fumes, her game is marked by fierce determination. . . . Whatever she can give during the World Cup, DiCicco said, he will take.*

"'Michelle is the first person that created universal acceptance of the women's game,' DiCicco said. 'People like Pelé and Franz Beckenbauer saw her play and realized that women could play the game as skillfully and tactically proficient as men could. She can put a player onto the ball with 40-yard passes, right- and left-footed, and score a goal from 25–30 yards.'"

The Times *article went on to quote teammates speaking of her value to the team: "'She taught us what it is like to be professional,' Mia Hamm said.*

"The National Team's co-captain Julie Foudy said, 'She leaves her heart and soul on the field, along with a few teeth and bone chips.'

". . . The question for the World Cup is not her talent, but her stamina. Akers said that she had tried antidepressants and birth-control pills in an attempt to stimulate her blood pressure, but she reacted adversely to both. Other medication that might help her is banned as performance-enhancing.

"She is trying to maintain her health through diet and rest. She carries water to remain hydrated and she avoids dairy products, to which she is allergic. Although she paved the way for endorsements for her teammates, Akers is the only star on the team currently without a shoe contract, refusing to expend excessive energy on public appearances.

"'I don't know what is going to happen,' Akers said. 'This is day by day. I can only do the best I can to conserve energy and prepare for the World Cup. If it's not there on the day I need it, it's not there.'

"But she added: 'I'm hanging tough. I'll get the job done.'"

☻ ☻ ☻

I continued to put a positive face on things with the media. And the truth was, I felt great about our team's prospects in the tournament because I had such confidence in my teammates. We had eight players on our roster with over one hundred caps (international game appearances) who brought incredible veteran leadership and exceptional skills.

My biggest doubts centered on my own ability to play. And not just to *play*, but to contribute.

Those days when I felt the most uncertainty and discouragement, when my CFIDS flared up at its worst, I called Sal or Jimmy. There were many tears shed on telephone receivers and lots of long-distance prayers as I came to rely heavily on their support in the days leading up to the World Cup.

I also took great comfort in something my pastor said in a sermon about spiritual obedience. He said that when God calls us to do something, it is not our place to worry about what's going to happen, or even how we're going to do what He asks us to do. If we're willing to be used, our first priority is to "just show up."

So that was my personal strategy going into the World Cup. I had no idea how well, or even if, I could perform through six grueling games over three intensely competitive weeks. But since I remained convinced that God's plan for my life included one more World Cup tournament, I was going to "just show up."

Then, like everyone else, I'd just have to wait and see what happened after that.

Part

SIX

Days in the Sun:
The 1999 Women's
World Cup

Chapter Nineteen

ROCK ON, USA!

*T*hroughout my entire soccer career, my basic strategy before big tournaments has been much the same. To shut out the distractions and maintain control over rising emotions, I focus even more than usual on my normal routine. I tell myself, *This is the same sport, these are the same shoes, that's the same ball—I've done this all a million times before. This is just one more game. Win or lose, life will not end when the final whistle blows.*

For a long time that was just a technique I used to help keep my nerves and my competitive juices under control. I said it, but I didn't actually mean it.

This time, it was different. Maybe because I had grown some as a Christian in recent years, I had gained a higher perspective. This time I could honestly say, *The result doesn't matter. These games are just a blink in eternity. All that matters is what matters to God—which is my effort and my heart.*

Most of you who have read this far probably know what happened in the '99 Women's World Cup. The tournament received extensive worldwide media coverage as illustrated by the sampling of excerpts included at the beginning of this book. So there is little point in a play-by-play recounting of the entire tournament here.

What I will share is a quick look at some very personal highlights drawn from what I wrote in the heat of the moment during the tournament on my own web page, in my personal journal, and for ESPN.com, which also asked for and posted a tournament diary.

WWC Opener, June 19, 1999
USA vs. Denmark, Giants Stadium

I dedicate each game to someone special by writing their name on my sock tape. This game was dedicated to Jimmy (my godly dude), so I wrote "SWEET" on the front of one sock and "JIMMY" on the front of the other with Romans 9:17. That Bible verse says, "I have raised you up for the very purpose of showing my power in you, so that my name may be proclaimed in all the earth." This is an especially close-to-the-heart verse for me when I am struggling big-time (with CFIDS or injury). I remind myself that God has chosen me (raised me up) specifically and allowed me to be in this position (on the soccer field or in a world of hurt) for the very reason of demonstrating His power to me and to the world. The weaker I am, the more I experience God (by relying on Him more) and the more He can be seen in me. Even though it stinks to be struggling at times, I always know God is prevailing, and this is a great comfort and inspiration for me to be strong, courageous, and to never give up.

Walking out of the tunnel is always one of my favorite parts of game day. The walkway to the field is usually lined with security, game officials, staff, and media. As you move past them, you hear words of encouragement, see cameras whirling and clicking, and have people sticking out their hands for high fives as you walk past. Jogging out of the tunnel, the stadium slowly wakes up to our entrance. At first, the clamor and crowd noise is soft. But then it slowly builds into one big, deafening noise. As the cheering increases, it almost physically lifts me up. It is cool to just stand there and let that sink in.

This crowd, though, was extra-special. First, it was the largest crowd for a women's sporting event ever (in the history of the world). And two, it was the largest sporting crowd ever for Giants Stadium. The only bigger event was for the Pope! Not bad for a bunch of girls, huh?

The kickoff came quick for us. I didn't feel totally settled in or ready to compete. The first minutes of the game were chaos. Thankfully, we were able to hold them off and finally settled down to play more of our game. The memories I have of this game are:

- Looking for my dad and friends and not being able to find them.
- How doggone hot it was on the field and how dry my mouth was.
- A jam-packed stadium of swirling banners and signs, and yelling, cheering fans.
- Bri (Brianna Scurry) getting the wind knocked out of her.

- Heading the ball about 6000 times.

- Tackling and tracking like a maniac.

- The ref yelling at me to let her take care of the fouls (meaning don't play extra rough to even things out).

- The goals by Lil, Mia, and Foudy. Wow.

- The final whistle. 3–0.

- The on-field celebration. Yipeeeeeeee.

- Waving and thanking the crowd for being so dang awesome.

After an evening with friends and family, we were all home (at the hotel) by 11 o'clock and getting packed up for the flight to Chicago the next morning. I went to bed exhausted, but satisfied.

We did it. One down, five more to go.

WWC Game 2, June 24, 1999
USA vs. Nigeria, Soldier Field, Chicago

Once we got into the locker room, I started the usual pregame routine. Got my shoes, socks, shinguards, wristbands, etc., on. Drank my usual cup of Joe to get my blood pressure up, along with tons of water, listened to my usual music (*dc Talk* rocks), and did my customary sock tape dedication. This game was dedicated to my little brother, Mike, as a birthday present. I wrote the words "HAPPY B-DAY" on the front, and "BIG MIKE" on the back. He is now officially one old dude at the ripe old age of thirty-one.

My verses for this game were from Isaiah 40:8 and 55:10–11. Isaiah 40:8 says, "The grass withers, the flower fades; but the word of our God will stand forever." And the second one, from Isaiah 55:11, states, " . . . so shall my word be that goes out from my mouth; it shall not return to me empty, but it shall accomplish that which I purpose, and succeed in the thing for which I sent it."

I took two thoughts from these passages into the Nigeria game:

First, God and His Word are rock solid to the end of time (Isa. 40:8). The stuff and fluff I (we) often deem so important in life (i.e., success, wealth, fame, career, etc.) diminishes and dissolves over time (like flowers and grass). Eventually, everything and everyone on earth fades away, dies, or is lost from memory. The only thing that stands forever unchanged and indivisible is God and His Word. Therefore, I need to focus on God, His pledge and promises to me, and the aim He has for my life—not the result of the game, the World Cup, or my personal performance on the field.

Second, God gets the job done (Isa. 55:10–11). No promise or word out of God's mouth fails or is halfway achieved. What God says and intends to happen ultimately happens. Period. This is a great confidence booster and peace to me as I face not only my illness, possible injury, and other setbacks, but the uncertainty of life in general. I know that if I am striving to be faithful and right with God, He will work out His purpose for me no matter what obstacles or situations I may encounter.

Once the opening whistle blew in this game, we were transformed instantaneously into a bunch of bungling idiots. We stumbled around, gave away the ball, collided with each other, chased frantically, and in general, lost control of our bodily functions and brain power.

In contrast to our nightmare beginning, the Nigerians came out on fire and scored in the first two minutes to put them up 1–0. Thankfully, we have enough veteran seasoning to know a game is a ninety-minute ordeal and that we had another eighty-eight minutes to rectify the situation. As we dug the ball out of the net, we collectively took a deep breath and set to the task of getting on the scoreboard. It didn't take long. We immediately rallied to score a bunch of goals (an "own" goal mistake by Nigeria, another blast from Mia, a Tiff Milbrett special, a header from me, and a bunch of others that, as usual, I can't remember for the life of me) which brought us into the clear for a seemingly easy win.

Notice I said seemingly. Scoring was not our only challenge in this game. If you saw the game, you undoubtedly witnessed one of the most brutal games of my and the team's fourteen-year National Team history. The Nigerians were not only extremely fast, quick, and built like brick houses, they were ferocious in their tackling.

I came out at the half to preserve my gas tank. Overall, the game was a great success for us. We won the game 7–1, incurred no injuries (a miracle), and we did it all in front of an electric and extremely appreciative crowd. Thank you, Chicago.

Two games down, four to go.

Rock on, USA.

WWC Game 3, June 27, 1999
U.S. vs. North Korea, Foxboro Stadium, Boston

Wow. Did you see the game? If not, you missed some serious highlight reel stuff.

Foxboro Stadium was sold out (another one! yeah, baby) and the crowd was great. We arrived early, so we got to watch a bit of the game before us. We stood in the paved pathway leading from the locker rooms to the field, and the fans lining the walkway went nuts. Millie and I joked that we felt like animals in the zoo. Everyone is staring at us and taking pictures of us like we are part of the local animal attraction. We laugh and start acting like elephants by turning our arms into trunks and making elephant noses. As we were taking our own pictures (of the fan zoo in the stadium) we got to see all kinds of cool spectacles, signs, and creative stuff. Some kid put out a sign asking me to marry him (sorry, dude), flags were everywhere, painted faces, crazy hats. One whole section had a block of people wearing red, white, and blue T-shirts. It looked very cool from the bench. Rock on, USA fans.

This game was dedicated to a church friend of mine from Orlando, Laurie, who with her family has been praying for me for since 1995. Laurie is battling cancer and has the most remarkable perspective and attitude toward life. When I am struggling (emotionally and physically), her example, words, perspective, and insight into dealing with chronic illness and adversity give me an unexpected and enlivened peace when I need it most.

I wrote Laurie's name on my sock tape with the reference Joshua 1:9, a verse which says, "I hearby command you: Be strong and courageous. Do not be frightened or dismayed, for the LORD your God is with you wherever you go."

Laurie gave me this verse the day before I left for the WC and I have not forgotten her slant on what God is saying to her (and me) through this incredible command and promise. Here's what I took into the game:

First, being strong and courageous is not optional. God demands courageous living from me and will not tolerate me wimping out because I am chicken. Therefore, in order to be obedient in my faith, I cannot let my fears, anxieties, etc., dictate my choice of action or state of mind.

Second, God is my strength and courage. I find that courage and strength because God will never fail or forsake me (Josh. 1:5) and is with me wherever I go. Rock on. The point of this is, I don't find strength or courage through my own resources (i.e., my knowledge, willpower, abilities), but I choose it because I know God is beside me—always. He becomes my strength, my confidence, my courage, and with Him at my side, I can overcome CFIDS, accept defeat or disappointment, fall in love, win a world championship, walk into an uncertain future, or face any circumstance with absolute confidence and boldness.

Knowing this promise and having this perspective gives me extraordinary freedom to really go for it in my life and on the soccer field. And this is what I try to carry with me as I walk onto the field to compete.

Tony and staff put out a different lineup against the North Koreans. The strategy for this game was to win, of course, but also to rest and protect various players for the quarterfinal vs. Germany. So I got stuck on the bench for the entire match.

Our first half was a bit boring, as we came out flat and North Korea built a formidable bunker in front of their goal. However, in the second half, our team absolutely exploded. The Great Wall of China couldn't have kept us out.

Brianna deserves some print for her performance in this game. Not that she isn't incredible all the time, but this game took my breath away. I stood in awe, watching her fly around to catch or smack or tip the ball out of our goal. One time she kick-saved a worm-burner laser shot, jumped to her feet to block a rocket rebound shot, then, on the cross from that deflection, she charged out, leaped over everyone, and, finally, grabbed the ball and tucked it safe in her albatross arms. I was standing on the bench yelling my head off the entire time. You go, Bri.

During the whole game, I sat on the bench not whiffing a second of playing time. I didn't even wear my shinguards because I knew even if everyone on the team keeled over, Tony still would not put me in this game.

At the end of the 3–0 game, the team did the usual victory lap to acknowledge the crowd. This is always a fun time because everyone goes nuts as you run past, and we get the opportunity to say thanks for being such stud fans. Well, I was running along the field by the stadium wall high-fiving people, totally enjoying the moment, when some dude grabbed my arm and jerked me off my feet. I landed on the pavement, and when I tried to catch myself, my shoulder gave way. I immediately knew I had sublexed it (meaning it quickly went out of and back into the socket) and my first thought was, *Great, now I have to tell my dad I got hurt high-fiving. He will absolutely die.* After the security guard picked me up, I jogged to our doc, and we went in the locker room to fix me up.

I don't know who did this, and I assume he didn't mean to hurt me. He probably thought it would be funny to grab me and was just being playful, but now I have to deal with an injured shoulder on top of everything else. Plus, now my dad is totally freaking out (he is on edge with tension and worry as it is, and this just about puts him over the edge), most of my friends are both ticked and trying not to laugh (because it is funny, but just not now), and the people who pray for me on a daily basis now have to add another hour on their already bruised knees. Not cool at all. Thankfully, I should be good to go on Thursday vs. Germany, but the fact I (we) have to deal with this at all is crazy. So, fans, if I don't get too close, please understand. It only takes one goofball to ruin a perfectly fun and innocent exchange. And unfortunately, I am running out of body parts.

Great game, good win, and super fans. Three down, and three to go.

Chapter Twenty

TIME TO COWBOY UP

*T*wo more of my personal diary reports from the Women's World Cup:

WWC Quarterfinals, July 1, 1999
U.S. vs. Germany, Jack Kent Cooke Stadium, D.C.

Wooooooooooooo weeeeeeeeeeeeeeeee. What a game. My heart is just now recovering from the drama and craziness of this one.

We expected the Germans to be tough. They always are. But knowing that (in our brains) and experiencing it (alive and down our throats) are two different things. Much of our team seemed flat for the kickoff and suddenly, off a mistake back pass to Bri, we are down one to a very good German team. We rallied a tying goal (by Millie) soon after, but German midfielder number 10 stuck a beautiful one in to put them up again 2–1 at the end of the first half. *Doggone,* I thought, *another hole to dig ourselves out of. We have got to stop doing this to ourselves.*

After Tony "encouraged" us at halftime to get our heads in the game with a poignant reminder that our dream was about to die right here and now if we didn't do something fast, we bucked up and set our faces to play a more committed, dynamic second half. My body was already exhausted from the defensive workload of the first half, but somehow I managed to find an inner reservoir that I hoped would be enough to carry me another forty-five minutes.

Time to "cowboy up" (as the rodeo dudes say). And cowboy up we did.

The second half was a whole new game for us. Our focus sharpened, our mentality hardened, and we fought tooth and nail to overcome our deficit. Brandi tied the game off a loose ball in the box. Then, Joy connected with Mac (a sweet header off a corner) to put us ahead by one goal. The last minutes of the game were agonizing.

The one thought that ran unceasingly through my head was, *Do not let them score, do not let them score, do not let them score, do not let them score.* I was so fearful of a freak goal in the last minutes of the game, all I could think of was to boot the ball (and the opponent if necessary) as far down the field or out of the stadium as possible. I was in my "destroy and deny" mode. Seeing that "look" on my face, Lil kept reminding me we were a goal up.

Finally, after the third time of "Mish, we are up a goal!" I said, "Yeah, I know, Lil, and your point is what?"

"Stay home," she yelled, "stay home." Meaning stay in the middle, organize, and keep my wits about me in order to keep us safe on defense. Which is totally contrary to my instinct of hunting down and demolishing every threat of attack no matter where it happens to be—especially in a time such as this. But, knowing she was right (doggone it), I took a deep breath and yelled, organized, and played smart, tough defense until time ran out and we hung on to eventually win 3–2. When the whistle blew, I am proud to say I stayed home (thank you, Lil), we had no freak accidents, and we are one step closer to realizing our dream.

Our postgame celebration was very emotional this time. We gathered in the middle of the field and exchanged some heartfelt, intense words before waving and acknowledging the crowd. When I found my dad on the other side of the stadium, I jumped the signage, climbed the stairs into the stands, and gave him a big hug. As per my game tradition of dedicating each game to someone special, I dedicated this game to him and wrote "Pops" on my sock tape. When I showed him, he cried. It was a neat moment.

I sure do love my Pops.

Now we face Brazil for the semifinal on Sunday. We played them recently in Orlando and won, but it was a dogfight to the end. It will not be easy.

Once again, time to "cowboy up."

WWC Semi-Final, July 4, 1999
U.S. vs. Brazil, Stanford Stadium

July 4, Journal Entry Prior to the Game

Game day vs. Brazil. We are ready. The eyes are the key. I know we will win if I see the resolve and absolute unwillingness to do anything other than win in my teammates' eyes. We have "set our faces like flint" and are determined to finish out our quest to be world champs.

Had great Bible study time today regarding Christ on the cross (Luke 23:32–39) and His temptations to settle for immediate superficial glory, taking the easy route, evading His specific call (and the suffering that comes with it). At times, I face those same temptations. There are many moments when the weight of the effort and the grit I need to muster to make it ninety minutes is daunting. I know the toll it will take on me, and how I will have to endure the consequences for days afterward . . . and I have to *choose* to do it. In comparison with Christ on the cross it is nothing, of course; but still, like Christ, there are times I am tempted to stop, to rest, to take the easy way out.

However, even in saying that, I also know, like Christ, I can endure and overcome whatever comes at me, because in light of what God has for me later, the momentary troubles and challenges of today are simply building blocks to something far greater in the future. I can "cowboy up" because I trust God is doing big time things in and through me in my toughest, most difficult times and challenges. Rock on.

I start off with this because so many people (through my web page, the media, etc.) have asked how or why I can keep going after so many setbacks, so much adversity, knee surgeries, an eight-year chronic illness, and, specifically, after getting hit in the head and face a couple times in the game vs. Brazil. What is my motivation? Where do I get my strength? What do I do with the pain?

Well, part of the answer comes from just being stubborn as a mule. When I want or don't want something, I set every ounce of strength, focus, and energy in achieving that. As a kid, that energy went toward finding the hidden Christmas presents before the big day, trying to persuade Mom to let me have a second bowl of ice cream for dessert, or getting off restriction a couple days (or weeks) early. Whatever the case, if I wanted it bad enough, nothing and no one could stop me.

Being an athlete, this kind of determination is a tremendous quality. It has enabled me to endure long hours of fitness, Tony DiCicco's training sessions, interminable flights, bad food, boring meetings, injuries, unending hours of rehab, illness, and a host of other things that go along with sports, high-level competition, and life in general. And as far as competing in a WC, forget about it. With the WC title so close, do you think I will let a little knot on the head, cleat to the face, or a few bumps, bruises, or anything for that matter, get in the way of us winning the championship? No way. With my mind set on the goal of being world champions on Saturday, I will fight tooth and nail (and on one leg if necessary) to propel my team past a strong Chinese team.

Another part of my answer to these questions has to do with my experience with CFIDS. Severe chronic illness (or any disability or limitation) does one of two things: it either totally defeats you or it takes you to an even higher level of perseverance, perspective, and strength of character. As soccer players, we train our bodies and minds to reach our limits (and beyond) by enduring grueling training sessions day after day with relentless competition and testing at every turn. Over time, our bodies and minds become accustomed to the demand and we begin to excel, even under the most demanding of circumstances. In living and playing with a chronic illness, I have done much the same thing in order to continue to live out my life. Yes, it gets hard and sometimes I can't do much other than lay in bed, but for the most part, I have learned to live with the pain or symptoms of CFIDS (or injuries) and have used it to spur me on to greater focus and purpose.

The last and foundational part of my perseverance is born out of my faith. When all those other things (above) run out or fall short, my faith is the thing that enables me to just show up and take one more step Without it, I would have quit long ago.

I also know that God has prepared me with perfect precision for this exact moment of challenge or adversity, and I am capable of taking on the job in confidence as long as I keep my eyes focused on Him. I can get knocked down time and again and still have the strength and desire to get up. And the even cooler thing is if I am living out God's will for my life and get totally slammed and my body is totally thrashed (which happens often), even though I might not be getting up on the outside, I am still standing up in triumph on the inside.

So with all that in mind, this is the mentality I have when I walk onto the field knowing I might get pummeled, take a hit in the head, or have to endure ninety minutes of soccer while I am sick as a dog. It isn't anything heroic or mind-boggling. It is simply a built-in stubborn streak, inclusive preparation, a steadfast faith, and an unswerving commitment and desire to run my race full out so I can cross my finish line with the pride and satisfaction of knowing I gave it (and God) my all.

This game is dedicated to Bob Major, the dad of my best friend from the fourth grade. My buddy, Amy (nicknamed Maj), and I grew up playing soccer together in Seattle and have managed to keep in touch over the years, despite our crazy schedules and lives. I spent half my childhood at her house (eating and sleeping over, talking about boys, etc.) and think of myself as one of the family. Well, I got news early Friday morning that Mr. Major had been killed in a head-on collision on July 1. I was (am) rocked to the core. Amazing how quickly our lives can be forever altered. I still can't comprehend the loss, but my heart is broken over the loss and for the sadness Maj and her family must feel at this time. So the Brazil game is dedicated to him.

Okay, so let's get to the game.

⚽ ⚽ ⚽

July 5, Journal Entry After the Game

We won!!! 2–0. Yippeeeeeeee. We are through to the finals. Another frantic, frenzied game for us, but we managed to pull it out with an awesome performance from Bri and an incredible defensive effort from the team as a whole. Bri made three incredible saves and got MVP of the game. She rocked big-time. CP (Cindy Parlow) got the first goal off a mishandled ball by the GK (in the first five minutes) and in the eightieth minute Mia got taken down and I scored a PK. Whew. I celebrated exactly like I did in the Olympics (jumping up and down) and then ran to the bench and jumped on Dainis, our team's equipment manager.

All right, let me address a couple of things here. Evidently the whole world read the *USA Today* story about Dainis (now an international mystery man) and that celebration. Just so there are no misunderstandings, let me explain the significance of my leap into his arms and the smooch on his head. Dainis got in a goal one day after practice and I realized he was quick as a cat and had ESP powers to boot. I figured if I could score on him, I could score on anyone. So he and I have been practicing PKs for months now and he was (is) an integral part of my preparation (and success) for exactly that moment. So in celebration of the goal and appreciation of all his time spent diving and blocking shots, I ran to my PK partner and jumped on him to say, "Yipppeeeeeee, Dainis, we did it!"

It's funny how easy scoring looks to the casual observer—especially, penalties. I mean, what's the big deal? You step up, kick it, and it goes in. Unfortunately, it's not that easy or simple. I have been practicing day in and day out for the past couple months for exactly that moment. After every practice Dainis puts on his gloves and I gather the balls and we go until I am satisfied with my progress. Specifically, I work on my starting point, my approach to the ball, my point of contact with the ball, the ball's placement, power, height, and most of all, on my mentality. Being a goal scorer, especially in crucial moments, takes a special mind-set, and if you don't cultivate and exercise it daily, the likelihood of having the nerve and composure to score under that kind of pressure is shaky at best. Even when you have done everything right, things still can go wrong in those kind of pressure moments. So I whacked PKs at Dainis every day, all the while working on my technical skill, but also conditioning myself mentally for the moment when the ref would make the call for a PK in the WC.

This game was a rough one for me. I got my bell rung (head to head collision) and have a big knot on the back of my head. And if that wasn't enough, I also got a cleat to the face (courtesy of Sissi). Thankfully, I got my arm up before she got me, and that took the brunt of it or it could have been bad news. As it is, I have a cleat mark on the bridge of my nose and a bruise/welt above my eye. And yes, it is the same eye/side of my face that got busted up before. Thank God I don't have to go through that again.

Brazil played their usual game of flair, dangerous one-on-one stuff, and drama. But we played tough and disciplined defense for the entire ninety minutes. I tell you what, defense is much harder than attacking. The effort, focus, discipline, vision, and intensity required is enormous. Not only do you have to physically be in the game, and ready to rock at any given moment, but the mentality and concentration must be laser-like as well. There is absolutely no room for error. One lapse and the player is open and the ball is in the back of the net.

I have said it 5000 times: I hate playing defense. And the reason why is because it is doggone hard work. After games like this (and Germany) my brain (and body) is totally and absolutely fried. The defensive concentration required of this game was intense. Sissi is the leading goal scorer and the Brazilians in general are scary on the attack, so to have so much on the line and me marking Sissi was a pretty intense assignment. Whew. My synapses were smoking by the end of the game, that's for sure. My brother was right all along (even though it kills me to admit it): Defenders are a special breed.

I hope I can continue to live up to the task.

So, now we go into the final vs. China. Hacker (our sports shrink) gave us a great quote by George Bernard Shaw. It says, "Our lives are shaped not as much by our experiences as by our expectations." This George dude was right on the money. Our experiences these past five games and beyond (i.e., the 1991 and '95 WCs, '96 Olympics, and countless other trips, training sessions, and tournaments) have indeed shaped us as soccer players, as a team, and as people. But it was, and continues to be, our expectations (and vision) that have propelled us into greatness . . . and will empower us to be world champs.

Five down, one to go.

⚽ ⚽ ⚽

Actually it's six games plus two overtimes down, and now one shoot-out to go. We're back at the World Cup final on July 10 in the Rose Bowl, where I left you at the first of this book. Like I said, it wasn't the end of my story . . .

Chapter Twenty-One

MY CUP RUNNETH OVER

*E*ven after ninety minutes of scoreless regulation time and two scoreless overtimes the World Cup final is not yet final. It's China 0, USA 0.

I am lying on that training table in the medical triage room, down in the gray bowels of that historic old stadium, when Doc Adams tells me we are going to a penalty kick shoot-out.

I don't remember actually watching the first nine kicks. After receiving two liters of IV fluids I was only starting to plug back in mentally. I couldn't see the television screen while lying on my back on the training table. I couldn't even tell for sure what was happening by the reactions of the medical team, most of whom had their backs to me as they huddled around the television to alternately groan and cheer every development.

They groaned when China's Xie Huilin buried the first shot and cheered moments later when Carla Overbeck answered. Qui Haiyan's PK prompted another groan. Joy Fawcett's more elation.

But nothing that came before it even rivaled the volume of screaming and celebrating that took place in that locker room when Liu Ying sent her shot toward the goal only to have Brianna Scurry step up, guess left, dive that way, and deflect the ball wide of the net. When Kristine Lilly converted her kick we suddenly had a very real advantage—three goals to two.

After Zhang Ouying, Mia Hamm, and, of course, Sun Wen, all made their shots, the score was tied 4–4, with one last American turn to come. I remember Doc Adams somehow propped me up in a sitting position so I could see the TV screen for Brandi Chastain's kick. The moment her left-footed blast rocketed past a late-diving Gao Hong and smacked the back of the net, Doc almost jumped through the ceiling. But not until he ran over, got right in my face and started yelling, "We won! We won!" did the reality finally begin to sink in.

I slumped down and started crying in relief.

Then I said, "Get this stuff out of me!" (meaning the IV). "I'm going out there!"

Once more, Mark Adams played the role of friend as well as medical expert. "Take the IV out," he ordered. I suspect some of the other medical people may have questioned the wisdom of his decision. But no one argued.

Someone handed me an official yellow world champion T-shirt to replace the game jersey that had been cut off. Doc helped me off the table and then walked me slowly out the locker room door for the now-familiar jaunt through the passageways winding under the stadium.

Only one problem: Secret Service agents now blocked our way. The President of the United States was waiting in the locker room to congratulate the team, and his security had cordoned off all the adjacent corridors.

Doc did some fast talking, trying to tell the agents who I was and what we were doing. They insisted we retreat and take the long way around. Doc insisted we didn't have time—that we'd miss the ceremonies. He also knew I didn't have any energy to spare for a longer trek.

The Secret Service finally agreed to let me pass. They must have detained Doc a few seconds longer though, because he wasn't with me when I reached the tunnel leading out to the field only to find a very large and imposing man in a blue police uniform blocking my way. "I'm not supposed to allow anyone out on the field," he told me.

Since I was wearing a yellow T-shirt instead of my game jersey I guess he didn't realize I was a team member. "But I'm a player," I explained. "I need to get out th . . ."

"They said 'No one!'"

I tried to step past him. He easily moved in front of me.

All I could think was, *I wanna see my teammates!* So I simply tried to shove my way through the cop. I obviously wasn't thinking too clearly yet; the guy was 6'5" and built like an ox. I was still so weak and woozy I'm not absolutely sure he realized I was trying to push him out of my way. I'd have had more luck trying to run through the Great Wall of China.

I can't believe this! I thought. *My team has just won the 1999 World Cup. My teammates are celebrating and receiving their championship medals this very moment, and I can't walk out on the field to join them.* I was so frustrated and fatigued I didn't know whether I was going to cry or pass out.

Just then, behind the policeman, at the mouth of the tunnel, someone with official credentials and obvious clout saw what was happening and recognized me. When they said, "Let her through!" the cop immediately stepped back. The next thing I knew Doc Adams had rejoined me, taking me by the arm to steady me as we traipsed down the tunnel together and out onto the end zone grass.

I could barely make out the awards platform through the blizzard of shredded paper spewing from confetti cannons positioned all around the stadium. It wasn't until I'd begun shuffling across the field on the thick blanket of torn paper and felt the strange sensation of confetti sticking to the bottom of my bare feet that I realized I'd come out without any shoes or socks on.

In the time it took Doc and me to make the slow, tiring journey to midfield, the official awards ceremony ended. The crowd roared as my victorious teammates stood on the podium waving their thanks and acknowledgement to our fans. This was still going on as Doc helped me up the steps at the end of the platform. FIFA president Sepp Blatter recognized me in the maelstrom. Walking quickly toward me, he draped a left-over medal around my neck, hugged me, and congratulated me while kissing me on both cheeks in formal European style.

As my teammates realized my presence, there was huge round of long celebratory hugs with more than enough shared tears to soak much of my new yellow T-shirt. By the time I'd hugged everyone, I was getting wobbly. I needed a place to rest. Immediately.

"Over here, Mish," Doc Adams said as he eased me back down toward the field until I was half leaning, half sitting against the edge of the awards platform. While the team took the victory lap I'd visualized on the drive to the stadium a few hours earlier, I was content to sit there alone in all that happy, milling madness, soaking in the continuing roar of the crowd and watching as my teammates raced frantically around the field, greeting well-wishers, waving to family and friends in the stands, and repeatedly hugging one another.

Suddenly Sal walked up and gave me a big hug. She'd been in the stands watching the game. "How'd you get out here, Sal?" I exclaimed in surprise, remembering the big policeman. Then I cried some more over the unexpected chance to share this moment with someone who knew, perhaps better than anyone else in the world, what this moment meant to me—and for what I knew it meant to Sal after her 1996 knee injury had ended her National Team career and shattered her own longtime dream of playing in this World Cup.

Sal grinned through her own happy tears. "You hear that, Mish?"

"Hear what?"

"The crowd!"

I tried to tune in the noise. "What do you mean?"

"Listen. They're calling your name, Mish."

Finally, I heard it too. From around the stadium. In a rising chant. "Aaa-kers! Aaa-kers! Aaa-kers!" It quickly spread and grew louder. "Aaa-kers! Aaa-kers! Aaa-kers!"

Tears started streaming down my face.

"Mish, you gotta acknowledge 'em," Sal said. "Go on."

"C'mon. Go with me." I wanted to share the moment with her. So Sal helped me to my feet and ushered me from the side of the awards platform and slowly out toward the very middle of the field.

The applause and the cheers grew louder. I trudged a little oblong loop, maybe ten yards across at the widest point. And as people continued to call "Aaa-kers! Aaa-kers! Aaa-kers!" I faced all four corners of the Rose Bowl, pointing and clapping and waving back at a world record crowd I couldn't actually see through my tears.

I stood there until I thought I'd keel over. Then Sal, who'd walked close behind to make sure I was all right, caught up and helped me off the field after what may have been the shortest victory lap in history.

"Let's get you back to the locker room," Doc Adams suggested. I didn't resist as he and Sal led me slowly toward the tunnel. Somewhere along the way I encountered Tony DiCicco, who gave me a giant bear hug. I don't know for sure that he was crying, but I know I was. We'd been through so much over so many years together.

Tony actually had the World Cup trophy. He happily handed it to me and then someone snapped our picture with us both holding it up.

The locker room celebration was well under way by the time I finally got inside. Cheers, laughter, and popping champagne filled the air. Doc and Sal ushered me through a crush of media, teammates, and soccer officials to the back of the locker room, where I dropped on an empty bench away from the happy horde. Doc stood in front of me, holding my hand and keeping a close eye because I was clearly empty and about to pass out.

A few blurry minutes went by before I realized President Clinton was making his way around the locker room to pay his personal respects. When I stood up to better see what was going on, the President noticed me secluded in the corner, walked toward me, and smiled.

We shook hands. "From someone who knows how to take a hit," he told me, "you played a heckuva game."

I thanked him. We chatted for a minute or two about the game and then he was gone.

I told Doc Adams I was gonna drop and needed to lie down again. "Come on, Mish," he said, "I think you need some more fluids."

He led me back to a training room area off the main locker room and out of sight. He helped me lie down right on the cool concrete floor and started yet another IV. "If you don't get your act together soon, Mish," he warned me, "we're going to have to take you to the ER."

A long time passed before most of the outsiders finally drifted out of the locker room and things grew gradually quieter. By then, the added fluids had begun to clear my head enough that I could come out for a quick meeting with just my teammates, a private time where the staff and Tony thanked and congratulated us all.

Looking around that locker room full of totally exhausted faces and ear-to-ear smiles, I knew we were sharing a moment and a feeling none of us would ever forget. *World champions again! Incredible!*

The meeting over, Doc Adams hooked me up to the IV once more. And there, lying on my back again in that victorious locker room, with the fourth and final liter of IV fluid running into my arm, I could finally think. I realized that as excited as I was to have achieved our team goal and won the 1999 World Cup, I felt an even greater sense of personal satisfaction knowing that I'd been faithful and given my all. I knew even then, that for me, the most lasting and powerfully meaningful memory of the entire day would be the incredible gift I'd received from the Rose Bowl crowd when they'd chanted my name.

I could still hear the echo in my mind. *Aaa-kers! Aaa-kers! Aaa-kers!* What a tribute! It was as if they'd seen my heart.

EPILOGUE

*I*t's amazing to see what God can do through us when we just show up. What in my mind was to be a fitting finish—one last world championship—has turned out to be an exciting beginning.

The aftermath of the World Cup has been absolutely mind-boggling for the U.S. Women's National Team, and for me personally. Because of the wear and tear of the tournament and previously made commitments, I turned down a zillion media opportunities and was unable to do all the appearances with my team, including the obligatory visit to the White House. I needed time to recover.

Since the World Cup, my most important commitment has been cheering on someone who has cheered me on more than a million times: my Pops. Just weeks after our victory, he had a cancerous tumor removed from his colon, and as I write today, he is facing aggressive chemotherapy with a good prognosis. Watching him struggle through this is heart wrenching. I hate it. Now I know what it's like when he helplessly sees me battle CFIDS and injuries. I'm also reminded again where I got a large measure of my own grit and guts.

Wheaties made me the first soccer player ever to appear on a box of "The Breakfast of Champions." I agreed to author this book and a second one about my life written for kids. A number of companies wanted to talk about endorsement deals. I continue to have to screen all these opportunities in order to conserve my energy and maintain my focus on those things that really matter. Faith. Family. Friends. And whatever God has in store for my future.

As of now I intend to show up at the 2000 Olympics in Australia and see what happens there. After that? We'll see.

I do know that God has bigger and better plans for my life than I could ever dream of. Soccer Outreach International is already working with other groups and churches to conduct outreach events in Australia around the Olympics—using the same model we used at World Cup venues around the U.S. during the 1999 tournament. After I retire, I expect to expand my involvement with SOI, working with kids, spreading the great game of soccer and an even greater message of faith and hope around the world.

I also know this: I have played and lived one way my whole life—full speed ahead, on my own terms, in my own strength, and brushing aside any hint of personal heartache, fear, or frailty. Looking back, it is easy to see why that approach was destined to leave me alone, empty, and without hope.

I now know there is a better way. God's way. And although His plan demands even greater courage and sacrifice, it also guarantees unparalleled adventure and reward. God promises me His strength if I place my trust in Him and dare to admit and face the deepest fears and hurts of my heart.

This is perhaps the toughest challenge I have ever faced. To accept and even celebrate my weaknesses. To allow everyone I encounter in life—on the soccer field and off—to see and know my heart.

No games. For His glory.

ACKNOWLEDGMENTS

*T*o my best buddies, loved ones, teammates, coaches, doctors, PT's, and fans: The words "thank you" do not come one hundred thousand million miles near enough to expressing my deep gratitude and appreciation to you who have walked with me through my life, my struggles, my triumphs, and my occasional bone-headedness. If it weren't for your ceaseless prayers and countless phone calls, letters, E-mails, and tough love, I would never have found the way. Nor would I be half the person I am today. Thank you for standing in the gap. I love you.

Special thanks: To my Pops and the Rocket, I love you. To Sally Mally, for being my pal, lylas. To Judy, for your invaluable insight in helping to tell my story with integrity, vulnerability, and authenticity. To Slainer, for your faithful friendship and support. To Sweet Jimmy, for encouraging and challenging me to "cowboy up" in my adventure with God. And to Gregg. They told me you were good, but you have proved them all wrong. You are great. I am forever grateful for your dogged perseverance in digging my story out of the archives of my brain and finding the words and style to capture the essence of who I am (the good, the bad, and the ugly) and the amazing things God has done in my life.

To my God, whose grace and love saves and strengthens me daily: Thank you for being my steadfast anchor, my surefire hope, my unshakable refuge, my Savior—and my friend. Replenish and forge in me the willingness and perseverance to be strong and courageous in my race, to uphold a humble and forgiving spirit, to seek and love You with all my heart, mind, soul, and strength, and to love wholly the people You have entrusted to me. Empower me to be radical in this adventure with You and to be faithful with the endowment of Your Son, Christ Jesus.

To my readers: I ask God, from the wealth of His glory, to give you power through His Spirit to be strong in your inner selves, and I pray that Christ will make His home in your hearts through faith. I pray that you may have your roots and foundation in love, so that you, together with all God's people, may have the power to understand how broad and long, how high and deep, is Christ's love. Yes, may you come to know His love—although it can never be fully known—and so be completely filled with the very nature of God. To Him, who by means of His power working in us is able to do so much more than we can ever ask for or even think of, to God be the glory in the church and in Christ Jesus for all time, forever and ever. Amen. (Ephesians 3:16–21)

If you would like to find out more about Michelle or her work with SOI, you can go to michelleakers.com or www.socceroutreach.com, or write:

Soccer Outreach International
PMB #605
2875 S. Orange Ave., Ste. 500
Orlando, FL 32806

We want to hear from you. Please send your comments about this
book to us in care of the address below. Thank you.

ZondervanPublishingHouse
Grand Rapids, Michigan 49530
http://www.zondervan.com